Yale Near Eastern Researches, 5

Indenture at Nuzi:

The Personal Tidennūtu Contract and its Mesopotamian Analogues

BY BARRY L. EICHLER

New Haven and London
Yale University Press
1973

Library of Congress catalog card number: 73-77148
International standard book number: 0-300-0-01467-8

Designed by Sally Sullivan
and set in Monotype Imprint type.
Printed in the United States of America by
The Murray Printing Co., Forge Village, Mass.

Published in Great Britain, Europe, and Africa by
Yale University Press, Ltd., London.
Distributed in Canada by McGill-Queen's University
Press, Montreal; in Latin America by Kaiman & Polon,
Inc., New York City; in India by UBS Publishers'
Distributors Pvt., Ltd., Delhi; in Japan by John
Weatherhill, Inc., Tokyo.

To the memory of
E. A. SPEISER
(*Qoheleth* 12:9–10)

Contents

Acknowledgments

This study was begun at the suggestion of the late E. A. Speiser, to whom I shall always be deeply indebted for the invaluable legacy which he bequeathed as teacher and scholar.

I wish to acknowledge with gratitude the assistance given me by Jacob J. Finkelstein and Moshe Greenberg, who guided me in this undertaking. This study has benefited greatly from their valuable advice and criticism. Also my sincere thanks are due to Ernest R. Lacheman for making available to me much unpublished Nuzi material, to A. Leo Oppenheim for his constructive comments and to William W. Hallo for his meticulous attention as series editor.

Jane Isay and Maria Ellis of the Yale University Press are due a special note of thanks for their thorough and skillful editing of the manuscript.

Finally, I wish to thank my wife, Linda, for her aid in preparing the manuscript, her helpful suggestions, and her constant encouragement.

B. L. E.

Abbreviations

AASOR	*The Annual of the American Schools of Oriental Research.*
AfO	*Archiv für Orientforschung.*
AHDO	*Archives d'histoire du droit oriental.*
AHw	W. von Soden, *Akkadisches Handwörterbuch.*
a.i.	lexical series ki.KI.KAL.bi.šè = *ana ittišu*, publ. *MSL, 1.*
AJSL	*American Journal of Semitic Languages and Literatures.*
AnOr	*Analecta Orientalia.*
AOS	*American Oriental Series.*
ARM	*Archives royales de Mari.*
ARMT	*Archives royales de Mari: Textes.*
ARN	M. Çig, H. Kizilyay, and F. R. Kraus, *Altbabylonische Rechtsurkunden aus Nippur.*
ArOr	*Archiv Orientální* (Prague).
AS	*Assyriological Studies.*
ASAW	*Abhandlungen der Sächsischen Akademie der Wissenschaften, philologisch-historische Klasse.*
BA	*Biblical Archaeologist.*
BASOR	*Bulletin of the American Schools of Oriental Research.*
Berkooz, *Nuzi Dialect*	M. Berkooz, *The Nuzi Dialect of Akkadian: Orthography and Phonology.*
BIN	*Babylonian Inscriptions in the Collection of J. B. Nies.*
BiOr	*Bibliotheca Orientalis.*

BSAW	*Berichte über die Verhandlungen der Sächsischen Akademie der Wissenschaften.*
CAD	*The Assyrian Dictionary of the Oriental Institute of the University of Chicago.*
CAH	*The Cambridge Ancient History.*
Cassin, *Adoption*	E. M. Cassin, *L'Adoption à Nuzi.*
CBS	Tablets in the collection of the Babylonian Section of the University Museum, University of Pennsylvania.
CH	Code of Hammurapi.
Cross, *Property*	D. Cross, *Movable Property in the Nuzi Documents.*
CT	*Cuneiform Texts from Babylonian Tablets in the British Museum.*
Draffkorn, *Hurrians*	A. Draffkorn, *Hurrians and Hurrian at Alalah.*
EA	J. A. Knudtzon, *Die El-Amarna-Tafeln* (= *Vorderasiatische Bibliothek*, 2).
EL	G. Eisser and J. Lewy, *Die altassyrischen Rechtsurkunden vom Kültepe.*
Falkenstein, *Gerichtsurkunden*	A. Falkenstein, *Die neusumerischen Gerichtsurkunden.*
GAG	W. von Soden, *Grundriss der akkadischen Grammatik.*
HG	J. Kohler *et al.*, *Hammurabi's Gesetz.*
Ḫḫ	lexical series *ḪAR.ra* = *ḫubullu*, publ. *MSL*, 5 ff.
HSS	*Harvard Semitic Series.*
ICK	*1:* B. Hrozný, *Inscriptions cunéiformes du Kultépé.* *2:* L. Matouš, *Inscriptions cunéiformes du Kultépé.*
IEJ	*Israel Exploration Journal.*
ITT	*Inventaire des tablettes de Tello conservées au Musée Impérial Ottoman.*
JA	*Journal Asiatique.*

JAOS	*Journal of the American Oriental Society.*
JBL	*Journal of Biblical Literature.*
JCS	*Journal of Cuneiform Studies.*
JEN	*Joint Expedition with the Iraq Museum at Nuzi. American Schools of Oriental Research, Publications of the Baghdad School.*
JENu	*Joint Expedition at Nuzi: Unpublished texts.*
JNES	*Journal of Near Eastern Studies.*
JRAS	*Journal of the Royal Asiatic Society.*
JWH	*Journal of World History.*
KAJ	E. Ebeling, *Keilschrifttexte aus Assur juristischen Inhalts.*
Kh	Tablets from Khafadje in the collections of the Oriental Institute, University of Chicago.
Kienast, *ATHE*	B. Kienast, *Die altassyrischen Texte des Orientalischen Seminars der Universität Heidelberg und der Sammlung Erlenmeyer-Basel.*
KlF	*Kleinasiatische Forschungen.*
Koschaker, *Bürgschaftsrecht*	P. Koschaker, *Babylonisch-assyrisches Bürgschaftsrecht.*
Koschaker, *Griech. Rechtsurk.*	P. Koschaker, *Über einige griechische Rechtsurkunden aus den östlichen Randgebieten des Hellenismus.*
Koschaker, *NRUA*	P. Koschaker, *Neue keilschriftliche Rechtsurkunden aus der El-Amarna-Zeit.*
Kraus, *Edikt*	F. R. Kraus, *Ein Edikt des Königs Ammi-Ṣaduqa von Babylon* (=SD, 5).
KTS	J. Lewy, *Die altassyrischen Texte vom Kültepe bei Kaisarīje.*
Lautner, *Personenmiete*	J. G. Lautner, *Altbabylonische Personenmiete und Ernte-arbeiterverträge* (=SD, 1).
LE	Laws of Eshnunna.
MAD	*Materials for the Assyrian Dictionary.*

MAOG	*Mitteilungen der Altorientalischen Gesellschaft.*
MDP	*Memoires de la Délégation en Perse, Mission Archéologique de Perse.*
MSL	B. Landsberger, *Materialen zum Sumerischen Lexikon.*
Muffs, *Elephantine*	J. Y. Muffs, *Studies in the Aramaic Legal Papyri from Elephantine* (=SD, 8).
MVAG	*Mitteilungen der Vorderasiatisch-Ägyptischen Gesellschaft.*
NPN	I. J. Gelb, P. M. Purves, and A. A. MacRae, *Nuzi Personal Names.*
OIP	*Oriental Institute Publications.*
OLZ	*Orientalistische Literaturzeitung.*
Or N.S.	*Orientalia* (New Series).
PAPS	*Proceedings of the American Philosophical Society.*
PBS	*Publications of the Babylonian Section. University Museum, University of Pennsylvania.*
Petschow, *Pfandrecht*	H. Petschow, *Neubabylonisches Pfandrecht.*
RA	*Revue d'assyriologie et d'archéologie orientale.*
RlA	*Reallexikon der Assyriologie.*
RSO	*Revista degli studi orientali.*
RT	*Recueil des travaux relatifs à la philologie et à l'archéologie égyptiennes et assyriennes.*
SANE	I. Mendelsohn, *Slavery in the Ancient Near East.*
SAOC	*Studies in Ancient Oriental Civilization.*
Saarisalo, *Slaves*	A. Saarisalo, *New Kirkuk Documents Relating to Slaves.*
SD	*Studia et Documenta ad Iura Orientis Antiqui Pertinentia.*
ŠL	A. Deimel, *Šumerisches Lexikon.*
SMN	Tablets in the Nuzi collection of the Harvard Semitic Museum, Harvard University.

Steele, *Real Estate*	F. R. Steele, *Nuzi Real Estate Transactions.*
StOr	*Studia Orientalia* (Helsinki).
SZ	*Zeitschrift der Savigny-Stiftung für Rechtsgeschichte.*
TCL	*Textes cunéiformes. Musée du Louvre.*
TuM	*Texte und Materialien der Frau Professor Hilprecht Collection of Babylonian Antiquities im Eigentum der Universität Jena.*
UCP	*University of California Publications in Semitic Philology.*
VAS	*Vorderasiatische Schriftdenkmäler der königlichen Museen zu Berlin.*
Wiseman, *Alalakh*	D. J. Wiseman, *The Alalakh Tablets.*
WO	*Die Welt des Orients.*
WZKM	*Wiener Zeitschrift für die Kunde des Morgenlandes.*
YBC	Tablets in the Babylonian Collection, Yale University.
YOS	*Yale Oriental Series, Babylonian Texts.*
ZA	*Zeitschrift für Assyriologie und verwandte Gebiete bzw. Vorderasiatische Archäologie.*

CHAPTER 1

Introduction

THE NUZI TABLETS AND HURRIAN CULTURE

The ancient city of Nuzi[1] is situated about ten miles southwest of modern Kirkuk in northeastern Iraq. Its proximity to Kirkuk was one of the main reasons for the excavation of the site. During the first two decades of the twentieth century, tablets from the vicinity of Kirkuk were being distributed by dealers in antiquities. In 1925, Edward Chiera, then annual professor of the American Schools of Oriental Research, accepted the invitation of Gertrude Bell, the first Director of Antiquities in Iraq, to investigate the provenance of the so-called Kirkuk tablets. With the assistance of William Corner, the resident civil surgeon, Chiera traced some of the tablets to a specific spot in the mound of Kirkuk. Plans to excavate the spot, however, were abandoned because such activity would have endangered the foundations of that part of the city that was built on the mound. Therefore, Chiera sought a site with similar remains in the environs of Kirkuk. Basing himself upon Corner's

1. The underlying nominative form of the city name is still questionable. The problem cannot be solved by reference to Akkadian morphology (D. Cross, *Movable Property in the Nuzi Documents*, American Oriental Series, 10 [New Haven, American Oriental Society, 1937], 1 n. 4 and C. H. Gordon, "The Dialect of the Nuzi Tablets," *Or*, N.S. 7 [1938], 32 n. 2), since the city name is non-Akkadian. Hurrian morphology, however, has also not yet led to an accord. J. Lewy ("Ḫatta, Ḫattu, Ḫatti, Ḫattuša and 'Old Assyrian' Ḫattum," *ArOr, 18*/3 [1950], 414) considered Nuzi and Nuzu to be allomorphs, the latter being an adjectival derivative. E. A. Speiser ("Nuzi or Nuzu?" *JAOS, 75* [1955], 52–55) postulated Nuzi to be the nominative form, and Nuzu to be the apocopated form of the genitive *Nu-zu-e* (*Nuzwe). But A. Goetze has maintained that the evidence supports a nominative form, Nuzu (Review of Lacheman, *JEN, 6* in *Language, 16* [1940], 171; and more recently "Hurrian Place Names in -*š*(*š*)*e*," *Festschrift Johannes Friedrich zum 65. Geburtstag am 27. August 1958 gewidmet* [Heidelberg, Winter, 1959], p. 200 n. 1). The form Nuzi would then be explained as an Akkadianized genitive used by scribes who mistakenly interpreted Nuzu as an Akkadian nominative.

Although the matter is by no means settled, the form Nuzi is used in this study because it is the one most commonly found in the Akkadian texts, and therefore the one most frequently used by scholars.

intimate knowledge of the area, he began preliminary excavations at Yorgan Tepe[2]—allegedly the source of a cache of "Kirkuk" tablets found some twenty-five years previously. The results of the first brief season confirmed Chiera's expectations. Excavation of the site continued during the years 1927–31, under the joint sponsorship of the American Schools of Oriental Research in Baghdad and Harvard University.[3]

The archeological investigations revealed that the site had been occupied from prehistoric times but had experienced a rapid decline after its subjugation by the Assyrians following the fall of the Mitannian empire.[4] Our concern is with the Nuzi period at Yorgan Tepe, when the site was dominated by Hurrians[5] and the entire area with its center at Arrapḫa (modern Kirkuk) was a province of Mitanni. It was in the later levels of the Nuzi Period that several thousand tablets similar to those found at Kirkuk were uncovered.[6] These constitute the main Assyriological discovery at Nuzi, and they form the major body of texts of this type. The name Nuzi tablets has therefore come to designate all such texts found in the general area of Kirkuk.

The tablets excavated at Nuzi span a period of about four generations, and can be dated to the second half of the fifteenth century B.C.[7] Some are from

2. The mound is locally called Yoghlan or Yolghan Tepe (I. J. Gelb, P. M. Purves, and A. A. MacRae, *Nuzi Personal Names*, Oriental Institute Publications, 57 [Chicago, University of Chicago Press, 1943], 1).

3. For a complete account of the expeditions and their finds see R. F. S. Starr, *Nuzi: Report on the Excavations at Yorgan Tepa near Kirkuk, Iraq, conducted by Harvard University in conjunction with the American Schools of Oriental Research and the University Museum of Philadelphia 1927–1931* (2 vols., Cambridge, Mass. 1939, 1937).

4. H. Lewy ("Miscellanea Nuziana," *Or*, N.S *28* [1959], 22) maintained that the final destruction of the city came at the hands of the Babylonian forces.

5. It is difficult to ascertain the beginning of the Hurrian settlement at Yorgan Tepe archeologically. However, since the city name Nuzi was in use during, but presumably not prior to, the Hurrian occupation, it is possible to glean information from epigraphic evidence. The occurrences of the gentilic "Nuzian" in the Mari letters *ARM*, *1*, 75 and *5*, 17 would support a Hurrian settlement as far back as the Old Babylonian period (cf. A. Draffkorn, *Hurrians and Hurrian at Alalakh: an Ethnic-Linguistic Analysis* [unpubl. Ph.D. diss., University of Pennsylvania, 1959], p. 9).

6. A much smaller body of epigraphic material was found in the underlying Old Akkadian, Ur III, and Old Assyrian levels, at which time the city was named Gasur. These documents have been published by T. J. Meek, *Old Akkadian, Sumerian, and Cappodocian Texts from Nuzi*, Harvard Semitic Series, 10 (Cambridge, Harvard University Press, 1935).

7. The source of this absolute date is a Nuzi letter bearing the seal of Saušš̌atar, king of Mitanni. The text, *HSS*, *9*, 1, was first discussed by E. A. Speiser, "A Letter of Saushshatar and the Date of the Kirkuk Tablets," *JAOS*, *49* (1929), 269–75. He

the private archives of influential Nuzi families, while others were part of the official archives of the palace. They are written in a dialect of Akkadian[8] influenced by the Hurrian background of the scribes.[9] The content of the texts is quite varied. They include business transactions, especially those involving real estate, loans, and contracts of servitude; family records of marriage, adoption, and property settlement; transcripts of litigations and court proceedings; administrative lists, receipts, and inventories; and a few scholarly texts.[10] This variety of documentation has made possible a comprehensive reconstruction of life in Nuzi during the middle of the second millennium B.C.

Although Nuzi was peripheral to both Babylonia and Assyria, the Nuzi tablets have been of great interest to students of the ancient Near East. They are one of the primary sources of knowledge for Hurrian customs and practices. The Hurrians played an active role in the ancient Near East from the middle of the third millennium to the end of the second millennium

---

correctly noted (ibid., p. 273 n. 8) that Sauššatar was succeeded by Artatama I who ruled Mitanni during the reign of the Egyptian king Thutmosis IV (cf. *EA* 29:16 ff.), but the order of the Thutmosid succession was not definitively established until the publication of W. F. Edgerton's monograph *The Thutmosid Succession*, Studies in Ancient Oriental Civilization, 8 (Chicago, University of Chicago Press, 1933). As a result of this study, Sauššatar is found to be a contemporary of Amenophis II (1450–1425 B.C.), rather than of Thutmosis III (1504–1450 B.C.) as stated by Speiser. Cf. E. M. Cassin, *L'Adoption à Nuzi* (Paris, Maisonneuve, 1938), p. 7.

The pertinent letter, sent by Sauššatar, was addressed to Itḫiya. According to Koschaker ("Randnotizen zu neueren keilschriftlichen Rechtsurkunden," *ZA*, *43* [1936], 201), Itḫiya is to be identified with Itḫi-tešub, son of Kibi-tešub, king of Arrapḫa (cf. *HSS*, *10*, 231:1, 2 and *JEN*, *3*, 289:31). Since Kibi-tešub is known to have reigned during the lifetime of Winnirki, mother of Teḫib-tilla (*JEN*, *1*, 82:26), Itḫi-tešub and Sauššatar must have been contemporaries of Teḫib-tilla, son of Puḫi-šenni, whose archives comprise a major portion of the Nuzi tablets.

8. See Berkooz, *The Nuzi Dialect of Akkadian: Orthography and Phonology*, Language Dissertations, 23 (Philadelphia, Linguistic Society of America, 1937); A. Goetze, "Some Observations on Nuzu Akkadian," *Language, 14* (1938), 134–43; C. H. Gordon, "Pronouns in the Nuzi Tablets," *AJSL, 51* (1934), 1–21; "Nouns in the Nuzi Tablets," *Babyloniaca, 16* (1936), 1–153; "The Dialect of the Nuzu Tablets," *Or*, N.S. 7 (1938), 32–63, 215–32; S. N. Kramer, "The Verb in the Kirkuk Tablets," *AASOR, 11* (1929–30), 63–119; G. Wilhelm, *Untersuchungen zum Hurro-Akkadischen von Nuzi*, Alter Orient und Altes Testament, 9 (Neukirchen-Vluyn, Kevelaer, 1970).

9. E. A. Speiser, "The Linguistic Substratum at Nuzi," *AASOR, 16* (1935–36), 136–42; contra A. L. Oppenheim, "Zur Landessprache von Arrapḫe-Nuzi," *AfO, 11* (1937), 56–65.

10. E. R. Lacheman, "An Omen Text from Nuzi," *RA, 34* (1937), 1–8; "Nuziana," *RA, 36* (1939), 81–85; and G. Dossin, "Le Vocabulaire de Nuzi SMN 2559," *RA, 42* (1948), 21–34.

B.C.[11] The Mitannian empire, of which they comprised the basic ethnic component, was their greatest political achievement. The most significant contribution of the Hurrians, however, was their cultural role as assimilators and disseminators of Mesopotamian civilization.[12] Their eclecticism and cultural adaptability are vividly portrayed in the Nuzi documents, which reflect the blending of native Hurrian traditions with assimilated Mesopotamian elements in the fields of law,[13] linguistics,[14] religion,[15] and art.[16]

It is the Hurrian setting of the Nuzi tablets which has also attracted the attention of biblical scholars.[17] The patriarchal homeland in the Middle Euphrates valley was the object of a substantial Hurrian penetration,[18] which must have influenced the life of the indigenous Semitic population. Since little pertinent epigraphic material has come to light from this region, scholars must look to Nuzi for data which would be valid by extension for the Hurrian area of Haran and Nahor.

11. Studies dealing with the history of the Hurrians include: A. Goetze, *Hethiter, Churriter und Assyrer* (Oslo, H. Aschehoug & Co. [W. Nygaard], 1936); A. Ungnad, *Subartu* (Berlin, de Gruyter, 1936); I. J. Gelb, *Hurrians and Subarians*, Studies in Ancient Oriental Civilization, 22 (Chicago, University of Chicago Press, 1944); R. T. O'Callaghan, *Aram Naharaim*, Analecta Orientalia, 26 (Rome, Pontificium Institutum Biblicum, 1948); E. A. Speiser, "Hurrians and Subarians," *JAOS, 68* (1948), 1–13; "Hurrian Participation in the Civilizations of Mesopotamia, Syria, and Palestine," *JWH, 1* (1953), 311–27; A. Goetze, *Kleinasien* (Munich, Beck, 1957); I. J. Gelb, "Hurrians at Nippur in the Sargonic Period," *Festschrift Johannes Friedrich* (Heidelberg, Winter, 1959), pp. 183–94; F. Imparati, *I Hurriti* (Firenze, Sansoni, 1966).

12. E. A. Speiser, *JWH, 1* (1953), 318.

13. Ibid., pp. 314 f., especially n. 24.

14. Ibid., pp. 316 f.

15. Ibid., p. 314, especially n. 23.

16. Ibid., pp. 315 f., especially n. 29.

17. Biblical studies utilizing Nuzi material include: A. Draffkorn, "Ilāni/Elohim," *JBL, 76* (1957), 216–24 (the reader's attention is also directed to M. Greenberg, "Another Look at Rachel's Theft of the Teraphim," *JBL, 81* [1962], 239–48); O. Eissfeldt, "Der Beutel der Lebendigen. Alttestamentische Erzählungs- und Dichtungsmotive im Lichte neuer Nuzi Texte," *BSAW, 105*/6 (1960); C. H. Gordon, "Biblical Customs and the Nuzu Tablets," BA 3 (1940) 1–12 (cf. J. van Seters, "The Problem of Childlessness in Near Eastern Law and the Patriarchs of Israel," *JBL, 87* [1968], 401–08); M. Greenberg, *The Hāb/piru*, American Oriental Series, 39 (New Haven, American Oriental Society, 1955), 65–70; O. Loretz, "Ex. 21:6; 22:8 und angebliche Nuzi-Parallelen," *Biblica, 41* (1960), 167–75; E. A. Speiser, "Of Shoes and Shekels," *BASOR*, 77 (1940), 15–18; "I Know Not the Day of My Death," *JBL, 74* (1955) 252–56; "The Wife-Sister Motif in the Patriarchal Narratives," *Philip W. Lown Institute of Advanced Judaic Studies, Brandeis University Studies and Texts, 1* (1963), 15–28.

18. For the presence of Hurrians in this area during the eighteenth century B.C., see Draffkorn, *Hurrians*, pp. 7 ff.; and J.-R. Kupper, "Northern Mesopotamia and Syria," *CAH*, 2/1, 24 ff.

The importance of the Nuzi material was recognized almost immediately, and since the beginning of the publication of the texts, articles, and monographs devoted to their elucidation have appeared. Included in these studies are discussions of the historical and political implications of the texts[19]; examinations of the various aspects of the economic and social life of Nuzi[20]; and treatments of diverse legal problems.[21]

Most of the Nuzi tablets have now been published,[22] and the time is there-

19. For example, E. Chiera and E. A. Speiser, "A New Factor in the History of the Ancient Near East," *AASOR, 6* (1924–25), 75–90; E. A. Speiser, "Ethnic Movements in the Near East in the Second Millennium B.C.," *AASOR, 13* (1931–32), 13–54; N. B. Jankowska, "Communal Self-Government and the King of the State of Arrapḫa," *JESHO, 12* (1969), 233–82.

20. For example, D. Cross, *Property*; F. R. Steele, *Nuzi Real Estate Transactions*, American Oriental Series, 25 (New Haven, American Oriental Society, 1943); E. M. Cassin, *Adoption*; C. H. Gordon, "Nuzi Tablets Relating to Women," *Le Muséon, 48* (1935), 113–32 and *AnOr, 12* (1935), 151–84; H. Lewy, "The Nuzian Feudal System," *Or*, N.S. *11* (1942), 1–40, 209–50, 297–349 (for a critique of this view, see P. Koschaker, "Drei Rechtsurkunden aus Arrapḫa," *ZA, 48* [1944], 202–14); Steele, *Real Estate*, p. 12 n. 12 and Purves, "Additional Remarks on Nuzi Real Property," *JNES, 6* [1947], 179 ff.); A. Saarisalo, "New Kirkuk Documents Relating to Slaves," *StOr, 5*/3 (1934), 1–101; A. Skaist, "The Authority of the Brother at Arrapḫa and Nuzi," *JAOS, 89* (1969), 10–17; N. B. Jankowska, "Zur Geschichte der hurritischen Gesellschaft," *Proceedings of the 25th International Congress of Orientalists, 1* (1960), 226–32.

21. For example, P. Koschaker, *Neue keilschriftliche Rechtsurkunden aus der El-Amarna-Zeit*, Abhandlungen der Sächsischen Akademie der Wissenschaften, 39 (Leipzig, Hirzel, 1928); "Fratriarchat, Hausgemeinschaft und Mutterrecht in Keilschriftrechten," *ZA, 41* (1933), 1–89; E. A. Speiser, "New Kirkuk Documents Relating to Family Laws," *AASOR, 10* (1928–29), 1–73; R. E. Hayden, *Court Procedure at Nuzu* (Unpubl. Ph.D. diss., Brandeis University, 1962).

22. The Nuzi tablets may be divided into two categories—those obtained from dealers on the open market, and those unearthed during the excavation of the site.
1. Tablets purchased from dealers, listed by purchasing institution:

(a) Archeological Museum, Athens: E. Ebeling, "Ein Brief aus Nuzi in Besitz des Athener Archäologischen Museums, *Or*, N.S. *22* (1953), 355–58. (b) British Museum, London: T. G. Pinches, *Cuneiform Texts from Babylonian Tablets, etc., in the British Museum, 2* (London, Oxford University Press, 1896), No. 21 (translated by Pinches, "Some Early Babylonian Contracts or Legal Documents," *JRAS*, [1897], 590 ff.); C. J. Gadd, "Tablets from Kirkuk," *RA, 23* (1926), 49–161; C. B. F. Walker, *Cuneiform Texts from Babylonian Tablets in the British Musem, 51* (London, British Museum, 1972), Nos. 1–14. (c) Königliche Museen, Berlin: A. Ungnad, *Vorderasiatische Schriftdenkmäler der königlichen Museen zu Berlin, 1*) Leipzig, Hinrichs, 1907), 106–11. (d) Koninklijke Akademie van Wetenschappen, Leiden: F. M. Th. de Liagre Böhl, *Mededeelingen uit de Leidsche verzameling van spijkerschrift-inscripties, 2: Oorkonden uit de periode van 2000–1200 v.Chr.*, Mededeelingen der Koninklijke Akademie van Wetenschappen, Afdeeling Letterkunde, deel 78, Serie B, Nr. 2 (1934), 44. (e) Musée d'Art et d'Histoire, Geneva: E. R. Lacheman, "Les tablettes de Kerkouk au Musée

fore appropriate for a systematic analysis of the Nuzi documents, and for a testing of previously advanced interpretations. However, the Nuzi material

---

d'Art et d'Histoire de Genève, *Genava, 15* (1967), 5–23. (f) Musée national du Louvre, Paris: G. Contenau, *Contrats et lettres d'Assyrie et de Babylonie*, Textes Cunéiformes du Louvre, 9 (Paris, Geuthner, 1926), 1–46 which includes the two tablets published by Scheil in his "Tablettes de Kerkouk," *RA, 15* (1918), 65–73; G. Contenau, "Textes et monuments," *RA, 28* (1931), 27–39; E.-M. Cassin, "Tablettes inédites de Nuzi," *RA, 56* (1962), 57–80 which include the personal names published by Contenau, "Textes et monuments," *RA, 35* (1938), 26–27. (g) Musées Royaux du Cinquantenaire, Brussels: L. Speleers, *Recueil des inscriptions de l'Asie antérieure . . . textes sumériens babyloniens et assyriens*, Bruxelles, 1925, 309 f. (h) Pushkin Museum of Fine Arts, Moscow, and the Hermitage, Leningrad: N. B. Jankowska, "Legal documents from Arrapha in the Collections of the U.S.S.R.," *Peredneagiatskii Sbornik: Voprosi Hettologii i Hurritologii* (Moscow, 1961), pp. 424–580. (i) University of California, Berkeley: H. F. Lutz, "A Legal Document From Nuzi," *UCP, 9* (1931), 405–12 (republished by Chiera, "A Legal Document From Nuzi," *AJSL, 47* (1930–1931), 281–86. (j) Yale University, New Haven: there are a few Nuzi tablets in the Yale Babylonian Collection which will be published by E. R. Lacheman. (k) Private Collections: (1) B. Meissner, "Thontafeln aus Vryan-sehir," *OLZ, 5* (1902), 245–46, republished by Scheil, "Nouvelles notes d'épigraphie et d'archéologie assyriennes," *RT, 31* (1909), 56–58. (2) Dr. Bachman—three texts which were published by P. Koschaker, "Drei Rechtsurkunden aus Arrapḫa," *ZA, 48* (1944), 161–87 (3) Dr. Serota—one text published by A. Shaffer, "*kitru/kiterru:* New Documentation for a Nuzi Legal Term," *Studies Presented to A. Leo Oppenheim* (Chicago, Oriental Institute, 1964), pp. 181–94.

2. Tablets excavated at Nuzi:

Tablets in this category are designated by either "Joint Expedition Nuzi (JEN)" or "Semitic Museum: Nuzi (SMN)" numbers. The JEN texts found during the first season of excavations are in the Oriental Institute of the University of Chicago. They have been published by E. Chiera, *Joint Expedition with the Iraq Museum at Nuzi, 1–3* (Paris, Geuthner, 1927–1931); *4–5* (Philadelphia, University of Pennsylvania Press, 1934); E. R. Lacheman, *Joint Expedition with the Iraq Museum, 6* (New Haven, American Schools of Oriental Research, 1939); and "New Nuzi Texts and a New Method of Copying Cuneiform Tablets," *JAOS, 55* (1935), 429–31, plates I–VI. The SMN texts, uncovered during the subsequent seasons, are housed in the Harvard Semitic Museum. They have been published by E. Chiera, *Excavations at Nuzi, 1: Texts of Varied Contents*, Harvard Semitic Series, 5 (Cambridge, Harvard University Press, 1929); R. Pfeiffer and E. A. Speiser, *One Hundred New Selected Nuzi Texts*, Annual of the American Schools of Oriental Research, 16 (New Haven, American Schools of Oriental Research, 1936); R. H. Pfeiffer, *Excavations at Nuzi, 2: The Archives of Shilwateshub Son of the King*, Harvard Semitic Series, 9 (Cambridge, Harvard University Press, 1932): E. R. Lacheman, "SU = Šiqlu," *JAOS, 57* (1937), 181–84; "An Omen Text from Nuzi," *RA, 34* (1937), 1–8; "Nuziana," *RA, 36* (1939), 81–95, 113–219 (these texts have been partially republished in HSS 14 and 15); *Excavations at Nuzi, 5–8*, Harvard Semitic Series, 14, 15, 16, and 19 (Cambridge, Harvard University Press, 1950, 1955, 1958, and 1962). A final volume, *Excavations at Nuzi, 9*, is currently being prepared for publication by E. R. Lacheman, to whom I wish to express my deep gratitude for having made copies of these new texts available to me.

must also be seen in the broader perspective of Mesopotamia; for, in addition to being a source for Hurrian culture, the Nuzi tablets provide an interesting commentary on Mesopotamian civilization, by enabling the scholar to measure the nature and extent of Mesopotamian influence upon an intrusive Hurrian element. The study of Nuzi legal institutions should be especially fruitful in this respect, since Mesopotamian law exerted a potent cultural influence upon other societies.[23] The Nuzi legal institutions may be discerned from the many legal documents, which the Nuzi scribes generally classified and provided with specific titles. Although these legal documents differ in language and formulary from their southern Mesopotamian counterparts, they reflect underlying principles and concepts of cuneiform law[24] which are demonstratively Mesopotamian.

THE TIDENNŪTU TRANSACTION

One of the most interesting legal institutions in Nuzi is that of *tidennūtu.*[25] The name is derived from those texts which the Nuzi scribes classified by the superscription "a document of *tidennūtu.*" All of these documents describe the same basic transaction, in which two contracting parties exchange certain property.

The first *tidennūtu* transaction was published in 1918 by Scheil, who understood the text to be a lease contract.[26] Eight years later, Gadd published eleven *tidennūtu* documents which he specified as "tablets of loan," describing the institution as one of mutual loan.[27] Cuq, in his thorough review of Gadd's article, interpreted the institution as one representing a type of pledge transaction which secures a loan.[28] Thus one party is the debtor, who borrows certain commodities from the other party, the creditor, who retains the person or real estate received from the first party as a pledge. Koschaker agreed with Cuq in the main,[29] but differed with him on the right the creditor held over

23. E. A. Speiser, "Cuneiform Law and the History of Civilization," *PAPS, 107* (1963), 536 f. See also P. Koschaker, "Cuneiform Law," *Encyclopedia of the Social Sciences, 9* (1932), 211–19.

24. Speiser, *PAPS, 107* (1963), 537 f.

25. The etymology and meaning of this term will be discussed below in Chapter 4.

26. V. Scheil, *RA, 15* (1918), 66, where he designates the tablet as a "contrat d'affermage."

27. C. J. Gadd, *RA, 23* (1926), 55 f.

28. E. Cuq, "Les Tablettes de Kerkouk," *Journal des Savants* (1927), pp. 396 f.; cf. also his *Études sur le droit babylonien, les lois assyriennes, et les lois hittites* (Paris, Geuthner, 1929), pp. 422–26.

29. Koschaker, *NRUA*, p. 131; *Über einige griechische Rechtsurkunden aus den östlichen Randgebieten des Hellenismus,* Abhandlungen der Sächsischen Akademie der Wissenschaften, 42 (Leipzig, Hirzel, 1931), p. 83.

the pledge. Cuq considered the right of the creditor to be that of a lessee, with the tablet representing a rental contract.[30] But on the basis of certain affinities to sale terminology, Koschaker regarded the right of the creditor to be that of a buyer, with the tablet representing a sale contract with power of redemption by the seller.[31]

A subsequently published Nuzi tablet forced Koschaker to qualify his understanding of *tidennūtu* as a redeemable sale. The tablet (*HSS*, *5*, 56) is a sale-adoption contract in which a person sells land held by another in *tidennūtu* to a third party. It is evident from this text that the original owner retained ownership of the property, even though it was given to another person in *tidennūtu*. Since a *tidennūtu* transaction can therefore not be an outright sale, Koschaker modified his original interpretation[32] to the view that the *tidennūtu* contract implies a type of divided ownership[33] in which the debtor retains the primary title, but sells his right of use to the creditor.

Speiser, in an analysis of *tidennūtu* transactions based upon tablets published in the first Nuzi volume of the Harvard Semitic Series (*HSS*, *5*), categorized them as "mortgages with antichresis."[34] Thus he agreed with Cuq and Koschaker that the institution of *tidennūtu* was a type of security transaction, although he differed with them on certain details.[35] A similar conclusion was reached by Steele in his investigation of Nuzi real estate transactions. His summation states that "*ditennūtu*, insofar as real estate is concerned, refers to loans secured by real estate, the usufruct of which covered the interest involved."[36]

30. E. Cuq, *Journal des Savants* (1927), p. 396.

31. Koschaker, *NRUA*, pp. 135 f.; *Griech. Rechtsurk.*, pp. 83 f. Another point of difference concerns the right of the creditor over the profits derived from the pledge. Cuq (*Journal des Savants* [1927], p. 397) maintained that they are to be used by the creditor in lieu of interest, and if in excess of the current interest rates, they should logically be applied against the principal sum. However, Koschaker (*NRUA*, p. 137) considered the profits to be applicable only against the interest since the pledge is redeemed by the return of the principal sum.

32. Koschaker, *Griech. Rechtsurk.*, pp. 85 ff.

33. The concept of divided ownership is foreign to classical Roman Law, but it is known in Germanic law. (R. Huebner, *A History of Germanic Private Law* (transl. by F. S. Philbrick, Boston, Little, 1918), pp. 232 ff.) Koschaker's belief that the creditor possesses partial ownership of the land is based upon the similarity of certain stipulations in the *tidennūtu* document with those of sale contracts (Koschaker, *Griech. Rechtsurk.*, pp. 83 f.)

34. E. A. Speiser, "New Kirkuk Documents Relating to Security Transactions," *JAOS*, *52* (1932), 356.

35. Ibid., p. 356 n. 22, and pp. 361 f.

36. Steele, *Real Estate*, p. 49. I. Mendelsohn accepted this interpretation of *tidennūtu* in his study, *Slavery in the Ancient Near East* (New York, Oxford University Press, 1949), p. 29. Cf. Purves' review of Steele's discussion in "Commentary on Nuzi Real Property in the Light of Recent Studies," *JNES*, *4* (1945), 79 ff.

This consensus of opinion was challenged by H. Lewy.[37] Her point of departure was those tablets in which both parties furnish each other with the services of persons. Both Koschaker[38] and Speiser[39] had already noted the difficulty in interpreting such *tidennūtu* transactions as secured loans, since they record an identical exchange of values, namely persons. According to Lewy, these texts are in fact exchange documents in which the working capacity of the persons is the exchanged value. She maintained that in *tidennūtu* transactions no distinction is made in principle between persons, real estate, and movable goods. These all merely represent values which can be exploited by another party. Hence these items may replace one another in the individual contracts. Nevertheless, the essence of the *tidennūtu* transaction is always "an exchange of values capable of producing profits."[40] Thus H. Lewy viewed the institution *tidennūtu* as a mutual exchange in which there is no debtor–creditor relationship.[41]

From the preceding summary of the history of its interpretation, it may be seen that the nature of the *tidennūtu* transaction is still not clearly defined.[42] With the publication of the Nuzi tablets now nearing completion, the available material relating to *tidennūtu* has almost doubled since the appearance of the last study on the subject. There are now over two hundred tablets known which refer to this institution.[43] These texts seem to fall into two classes. The first group may be designated as real estate *tidennūtu*, in which land or buildings represent one of the exchanged values. The other may be designated as personal *tidennūtu* in which a person or persons represent one of the exchanged values. This entire corpus of material must be thoroughly analyzed. The two classes of *tidennūtu* contracts should at first be studied independently, since a distinct set of clauses, reflecting inherently different situations, is to be found in each group of documents. With each class serving as a countercheck to the other, a conclusive definition of *tidennūtu* may then be obtained by correlating the results of the two separate investigations. The Nuzi *tidennūtu* transaction should also be placed in the wider spectrum of Mesopotamian legal institutions, in order to broaden our understanding of it.

37. H. Lewy, "The *Titennūtu* Texts from Nuzi," *Or*, N.S. *10* (1941), 313–36.

38. See Koschaker, *NRUA*, 131 n. 7.

39. See Speiser, *JAOS*, *52* (1932), 355 n. 22.

40. Lewy, *Or* N.S., *10* (1941), 324.

41. Although Koschaker (Review of *JEN 6* in *OLZ*, 47 [1944], 103; *ZA*, *48* [1944], 192 n. 55) did not accept H. Lewy's proposed interpretation, I have been unable to find a formal rebuttal of her position in the subsequent literature. Cf. H. Petschow, *Neubabylonisches Pfandrecht*, Abhandlungen der Sächsischen Akademie der Wissenschaften, 48 (Berlin, Akademie-Verlag, 1956), 76 n. 226.

42. Cf. V. Korošec, "Keilschriftrecht," *Orientalisches Recht*, Handbuch der Orientalistik, *1*/3 (Leiden, Brill, 1964), 169 f.

43. For a listing of the Nuzi *tidennūtu* transactions, see Table 1.

The present study begins this undertaking. Its scope is limited to the class of personal *tidennūtu* and its purpose is fourfold: to present a detailed analysis of the personal *tidennūtu* contracts; to determine the nature of the transaction represented by these contracts; to bring this transaction into relationship with similar Mesopotamian institutions; and to consider the etymology and meaning of the term *tidennūtu*.

CHAPTER 2

The Institution of Personal Tidennūtu

METHODOLOGY

The corpus of Nuzi texts from which information concerning the institution of personal *tidennūtu* may be gleaned consists of fifty-two tablets. Determination of the nature of the personal *tidennūtu* transaction requires a detailed analysis of these texts. Since until now only a few more than half of these texts have been treated in various articles and monographs, the entire corpus is appended in translation, with pertinent textual notes. It may be formally divided into three categories (the texts are cited by the numbers under which they appear in the appendix, below):

1. *Tidennūtu* contracts
   Nos. 1–3, 5–10, 12, 14–16, 19–20, 22–26, 28–30, 32–36, 38–40, 42–52.
2. Declarations concerning *tidennūtu* transactions [1]
   Nos. 4, 11, 13, 21, 27, 31, 37, 41.
3. Lawsuits concerning *tidennūtu* transactions
   Nos. 17, 18.

An examination of the *tidennūtu* contracts reveals that they do not exhibit a uniformly complete set of clauses.[2] The question then arises as to what is the relation of each clause to the whole transaction; in other words, what inferences, if any, may be drawn from the presence or absence of certain clauses?[3]

1. The Nuzi *lišānu* documents take the form of personal, oral declarations before witnesses. This type of deed and its abbreviated "*umma* PN" form were discussed by Koschaker, *NRUA*, pp. 21 ff. For the relationship of the *lišānu*-document to the subjectively formulated deeds of Susa, Kultepe, Alalakh, and Ras Shamra, see Y. Muffs, *Studies in the Aramaic Legal Papyri from Elephantine*, Studia et Documenta ad Iura Orientis Antiqui Pertinentia, 8 (Leiden, Brill, 1969), 175 f.

2. For a distribution chart of the various clauses see Table 2.

3. Cf. Greenberg's treatment of a similar problem with regard to the Nuzi *ḫāpiru* texts (*The Ḫāb/piru*, p. 66).

The key to this problem is to be sought in our understanding of the legal position of the written contract at Nuzi.

It emerged from H. Liebesny's treatment of legal procedure in Nuzi[4] that the written contract had secondary value as evidence in the Nuzi courts. Liebesny concluded that "the preeminence of the document as proof in legal procedure seems as foreign to the law of Nuzi as it was to Babylonian law."[5] In Nuzi, witnesses were the principal means of proof,[6] and in case of a lawsuit it was the responsibility of the witnesses to report on the details of the original transaction.[7] Thus the Nuzi legal document seems to have served as a summary of the transaction, recording the names of the witnesses, and not as a carefully formulated, all-inclusive written contract. If this be so, there is some justification for combining the various clauses appearing in the personal *tidennūtu* documents in order to obtain a synoptic view of the institution as a whole. But one must not lose sight of the individuality of every contract: each text should be judged separately as to whether its provisions are applicable to the other documents, or whether they represent isolated elements operative in it alone.

In this chapter the personal *tidennūtu* transaction is analyzed by examining the various clauses incorporated in the documents, and by attempting to determine the relevance, to the class as a whole, of provisions specific to an individual contract. A unified characterization of personal *tidennūtu* will then be offered, based on the analyses of the individual clauses.

THE ELEMENTS OF PERSONAL TIDENNŪTU CONTRACTS

All of the personal *tidennūtu* contracts exhibit the same basic scheme, in which the two contracting parties exchange certain property: PN receives certain commodities[8] from PN_2; PN_2, in turn, receives a person or persons from PN. When PN returns the given commodities, he reclaims the person or persons from PN_2.

In the analysis which follows, PN has been designated as Party D—the contracting party who has the right to dissolve the transaction by returning the

4. This study has been published in the following three articles: "The Oath of the King in the Legal Procedure of Nuzi," *JAOS*, *61* (1941), 62–63; "Evidence in Nuzi Legal Procedure," *JAOS*, *61* (1941), 130–42; "The Administration of Justice in Nuzi," *JAOS*, *63* (1943), 128–44. See also Hayden, *Court Procedure at Nuzu*, pp. 26 ff.

5. Liebesny, *JAOS*, *61* (1941), 131; Hayden, *Court Procedure at Nuzu*, p. 29.

6. Liebesny, *JAOS*, *61* (1941), 132. This is demonstrated by those cases in which the witnesses are called to testify even though a document exists (*AASOR*, *16*, Nos. 30 and 33); and by those cases in which the defendant is requested to produce witnesses even though the accusation of the plaintiffs is supported by a document (*JEN*, *6*, 662).

7. Ibid., p. 131.

8. These commodities usually consist of metals, grains, domestic animals, cloth, and the like; occasionally, slaves are also given.

received commodities; PN_2 has been designated as Party C—the other contracting party.

Title of the Tidennūtu Contract

Objectively formulated contracts.[9] Of the forty-one contracts whose opening lines are preserved,[10] eight do not bear any title.[11] All of the rest are expressly titled *ṭuppi tidennu* "a *tidennu* document" (twice),[12] or *ṭuppi tidennūti* "a document of *tidennu*-ship" (thirty times).[13] This title stands alone in three contracts;[14] elsewhere it is augmented by various details. Six times it is described as *ṭuppi tidennūti* of Party C[15]; once (text 2) it is called the *ṭuppi tidennūti* of both contracting parties; but in most cases (twenty-three times) it is named as the *ṭuppi tidennūti* of Party D. The variations in title do not depend on differences among scribes, since contracts written by the same scribe exhibit different formulations,[16] and the title, though common, was not essential to the contract. If the title reflected the commissioning parties, every title should have contained the name of one of the contracting parties, and all texts should have had titles. If anything more than the whim of the moment determined these divergences, it is not evident.

Subjectively formulated declarations.[17] These documents contain either the introductory formula *lišānšu ša* PN . . . *iqtabi* "Tongue of PN—he has declared . . ." or its abbreviated form *umma* PN "thus (declares) PN." All of the declarations concerning *tidennūtu* are made by Party D, with the exception of text 27, in which the declaration is made by the sons of Party D, who are being handed over to Party C.

Contracting Parties

Party C. In all of the *tidennūtu* transactions Party C is represented by a single person. The role of Party C is threefold: to provide Party D with certain commodities; to hold the person given to him by Party D until the contract is terminated; and then to get back the given commodities from Party D.

9. For a complete listing of these *tidennūtu* contracts, see above, p. 11.
10. The opening lines of texts 10 and 47 are broken.
11. Texts 3, 7, 14, 20, 28, 30, 32, and 49.
12. Texts 25 and 29. This may, however, be a scribal error of omitting the final *ti* syllable.
13. Text 34 offers the variant form, *ṭuppi tidennāti*, in which the suffix-*ātu* (identical with that of the feminine plural) is used in the formation of the abstract noun, rather than the more common -*ūtu* suffix.
14. Texts 25, 43, and 50.
15. Texts 16, 23, 24, 26, 36 and 44.
16. Cf. texts 12, 20, and 24.
17. For a complete listing of these tablets, see above, p. 11.

One contract, however, records an exceptional procedure. In text 49, Party D receives certain commodities from two people (A and B). But instead of returning these commodities to them, he must return them to a third party who is holding the person given by Party D. Thus it is the third party who performs the role of Party C by holding the person and by getting back the commodities. If this be so, what is the role of A and B? It would seem that they are in debt to the third party (C), and in payment of this debt they deliver certain commodities to Party D, on behalf of Party C.[18]

Party D. In most of the *tidennūtu* transactions Party D is also a single person. There are four contracts, however, in which Party D consists of two individuals, either two brothers,[19] or a mother and son.[20] The role of Party D is threefold: to provide Party C with a person or persons; to receive commodities from Party C; and to return these commodities to Party C.

Here, too, there is one contract which records an exceptional procedure. In text 50, one party provides Party C with a person and obligates himself to return the received commodities to Party C. Nevertheless, another party (E) receives the commodities given by Party C. It is evident that the first party performs the main role of Party D by providing a person and by returning the given commodities. The other party (E) may then be supposed a prior creditor of Party D, to whom Party C is authorized by Party D to deliver the commodities.[21]

It may be stated here that, with regard to the lawsuits, the litigants in text 17 are the sons of Party C vs. the person given by Party D. In text 18, the litigants are Party C vs. the *ewuru*-heir of Party D. In both lawsuits, Party C wins the case.

Property Given by Party C

The corpus of *tidennūtu* texts furnishes forty-eight complete lists of the commodities given Party D by Party C. For the most part they consist of property clearly representing capital[22]: metals (gold, silver, tin, copper, bronze); domestic animals (cattle, asses, sheep, goats); produce (barley, wheat, emmer, oil); manufactured goods (cloth); implements (wheels); or a combination of the above commodities. In nine of the documents Party C

18. Cf. text 52 in which Party D receives the given commodities from the representative(?) of Party C.

19. Texts 5 and 35.

20. Texts 6 and 39.

21. Cf. text 20 in which Party D, upon his receiving certain commodities from Party C, assigns them to a third party.

22. Note the use of the term kù-babbar-meš: *kaspū* "money" when referring to the commodities given by Party C in texts 14, 34, 38, 42, and 51.

provides Party D with slaves, raising the question whether these transactions, in which each party provides the other with persons, are similar to the other personal *tidennūtu* contracts. This issue is important for determining the nature of the personal *tidennūtu* transaction, and it will be dealt with in its appropriate place.[23]

In order to compare the values of these commodities, a common unit of exchange is required. Cross, in her treatment of the economic aspects of the Nuzi texts, has already related the different kinds of movable property to a uniform standard of silver wherever possible.[24] The following table of relative values is based primarily on her study:

Metals:	1 shekel of gold ~ 9 shekels of silver[25]
	1 shekel of tin ~ .005 shekel of silver[26]
	1 shekel of copper ~ .0025 shekel of silver[27]
	1 shekel of bronze ~ .0025 shekel of silver[28]
Produce:	1 homer of barley ~ 1.5 shekels of silver[29]
Livestock:	1 goat ~ .95 shekel of silver[30]
	1 sheep ~ 1.33 shekels of silver[31]
	1 ass ~ 6.67 shekels of silver[32]
	1 ox ~ 10 shekels of silver[33]

23. Below, pp. 41–43.

24. For a summary presentation, consult Cross, *Property*, p. 62 or Steele, *Real Estate*, pp. 34–35.

25. The tablet SMN 2615, by which Cross has established this ratio (*Property*, p. 39), has recently been published as *HSS*, *19*, 127.

26. The second half of *HSS*, *19*, 127, which was not utilized by Cross, discusses the relation of tin to silver. Line 9 reads *šum-ma* a n - n a - m e š 3 - t a - a n m a - n a - t a - a n, "If (the aforementioned 27 shekels of silver are to be paid in) tin, (it is to be calculated as) three minas per (shekel of silver)." Accordingly, the ratio of tin to silver is 180:1. However, in a similar formulation *HSS*, *14*, 37:15 states that the ratio of tin to silver is 240:1. Hence Cross' conclusion of at least 200:1 (*Property*, p. 47) will be maintained.

27. Ibid., p. 44.

28. The cost of bronze was only slightly higher than that of copper (ibid. p. 46). Note, however, the ratio given in *HSS*, *14*, 37:16.

29. Ibid., p. 35. *HSS*, *19*, 126 gives the price of one shekel of gold for nineteen homers of barley. This low rate of .47 shekel of silver for one homer of barley is to be compared with the texts cited by Cross in *Property*, p. 35 n. 75. Note that in *HSS*, *19*, 126, the barley is to be delivered in the month of *Ulūlu*. At pre-harvest rates, one homer of barley might be as high as 4 shekels of silver (*Property*, p. 36, n. 81).

30. *Property*, p. 31.

31. Ibid., p. 28.

32. Ibid., p. 21.

33. Ibid., p. 19.

Cloth: 1 cloth ~ 5 shekels of silver[34]
Slaves: 1 slave ~ 30 shekels of silver[35]

The relative value at Nuzi of oil and of a set of wheels is unknown, as is the relative value of wheat and of emmer. However, for the present study the value of these grains will be assumed to be at least equal to that of barley.

The above table represents only an approximation to the standard value of these commodities. Prices of produce are difficult to evaluate because they fluctuate according to the time of the year. The values of livestock and slaves likewise vary with sex, age, and condition. The cost of cloth depends upon its quality, measurements, weight, and processing. Nevertheless, these approximate figures for converting the commodities given by Party C into a common unit of exchange yield comparative data which can be used to determine the nature of the personal *tidennūtu* transaction.

The following chart presents the forty-eight complete lists of the property given by Party C, and their relative value in shekels of silver:

Text	*Property given by Party C*	*Value*
44	20 shekels of gold	180
45	20 shekels of gold	180
46	20 shekels of gold	180
47	20 shekels of gold	180
48	20 shekels of gold	180
29	30 shekels of silver; 2 homers of barley	33
10	50 minas of tin	15

34. Texts presented by Cross (ibid., p. 53) show the value of cloth strips to range from 2 to 7.5 shekels of silver. It should be noted that the *ṣubātu* in Nuzi is quite standardized as to size and weight of wool.

35. As correctly interpreted by Saarisalo (*Slaves*, p. 70), *JEN*, *2*, 195 seems to reflect a royal decree setting the price of an imported Lullian slave at 30 shekels of silver. The price of male slaves in Nuzi slave-sale documents support this value (ibid.). However, Saarisalo's estimated value of a slave boy at 2 minas of gold and 2 minas of silver (ibid., p. 71) is based on an erroneous reconstruction of *JEN*, *2*, 113:10–11 (ibid., p. 36). The lines should read: 1 *ṣu-ḫa-ru ša* 2 [*i*]-*na* [*a*]*m-ma-ti*! [*u*] 3 + [?] *ú-ba-ni*.

Text *JEN*, *5*, 515 sets the price of a slave boy at 30 shekels of silver and that of a female slave at 40 shekels (*Property*, p. 23; cf. *HSS*, *14*, 37:13–14). It should be noted, however, that *HSS*, *9*, 25 records the sale of a female slave for 20 shekels of silver. Therefore the value of 30 shekels will be used for a female slave. The value of a slave girl will also be assumed to be 30 shekels of silver.

The price of a slave girl in *HSS*, *19*, 112 (8 seah of barley) and that of a female slave and her son in *HSS*, *19*, 113 and 114 (2 homers 4 seah of barley) are extremely low. These recorded transactions were probably not normal ones. On the other hand, *AASOR*, *16*, no. 95 records the extremely high rate of 60 shekels of silver for the delivery of a female slave.

Text	*Property given by Party C*	*Value*
40	40 minas of tin; 10 minas of bronze	13.5
34	35 minas of tin; 1 homer of barley; 1 homer of wheat	13.5
41	30 minas of tin; 2 cloths	19
5	20 minas of tin; 16 homers of barley; 10 sheep; 1 cloth	48
12	20 minas of tin	6
31	12 minas of tin	3.6
50	12 minas of tin	3.6
6	10 minas of tin; 2 sheep	5.66
38	30 minas of bronze; 8 sheep; 8 goats	13.59
35	29 minas of bronze	4.35
2	4 talents, 20 minas of copper	39
30	3 talents of copper	27
49	3 talents of copper	27
15	1 talent of copper	9
32	30 minas of copper	2.25
11	20 minas of copper; 2.5 homers of barley	4.05
1	11 homers of barley	16.5
51	10 homers of barley; 1 ox; 1 sheep; 1 cloth; 2 *tallu* of oil	31.33+ oil
3	10 homers of barley	15
36	10 homers of barley	15
16	8 homers of barley	12
7	3 homers 50 *qa* of barley; 1 cow	15.25
52	3 homers of emmer; 1.5 homers of barley	6.75
4	3 homers of barley	4.5
28	3 homers of barley	4.5
14	2 homers of barley; 1 sheep; 1 cloth	9.33
43	1 homer of barley	1.5
9	8 asses; 1 set of wheels	51.16+ wheels
39	11 sheep; 4 goats	18.46
8	10 sheep	13.33
42	5 sheep; 1 cloth	11.66
18	12 sheep; 1 male slave	45.99
19	2 male slaves; 2 female slaves	120
20	1 slave boy; 1 slave girl	60
21	1 male slave	30
22	1 male slave	30
25	1 male slave	30
26	1 male slave	30

Text	*Property given by Party C*	*Value*
27	1 slave boy	30
23	1 female slave	30
24	price of 1 male slave	30

The value of the property given by Party C ranges from 1.5 to 180 shekels of silver. The mean value is 38.5 shekels of silver, with a standard deviation of 52.1, which reflects the great variation among the individual values. The mode is 30 shekels of silver, and the median is 17.5 shekels of silver.

Party D may dissolve the *tidennūtu* relationship by returning the received commodities and reclaiming the given person from Party C. However, it is not clear whether these commodities must be returned in kind or in value.[36] Most of the contracts state that Party D shall return the specified commodities so that the property given by Party C is probably to be returned in kind. Nevertheless, other contracts state that Party D shall return the capital (*kaspū*), which seems to indicate that any commodities of equivalent value would be acceptable.

The terms describing the transfer of the property given by Party C are these: Party C "gives" (*nadānu*) it to Party D, who "receives" (*leqū*) it. In fourteen of the forty-eight instances[37] this terminology is augmented by the expression *ana tidennūti* "(to give or receive the property given by Party C) in *tidennu*-ship."

Property given by Party D

In all personal *tidennūtu* transactions the property given by Party D is a human being. In twenty-five of the fifty-two transactions Party D gives himself to Party C,[38] while in eighteen cases Party D delivers his son.[39] There are single instances in which a brother (text 5), a brother/son (text 6), and a sister/daughter (text 39) is given to Party C. In only two texts is a slave of Party D given to Party C.[40]

In four transactions more than one human being is delivered to Party C. In these cases the persons are respectively: two sons (text 27); sons (text 50); Party D and his two sons (text 2); Party D, his sons and his household (text 20).

It may be inferred from text 37 (line 4), in which the person declares

36. The right of a debtor to repay his debt by a different medium of exchange is discussed in the Laws of Hammurapi, §§ 51, M, and R. (Cf. Driver & Miles, *The Babylonian Laws, 1*, 147 ff.).

37. Texts 1, 2, 7, 11, 13, 15, 19, 22, 32, 34, 35, 39, 40, and 49.

38. Texts 1, 7, 8, 10–12, 15, 19, 22, 24, 26, 28, 31–38, 44, 46, 47, 49, and 51.

39. Texts 3, 4, 9, 13, 14, 16–18, 23, 25, 30, 40–43, 45, 48, and 52.

40. Texts 21 and 29.

tidennāk "I am a *tidennu*," that the technical term for the person given in exchange by Party D is *tidennu*. This is corroborated by the occurrence of *tidennu* in text 21 (line 16), and of *tidenna* in text 35 (line 11).

The terminology describing the transfer of persons to Party C is more varied than that describing the delivery of commodities to Party D. In twenty transactions[41] the verb *nadānu* "to give" is employed. However, twenty-eight texts describe the transfer of the person by referring to his subjection to the authority of Party C, expressed by the phrases *ina bīt*(*i*) PN *wašābu*[42]/*erēbu*[43] "to stay in/enter the house of PN (Party C)." In thirty-four instances the delivery of an individual to Party C is further specified by the phrase *ana tidennūti* "for *tidennu*-ship."[44]

Since no pattern can be established between the different phrases describing the transfer and the distribution of the other clauses, it may be assumed that the differences in terminology do not reflect any inherent differences in the nature of the transaction. The variation in phraseology is rather to be ascribed to the stylistic preference of individual scribes.[45]

Only six tablets[46] state plainly that the person given by party D is to perform certain services while under the authority of Party C. Twenty-six other contracts[47] stipulate provisions in case of the person's delinquency in serving Party C although his obligation to work is not explicitly stated. Furthermore, text 30, which contains neither the work obligation nor the delinquency clause, clearly indicates by its penalty clause that the services of a weaver are one of the main elements of the contract. Thus thirty-three out of the forty-five completely preserved contracts (73%) clearly refer to the services of the person given by Party D. As for the remaining twelve documents,[48] it may be assumed on the strength of text 30 that the rendering of services by the person given by Party D is probably implicit in the *tidennūtu* transaction.

41. Texts 3–6, 9, 13, 14, 18, 21, 23, 25, 29, 30, 39, 40–43, 48, and 52.

42. Texts 2, 10, 15–17, 19, 22, 24, 32, 35, 36, 44–46, 49, and 50.

43. The verb *erēbu* appears in both the G and Š stems. Texts 1, 8, 12, 20, 26, 27, 31, 33, 34, 38, and 51.

44. In connection with the verb *wašābu*, the phrase occurs six times (texts 10, 24, 32, 44, 45 and 50). With the exception of text 48, it always modifies the verb *nadānu*; and with the exception of texts 20, 27 and 33, it always modifies the verb *erēbu*.

45. Note that the scribe Tarmi-tešub uses the terms *ana tidennūti nadānu* (texts 29 and 40), while Taya shows preference for the expression *ina bīt*(*i*) Party C *wašābu* (texts 19, 22, 46, and 47). However, the scribes were not always consistent in their terminology, as is evident from the documents written by the above-mentioned Taya (text 48) and by Sunzu (texts 12, 20, and 24).

46. Texts 12, 27, 28, 31, 32, and 35.

47. Texts 7–11, 13, 15, 16, 20, 22–24, 26, 29, 33–36, 38–40, 42, 46–48, and 52.

48. Texts 1–5, 19, 21, 25, 41, 44, 45, and 51.

The stipulated work is most often described simply as kin: *šipru*[49] "task, work." Occasionally it is defined more closely as harvesting (texts 31, 32), orchard work (text 28), meadow work (text 27), weaving (texts 30, 37), or carpentry (text 29).

The value of services performed by the person given by Party D may be calculated on the basis of the daily compensatory payment which Party D must give Party C in case of the person's failure to work. This payment—one mina of copper—is specified as the person's daily hire. On a yearly basis then, these services would be valued at about 360 minas of copper which is equivalent to approximately 54 shekels of silver.

When Party D returns the commodities received from Party C, the person is freed from the authority of Party C. Some contracts[50] state simply that Party D takes back (*leqū*) the person, but most of the documents employ terms denoting liberation from servitude: *waṣū* "to go out," in the G and Š stem[51]; *ašar ḫadū alāku*[52] or *ašar libbišu alāku* "go where one pleases" (text 10); and *rēqu* "to distance oneself" (text 51). The choice of terminology again seems to be at the discretion of the scribe,[53] since consistent differentiation affecting the other clauses cannot be discerned.

Duration of the Arrangement

Indefinite duration clause

immatimē kaspī ša pī ṭuppi annī PN *ana* PN_2 *utarru u* PN_3 *ileqqe.*
Whenever PN returns the money specified in this document to PN_2, he shall then take back PN_3.

This and similar clauses imply that the contract is of indefinite duration, since the *tidennūtu* arrangement is terminated whenever Party D returns the received commodities to Party C. Twenty-two contracts contain such a clause allowing Party D to terminate the contract at will.[54]

Definite duration clause

immatimē x *šanāti imtalū kaspī ša pī ṭuppi annī* PN *ana* PN_2 *utār u* PN_3 *ileqqe.*

49. Texts 7–11, 13, 16, 17, 20, 22–24, 26, 33–36, 38–40, 42, 43, 46–48, and 52.
50. Texts 3, 4, 16, 21, 23, 25, 39, 42, 43, and 52.
51. Texts 1, 2, 7, 11, 12, 15, 20, 22, 24, 26–31, 34–36, 38, 40, 41, and 46–48.
52. Texts 8, 19, and 45.
53. The scribe Elḫib-tilla (texts 4 and 52) uses the term *leqū*, while Sunzu (texts 12, 20, and 24) and Tarmi-tešub (texts 29 and 40) prefer *waṣū*. Note that Taya who generally employs the term *waṣū* (texts 22, 46–48) also uses the term *ašar ḫadū alāku* (text 19).
54. Texts 1, 2, 4, 7, 8, 10, 15, 19, 21–24, 27, 38, 39, 41, and 44–49.

Whenever x years have elapsed, PN shall return the money specified in this document to PN_2 and thus take back PN_3.

Twenty-four contracts stipulate a definite term during which the *tidennūtu* arrangement is to remain in effect. These terms are: to the completion of the harvest (texts 31, 32); two years (text 9); three years (texts 11, 42); four years (texts 6, 35); five years (texts 40, 52); six years (texts 14, 43); eight years (text 16); ten years[55]; twenty years (texts 3, 26); fifty years (texts 30, 51); and the death of the person given by Party D.[56]

Text 33 is the only contract which does not have a duration clause. But neither does it contain a statement that the exchange of properties between the contracting parties was to be permanent. It may therefore be assumed that the arrangement was for an indefinite period of time which was not stipulated in the document.

The question of whether the definite and indefinite duration clauses represent two different types of *tidennūtu* transactions will be dealt with in a later section.[57]

Delinquency Clause

šumma ina 1 *ūmi šipiršu ša* PN_2 PN_3 *izzib* 1 ma-na urudu *uriḫulšu ša ūmi u ūmi* PN *ana* PN_2 *umalla.*

If PN_3 neglects the work of PN_2 for a single day, PN shall pay to PN_2 one mina of copper, his daily *uriḫul.*

Responsibility. Thirty-one of the forty-five fully preserved *tidennūtu* transactions (70%) include provisions concerning the failure of the person given by Party D to work for Party C.[58] An obligation to compensate Party C for the person's delinquency is always imposed on Party D.[59] If Party D consists of two people, the obligation to compensate falls on both.[60]

Although text 16 clearly obligates Party D to bear responsibility for his son's default, nevertheless in the lawsuit, text 17, based on the above contract, it is the son who is sued for his own delinquency. It may therefore be assumed that Party D had already died,[61] but the contract remained in force as a self-*tidennu* transaction. In self-*tidennu* transactions, the person given to Party C is identical with Party D and assumes the responsibility for his own failure

55. Texts 12, 25, 28, 29, 34, and 36.

56. Text 5; text 20 terminates the arrangement at the death of Party D who, together with his sons and household, is being held as *tidennu.*

57. Below, p. 36.

58. Texts 7–11, 13, 15–17, 20, 22–24, 26, 28, 29, 31–36, 38–40, 42, 43, 46–48, and 52.

59. Texts 9, 13, 16, 23, 29, 35, 40, 42, 43, and 52.

60. Texts 35 and 39.

61. Note that it is the sons of Party C who prosecute the case.

to work.[62] Text 36 records the appointment of a guarantor (*māḫiṣ pūti*)[63] who is responsible for compensation in case of Party D's delinquency. In text 34, Party D declares that if he neglects the service of Party C, his wife and children may be seized for compensation.

Terminology. In the contracts containing a delinquency clause, failure to work is expressed by the following terminology: *šipra ezēbu* "to leave or neglect the work[64];" *ina šipri rēqu* "to distance oneself from work[65];" *ina šipri paṭāru* "to depart from work[66];" *ištu šipri ḫesū* "to conceal oneself from work[67];" *šipra wuššuru* "to abandon the work" (text 38); and *lā ašbu* "not be present" (text 15).

Since the semantic range of these terms is so closely related, it is very difficult to conceive that each term represents a different type of delinquency.[68] The variation in terminology seems rather to be another example of the lack of rigidity in the formulation of Nuzi legal documents. Nevertheless, the problem still exists as to what circumstances caused the delinquency of the person given by Party D. Failure to work may result from either the physical absence of the person from the estate of Party C; the inability of the person to work, most commonly due to illness or accident; or the refusal of the person to perform the assigned work. The terminology clearly indicates that physical absence is the major concern of this provision, and it cannot be decided with any degree of certainty whether the other two circumstances are also to be included within the purview of the delinquency clause. Which party is to bear the loss caused by an accidental incapacitation of the person cannot be determined from the evidence at hand. Whether or not the deliquency clause also covered refusal to work may depend upon the degree of the person's subservience to Party C. If Party C does not have the authority to discipline the person, it seems likely that Party C should be able to claim compensation from Party D for the person's refusal to work. But if Party C does have such authority, Party D may perhaps not be held responsible for the person's refusal to work.

Meaning of the term uriḫul. With the exception of three contracts,[69] the failure

62. Texts 7, 8, 10, 11, 15, 20, 22, 24, 26, 28, 31–33, and 38.
63. The role of the guarantor in Nuzi has been studied by Cassin, "La Caution à Nuzi," *RA*, *34* (1937), 154–68.
64. Texts 8–11, 13, 22, 24, 26, 29, 31, 33, 34, 39, 40, 42, 46, and 52.
65. Texts 17, 20, 23, 32, and 48.
66. Texts 16, 17, 28, 36, and 43.
67. Texts 7, 8, and 35.
68. Note the use of *ina šipri paṭāru* together with *ina šipri rēqu* in the same document, text 17 (lines 13 and 16). Text 8 (lines 17–18) employs the verbs *ezēbu* and *ḫesū* in formulating this clause.
69. Texts 46–48.

of the person given by Party D to work entails monetary payment to compensate Party C for the loss of service. This compensatory payment is called *uriḫul* and occurs most frequently with the possessive pronominal suffix as *uriḫulšu/ša* "his *uriḫul*."[70] That the pronominal suffix refers to the person given by Party D, appears from a similar usage in a non-*tidennūtu* contract: *JEN*, *3*, 273:18 ff. stipulates that, in case of a breach of contract, the oxen which had been withheld from their original owner must be returned together with their *uriḫul*. The pronominal suffix thus refers to that property of whose use the injured party has been deprived.

The term *uriḫul* was first translated by Speiser as "upkeep."[71] But on the basis of new occurrences of the term, Koschaker reinterpreted it as the sum representing the loss of profits due to non-possession of a property.[72] Subsequently, Speiser confirmed this meaning and translated the term as "compensation."[73] However, a more exact delineation of the meaning of *uriḫul* can now be offered.

The context in which *uriḫul* most frequently appears is the delinquency clause of the personal *tidennūtu* transactions. Occurrences in contexts other than the personal *tidennūtu* contracts[74] bear out the main purport of the term, i.e. compensation for losses resulting from non-possession or non-use. But such a meaning leaves undetermined the method by which compensation is to be calculated, and it is especially difficult to ascertain the compensation for losses resulting from the non-possession of a bow (*JEN*, *4*, 374:9).

An important clue to the meaning of the term *uriḫul* is provided by the personal *tidennūtu* contract text 48. Lines 9–10 stipulate: guškin máš nu *išu u* PN *uriḫulša* nu *išu* "the gold does not bear interest and PN does not receive his *uriḫul*." This passage recalls the Neo-Babylonian antichretic clauses which state: *idī amēlūtu yānu u ḫubulli kaspi yānu* "There is no *idū* for the slave and no interest on the silver."[75] If the two are equivalent, *uriḫul* stands for *idū* "wages, hire." The use of the term *uriḫul* (wages, hire) in the personal *tidennūtu* delinquency clauses, as well as in the other contexts mentioned, would then signify that the compensation is to be based upon the

70. Texts 7, 9, 10, 22–24, 33–35, 39, 40, 42, 43, and 48.

71. *JAOS*, *47* (1927), 47. This interpretation was accepted by Koschaker (*NRUA*, p. 16) and by Saarisalo (*Slaves*, p. 52).

72. *OLZ*, *35* (1932), 405. Cf. Chiera, *AJSL*, *47* (1930), 285.

73. *AASOR*, *16* (1935–36), 128.

74. Mention is made of the *uriḫul* of slaves (*HSS*, *19*, 118:13, 128:20), of animals (oxen: *JEN*, *3*, 273:19, *JEN*, *4*, 349:23, 374:7; horse: *JEN*, *4*, 361:35; ass: *UCP*, *9*, 1:53), and of a bow (*JEN*, *4*, 374:9), in compensation for these having been withheld from their owner.

75. For variations of the antichretic clause, see Petschow, *Pfandrecht*, p. 103 and n. 314.

hire of the delinquent person, i.e. the amount which the injured party would have to spend in order to hire a replacement during the period of delinquency. That the compensation is based on hire seems to be confirmed by the following lexical entry dealing with pledge law (*Ḫḫ*, *1*, 367 ff. [*MSL*, *5*, 40:2 ff.]) which states: u_4 GÀN-ba-an-dag u_4 1-kam bán-še-ta-àm á-bi ì-ág-gá = *u_4-mu ša ip-par-ku-ú u_4-mu-kal* bán-ta-àm *še-im i-di-šu i-man-da-ad* "for the time when he (the pledged slave) has discontinued working, he (the debtor) will measure out one seah of barley for each day as his wages (i.e. in order to pay a replacement)."[76] Comparison of this lexical entry with the delinquency clause of the personal *tidennūtu* contracts reveals a close parallelism between the use of *uriḫul* and *idū*. Both terms also appear with the third person possessive pronominal suffix.

Penalties incurred by delinquency. In the delinquency clause of the personal *tidennūtu* transactions, the term *uriḫul* usually occurs in apposition to a specified sum.[77] In one contract (text 31) this sum is set at one seah of barley per day, which, according to Nuzi text *HSS*, *19*, 118:13 f., is the daily hire (*uriḫul*) of a slave.[78] It is interesting that this sum is identical to the compensatory payment stipulated in the lexical entry *Ḫḫ 1*, 369, mentioned above. The sum most commonly imposed in the delinquency clauses of the personal *tidennūtu* contracts, however, is one mina of copper. That these two amounts are equal in value may be shown by converting them into silver[79]; the result in each case is approximately .15 shekel of silver.

Three tablets do not specify the compensatory payments in terms of a definite monetary sum. Text 7 states that Party D shall make compensation on the basis of the daily wage of the person given to Party C, and text 22 similarly prescribes that payments are to be calculated on the basis of the hire

76. Cf. *CAD*, I–J, p. 17a. The equation in the Ḫurro-Sumerian vocabulary of Ras-Shamra (F. Thureau-Dangin, "Vocabulaires de Ras-Shamra," *Syria*, *12* (1931), 242) á = *ut-ḫu-ru* = *i-du* does not negate the thesis that *uriḫul* corresponds to Akkadian *idū*; the preceding entries in the vocabulary (*pūtu*, *šuplu*, *mīlu*, and *rupšu*) clearly show that in this context á = *idu* refers to "side" and not to "wages."

77. In texts 15, 16, and 36 the term *uriḫul* is omitted.

78. Cf. *MSL*, *1*, 103:20 which also designates this amount as the daily hire (*idū*) of a slave. This data adds further weight to the equating of *uriḫul* with *idū*.

According to text *HSS*, *5*, 6:8–9 one seah of barley represents the hire (*igru*) of a man. If this stipulated sum refers to a daily wage, then the use of the term *igru* in connection with this sum would clearly indicate that *uriḫul* is the equivalent of the Akkadian terms *idū* and *igru* (wages, hire).

79. Cross, *Property*, pp. 35, 44. Also compare *AASOR*, *16*, No. 95:10 ff. with *HSS*, *19*, 128:20 ff.; both contracts stipulate fines for an identical breach of contract, i.e. non-delivery of a purchased slave at the specified time. In *AASOR*, *16*, No. 95 the fine is given as one mina of copper per day while in *HSS*, *19*, 128 it is one seah of barley per day.

of a slave. The clause in text 20 (line 20) is partially broken, but it may be safely restored as [*ú-ri-ḫul*] *ša* 1 anše *ú-ma-al-la* "he shall pay the hire of an ass." However, the incongruousness of this compensation recommends a reading *uriḫul ša* 1 ⟨ìr⟩^{du_4} [80] *umalla* "He shall pay the hire of a slave."

In three contracts, each with the same Party C and the same property given by Party C, the delinquency clause differs from all the other documents. Texts 46–48 stipulate that, if the person given by Party D shirks from the service of Party C, the commodities given by Party C will begin to accrue interest. In these cases, therefore, the delinquency of the person nullifies the *tidennūtu* transaction and the contract automatically assumes the nature of a regular loan with interest.

Whether the penalty for delinquency applies in those *tidennūtu* contracts which lack a delinquency clause remains to be discussed. In view of the summary, non-inclusive nature of the Nuzi legal documents, mere absence of the clause does not prove that the penalty did not apply. Since the services of the person given by Party D are such an integral part of the transaction, and since the amount of the compensatory payments is so uniformly established, it seems very likely that these provisions do apply to these other *tidennūtu* transactions. Nevertheless, one point remains problematic. It has already been noted that texts 46–48 exhibit a unique provision in their delinquency clause: upon the person's failure to work, items given by Party C begin to accrue interest. These texts form a group with texts 44 and 45; all texts have the same Party C and the same highly valued commodities given by Party C. Yet the latter two texts lack a delinquency clause. Did these transactions also include the unique provision for the accumulation of interest, in these cases attested to aurally by the witnesses but not recorded in the contract? Or did they include the more common penalty of one mina of copper per day? Although it would seem reasonable to interpret these two contracts as interest-accruing, together with the others of their group, no definite conclusion can be reached on this point.

Flight, Disappearance, or Death of the Person given by Party D

This section will deal with those documents which do not record self-*tidennu* transactions. The corresponding clause in self-*tidennu* transactions will be discussed in connection with the flight, disappearance, or death of Party D.

Only four documents make reference to the flight, disappearance, or death of the person given by Party D. Since two of them (texts 16 and 40) contain a delinquency clause as well, a distinction must be made between the clauses.

80. The writing of *ardu* as a logogram with an accompanying phonetic complement is quite common in Nuzi texts, e.g. Gadd, *RA*, *23* (1926), No. 54:5; *HSS*, *9*, 13:5; *HSS*, *19*, 121:2, 128:6.

The most apparent difference is that flight, disappearance, and death represent the permanent, as opposed to the temporary, absence of the person given by Party D. If correctly restored, text 16 stipulates that, upon the death of the person (a son), Party D is to provide Party C with another son. According to this contract then, Party C will accept monetary compensation for the temporary absence of the person, but in the event of a permanent absence, he demands to be furnished with another person. In text 40, the formulation of the flight or disappearance clause is very general: in case of the flight or disappearance of the person, Party D must make full payment (*umalla*). Since this text also contains a delinquency clause, the most likely interpretation seems to be that this contract also differentiates between temporary and permanent absence. In the former case, compensatory payment must be made; but in the latter, Party D must make full payment, i.e. give back the commodities received from Party C, thus terminating the contract.

The remaining two contracts which refer to the permanent absence of the person given by Party D do not contain the usual delinquency clause. In text 5, the person's death entails the return of commodities received from Party C, thus terminating the transaction. This contract therefore supports the interpretation of text 40 advanced above. Text 21 stipulates that Party D bears the responsibility for the death, disappearance, and flight of the person, but does not specify what action this entails.

For the status of all of the other contracts which do not contain a clause on the flight, disappearance, or death of the person given by Party D, we must depend on inference. Since it is hard to believe that Party C would protect himself against the temporary absence of the person but not against his permanent absence, it must be assumed that Party C is also protected in the case of flight, disappearance, or death. This protection may take the form of compensatory payments (in which case the flight, disappearance, or death is treated as a failure to work),[81] or the provision of another person. Texts 5 and 40 indicate that the permanent absence of the person given by Party D may at times cause the termination of the *tidennūtu* transaction.

Clear Title Clause

šumma PN_3 *pāqirāna iraššši* PN *uzakkama ana* PN_2 *inandin*
If PN_3 has a claimant, PN will clear (him) for PN_2.

Five contracts[82] contain a clause referring to a possible prior encumbrance of the person given by Party D: if an actionable claim is brought against the

81. The delinquency clause in a.i. 7 IV 13–22 (*MSL*, *1*, 103–4) does not differentiate between temporary and permanent absence. Both are to be covered by compensatory payments of one seah of barley per day.

82. Texts 29 and 39–42.

person, Party D is under obligation to clear him for Party C. The purpose of this clause is to give Party C a clear title to the person's services, without which Party C's interest could never be safe. Since Party C is protected against the physical absence of the person, it may be assumed that, despite the infrequent recording of the clear title clause in the contracts, it was operative in all personal *tidennūtu* transactions.

Support of Person given by Party D

There are only three contracts which discuss the support of the person given by Party D while under the authority of Party C. In text 43, Party C bears the responsibility of providing the person with barley and wool rations. If reconstructed correctly, text 44 makes a similar provision. The low value of the commodities given by Party C in text 43 (1.5 shekels of silver) in contrast to the high value of the given items in text 44 (180 shekels of silver) should be noted. This clearly indicates that the support provision is independent of the value of the commodities given by Party C. The third contract, text 42, records only the obligation of Party C to provide Party D with two minas of wool each year as the wool ration of the person given by Party D.

There is no reason to suppose that Party C's responsibility for the maintenance of the person did not apply in all the contracts. The physical presence of the person working in the house of Party C, especially in self-*tidennu* transactions, also argues for its general applicability. Furthermore, in Mesopotamian contracts of hire and in those pledge documents in which the pledge performs services for the creditor it is understood that the hirer or creditor provides for the needs of the hireling[83] or pledge.[84] It may therefore be assumed that as long as the person serves Party C, Party C bears the responsibility for his food and clothing.

A modification of this situation, however, merits attention. In text 42, Party C allots wool to Party D, rather than to the person given by Party D; this seems to imply that the primary obligation to clothe the person was incumbent upon Party D, who in this contract is reimbursed by Party C. If this be correct, the rarity of an explicit support clause in the contracts may be accounted for as follows: it was in all instances the responsibility of Party C

83. See *MSL*, *1*, 83:18 ff.; Lautner, *Altbabylonische Personenmiete*, Studia et Documenta ad Iura Orientis Antiqui Pertinentia, 1 (Leiden, Brill, 1936), 110; Goetze, *The Laws of Eshnunna*, Annual of the American Schools of Oriental Research, 31 (New Haven, American Schools of Oriental Research, 1956), 46 f. Cf. Simmons, "Early Old Babylonian Texts from Tell Harmal and Elsewhere," *JCS*, *13* (1959), 92.

84. See Petschow, *Pfandrecht*, p. 111. Cf. B. Parker, "Economic Tablets From the Temple of Mamu at Balawat," *Iraq*, *25* (1963), 87 f.

to feed the person given by Party D[85]; in a few instances only, however, Party C also accepted the responsibility of clothing the person given to him by Party D. The support clause in the three contracts mentioned above may thus be due to the unusual circumstances of Party C's undertaking to clothe the person as well as feed him.

Death or Disappearance of Party D

Ten contracts, including eight self-*tidennu* transactions,[86] contain clauses which deal with the death or disappearance of Party D. In the two documents which are not self-*tidennu* transactions (texts 23 and 41), Party D has given his son to Party C in *tidennūtu*. Should Party D die, the right to terminate the contract by returning the commodities, thereby freeing the person held by Party C, is to pass to his sons. That this right belonged to the inheritor of Party D's estate, whoever he might be, may be seen from the lawsuit text 18. According to this lawsuit, Party D had given his son to Party C in *tidennūtu* and had designated his brother as the *ewuru*-heir. Upon the death of Party D his brother inherited his estate; it is for this reason that the brother of Party D is held responsible for the return of the commodities to Party C.

In the self-*tidennu* transactions the balanced relationship of the transaction is upset by the death of Party D, since he is also the person held by Party C. Texts 46, 47, and 48 stipulate that upon the death of Party D his sons "may return the received commodities to Party C and thus go (wherever they please)." Thus the same *tidennūtu* transaction is continued by the sons of Party D who assume their father's role as Party D (made explicit by the statement "they may return the received commodities"), and also as the person held by Party C (shown by the statement "and thus go wherever they please").[87] Text 45, which does not specifically mention the death of Party D, confirms this interpretation. According to this text, if Party D is unable to return the commodities to Party C, this right or obligation will rest upon Party D's son and subsequently upon his son's children. On the other hand, text 15 states merely that upon the death of Party D, the sons of Party D "may (or must) return the received commodities in full." This document may be interpreted in the same manner as the texts just mentioned. Nevertheless,

85. According to the Nuzi ration lists a male worker received 3 seah of barley per month (H. Lewy, "The Origin and Development of the Sexagesimal System of Numeration," *JAOS*, *69* [1949], 6–7). Thus the expense of the *tidennu*'s food upkeep amounted to 3.6 homers of barley or 5.4 shekels of silver per year.

86. The self-*tidennu* contracts are texts 15, 32–35, 46, and 47. Although text 48 records the receipt of the commodities by the father of the *tidennu*, it is also to be included in this category since lines 5–7 indicate that the *tidennu* may take the initiative to terminate the contract by returning the commodities (cf. text 27).

87. Text 27 may reflect such a situation.

since the statement "and thus go wherever they please" is omitted in this text, another possibility exists: the omission may indicate that the sons of Party D do not assume his role as the person held by Party C. Then the death of Party D would terminate the *tidennūtu* relationship, and his sons would be obligated to return the commodities to Party C immediately. According to this interpretation, the force of this clause is identical to that of the clause dealing with the death of the person given by Party D in texts 5 and 40.

The other four self-*tidennu* contracts specify guarantors (*māḫiṣ pūti*), whom Party C may seize in the event of the disappearance or death of Party D. Text 35, in which Party D consists of two people and which therefore names two guarantors, expresses their role in the following way: "If they (the guarantors) cannot find them (Party D), then Party C may seize them (the guarantors)."[88] Text 32 indicates that the guarantor is responsible for the presence of Party D in the house of Party C, as well as for the eventual return of the commodities. Text 33 applies the distinctively personal concept of *māḫiṣ pūti* (literally "one who strikes the forehead") to real estate: specified land, designated as *māhiṣ pūti*, is to serve as the object of a potential future foreclosure by Party C. Text 34 also seems to exhibit the same usage of *māḫiṣ pūti* with reference to Party D's estate (é^{ḫi}).[89] But this is the second of two related statements: first, Party D declares that in case of his absence his wife and children are to be held responsible for the compensatory payments, and for the return of the commodities to Party C; then the contract designates his estate (é^{ḫi}) as his *māḫiṣ pūti*. The difficulty in distinguishing between the role of his family and that of his é^{ḫi} warrants the interpretation of é as household[90] rather than estate, and Party D's second statement would then be a recapitulation of his first declaration.

The majority of *tidennūtu* contracts do not contain clauses dealing with the death or disappearance of Party D. It nevertheless seems reasonable to infer from the documents just discussed that the responsibility of terminating or perpetuating the *tidennūtu* arrangement rested upon the heirs of Party D, unless a special guarantor had been designated.

Breach of Contract

Types of penalty clauses. Sixteen personal *tidennūtu* contracts include a penalty clause covering breach of contract. These clauses may be divided into

88. This clause clearly shows the main difference between Roman and Mesopotamian suretyship. Unlike Roman law, in which the guarantor is an accessory debtor, Mesopotamian law views the main function of the guarantor to be ensuring the presence of the debtor for personal prosecution by the creditor (Bereitsexecution). See Koschaker, *Bürgschaftsrecht*, pp. 76 ff.

89. Noted by Speiser, *AASOR, 16* (1936), 110.

90. Cf. *CAD*, B, 293–94, especially meaning 6 h.

two main groups: in the first the penalty clause is directed against either party,[91] and in the second the penalty clause is directed against Party D.[92]

Against either party

mannu ina berīšunu (*ištu* x *šanāti*) *ibbalakkat . . . umalla*
Whoever between them violates the agreement (within the x years) shall pay a fine of . . .

This group consists of eight contracts. The formulation of this clause is always general. Two contracts, texts 9 and 29, mention within the penalty clause a period of time identical to the definite duration of the contract.

Against Party D

šumma PN *ibbalakkat . . . umalla*
If PN violates the agreement, he shall pay a fine of . . .

Eight contracts fall into this category. In five of them the penalty clause is formulated in general terms, but three contracts define the breach of contract explicitly.

The penalty clause in text 30 specifies that by returning the copper and demanding his son Party D will violate the agreement. Since the contract states that after fifty years Party D may return the money and take back his son, the breach of contract must consist of returning the money before the end of the fifty-year period. Thus the penalty clause protects Party C against the premature termination of the relationship and clearly indicates that the *tidennūtu* arrangement automatically terminates with the return of the commodities to Party C.

Similarly, the penalty clause in text 20 (a self-*tidennu* contract) specifies that by freeing himself from the house of Party C, i.e. by severing all obligations through the return of the commodities, Party D will violate the agreement. Thus the penalty clause ensures the fulfillment of the clause in lines 8 f., in which Party D promises not to free himself from the service of Party C. According to the contract, only the death of Party D allows his children to return the commodities and thus go free. This penalty clause, too, protects Party C against the premature termination of the *tidennūtu* arrangement.

The penalty clause in text 24 specifies that by returning the commodities—in this instance the purchase price of a slave—Party D will violate the agreement. This *tidennūtu* contract is similar to those non-*tidennūtu* transactions which record the advance payment of a purchase price. One such text, for

91. Texts 6, 9, 13, 29, 31, 33, 40, and 42.

92. Texts 16, 19, 20, 22, 24, 30, and 46. In text 36, the clause is directed not only against Party D, but also against his guarantor.

example, records the payment of sixty shekels of silver for a slave girl who is to be delivered to the buyer at a future date.[93] Text 24 differs from that transaction only in that a person given by Party D is to remain in the house of Party C until the slave is delivered. The penalty clause ensures Party D's delivery of the slave, rather than the return of the money advanced by Party C as the purchase price of the slave.

The breaches of contract explicitly mentioned in texts 20 and 24 are too specific to be applied to the penalty clauses of other transactions. But the breach in text 30, which is also implicit in text 20—namely, the premature termination of the *tidennūtu* arrangement—may very well be one of the primary concerns of the other penalty clauses. This seems to be implied in those penalty clauses which state that "whoever violates the agreement within the specified duration shall pay the stipulated fine," since the premature termination of the contract is an action which represents a breach of contract during, but not after, the definite duration set for the rendering of services by the person given to Party C.

That the premature termination of the *tidennūtu* arrangement was not the only concern of the penalty clause may be seen from the fact that four tablets[94] which do not contain a definite duration clause nevertheless contain a penalty clause. Thus, as one would expect, the penalty clause protected the parties against the non-fulfillment of any of the provisions of the contract. This is evident from text 36, whose penalty clause is also directed against the guarantor. In this contract the only obligation of the guarantor was to ensure the compensatory payments in case of the absence of the person given by Party D.

Imposed fines. The penalty clauses impose the following payments upon the party which violates the agreement: one ox[95]; two oxen (text 13); one mina of silver and one mina of gold (text 20); one mina of silver (texts 22 and 46); one weaver (text 30); two slaves (texts 24 and 29); and four male and four female slaves (text 19).

In only a few instances can a definite pattern be discerned. The penalties in texts 19 and 24 are double the exchanged item given by Party C, while in text 29 it is double the person given by Party D. The penalty in text 30 is an exact replacement of the person given by Party D. This pattern of relating the fines to both exchanged items suggests that the penalty clause is primarily concerned with the premature termination of the *tidennūtu* arrangement by Party D.[96]

The remaining fines consist of payments of oxen and minas of silver and

93. *AASOR, 16,* No. 95.

94. Texts 19, 22, 24, and 46.

95. Texts 6, 9, 31, 40, and 42.

96. It must be noted that text 19 does not record a definite duration period.

gold, such as are commonly imposed in Nuzi transactions. There is no apparent overall correlation between the values of commodities given by Party C and the penalty.[97]

Four documents,[98] whose penalty clause is directed against Party D specifically, state that the penalty is to be paid to Party C. It is thus paid to the protected party rather than to a royal or temple treasury.

Twenty-seven contracts do not contain a penalty clause. It is impossible to determine whether these parties were protected by a non-recorded penalty clause; if so, the penalties cannot be determined since the evidence does not show a pattern.

Šūdūtu Clause

ṭuppu ina arki šūdūti ina pāni abulli šaṭir

The document was written after a proclamation before the gate.

The use of the *šūdūtu* clause is not restricted to *tidennūtu* contracts; it is found at the end of many different types of transactions in the Nuzi documents.[99] Only eleven personal *tidennūtu* contracts[100] contain this clause, which specifies that they were written after the *šūdūtu*–proclamation. Four other *tidennūtu* documents[101] give the place in which the contract was drawn up, but fail to say whether the writing took place after the *šūdūtu*.

Although the translation of the term *šūdūtu* "public proclamation"[102] is certain, the legal and social implications of the *šūdūtu* clause are still obscure.

97.

Text	*Value of commodities**	*Value of fine**
6	15.66	10 (less than 1x)
9	51.16+	10 (less than 1x)
40	13.5	10 (less than 1x)
42	11.66	10 (1x)
31	3.6	10 (3x)
36	15	60 (4x)
16	12	60 (5x)
20	60	600 (10x)
22	30	1080 (36x)
46	30	1080 (36x)

* expressed in shekels of silver

98. Texts 19, 20, 22, and 24.

99. The *šūdūtu* clause appears in certain sale adoptions (*HSS*, *5*, 56), real adoptions (*HSS*, *5*, 60), *šimtu*-depositions (*HSS*, *19*, 16), *tamgurtu* agreements (*JEN*, *5*, 470), *šupe'ultu* exchanges (*JEN*, *5*, 485), *makannūtu* contracts (*HSS*, *19*, 146), lawsuits (*JEN*, *4*, 345), etc.

100. Texts 3, 8–10, 13, 24, 26, 29, 38, 40, and 41.

101. Texts 6, 31, 39, and 52.

102. This meaning was first proposed by Landsberger *apud* Koschaker, *NRUA*, pp. 77–78.

The term is used in connection with royal decrees,[103] and is sometimes modified by the adjective *eššu* "new."[104] Occasionally, the terms *andurāru* "a release"[105] and *kirenzi* "a decree(?)"[106] appear in parallel with *šūdūtu*. Koschaker understood the *šūdūtu* clause to refer to an act of publicity which preceded a final release of property, the legal function thus being equivalent to the Middle Assyrian *ṭuppu dannatu* which marked the final alienation of property no longer subject to outside claims by a third party.[107] However, this equation was rejected by San Nicolò.[108] C. H. Gordon attempted to connect *šūdūtu* with the biblical year of release,[109] and more recently H. Lewy suggested that the *šūdūtu* clause may have nothing to do with the contents of the documents, but may have been intended as a date formula.[110]

The use of the *šūdūtu* clause in the personal *tidennūtu* contracts does not provide any new insight into its purpose. Its bearing on the transactions, if any, cannot be determined, nor can a correlation between it and other personal *tidennūtu* clauses be made. It might be argued that publicity marking a final

103. *AASOR, 16*, No. 51:1 and *JEN, 2*, 195:12; Speiser's equation of *šādūtu* with *šūdūtu* (*AASOR, 16* [1936], 103) was challenged by H. Lewy (*Or*, N.S. *11* [1942], 26 ff.). For a critique of Lewy's position, see Koschaker *ZA, 48* (1944), 187 n. 44. The decree of a *ḫazannu* is not termed *šūdūtu* but rather *ṭēmu* (H. Lewy, "Notes on the Political Organization of Asia Minor at the Time of the Old Assyrian Texts," *Or*, N.S. *33* [1964], 186 n. 4 and 192 n. 2).

104. *JEN, 2*, 116:11 f; *HSS, 9*, 35:29; *HSS, 19*, 97:32; Gadd, *RA, 23* (1926), No. 47:33. Previous explanations for the term *šūdūtu eššu* were offered by Landsberger (Koschaker, *OLZ, 35* [1932], 404) and Cassin (*Adoption*, p. 243).

105. *HSS, 5*, 25:24 and *HSS, 9*, 102:30 f. See Speiser, *AASOR*, 10 (1928–29), 12; P. Koschaker, Review of *HSS, 5*, in *OLZ, 34* (1931), 225; and H. Lewy, *Or*, N.S. *28* (1959), 129 n. 1.

106. *HSS, 19*, 118:17. See A. Shaffer, "Hurrian **kirezzi*, West-Semitic *krz*," (*Or*, N.S. *34* [1965], 32–34), who equates *šūdūtu* with *kirenzu*. However, an unpublished real estate *tidennūtu* contract (SMN 2649:21–24) records the following clause: [*ṭup-p*]*í i-na* [egi]r *šu-du-ti i-na* [ká-gal] *ša šu-pa-*[*li*] *i-na* mu [*ša*] [*ki*]-*re-en-zi ša-ṭì-ir* "The document was written after the public proclamation at the lower gate in the year of the decree (?)." This would seem to argue against the equation of *šūdūtu* with *kirenzu*.

107. *NRUA*, pp. 67 ff. and in his review of Speiser, *AASOR* 10, in *OLZ, 35* (1932), 403; see Speiser, *AASOR, 10* (1928–29), 12; *JAOS, 52* (1932), 367; Oppenheim, "Ein Beitrag zum Kassitenproblem," *Miscellanea Orientalia dedicata Antonio Deimel Annos LXX complenti*, Analecta Orientalia, 12, (Rome, Pontificium Institutum Biblicum, 1935), 271; and Purves, *JNES, 6* (1947), 183 n. 5.

108. Review of Koschaker, *NRUA*, in *SZ, 49* (1929), 536.

109. "Parallèles nouziens aux lois et coutumes de l'ancien testament," *Revue Biblique, 44* (1935), 38 ff.

110. *Or*, N.S. *28* (1959), 5 n. 3. Cf. Lacheman, "The Word *šudūtu* in the Nuzi Tablets," *Proceedings of the 25th International Congress of Orientalists, 1* (1960), 233–38; and Hayden, *Court Procedure at Nuzu*, pp. 188 f.

alienation of property in order to ensure its non-encumbrance is inappropriate in *tidennūtu* transactions, which seem to be only temporary exchanges; nevertheless, the closely related clear title clause also appears in the personal *tidennūtu* transactions.

THE INSTITUTION OF PERSONAL TIDENNŪTU

Correlation Between Exchanged Properties and Duration of Contract

The following summary lists the value of the commodities given by Party C expressed in terms of shekels of silver, the person given by Party D, and the duration of the contract:

Text	*Value of commodities*	*Person*	*Duration*
43	1.5	son	6 yrs.
32	2.25	self	after harvest
31	3.6	self	after harvest
50	3.6	sons	—
11	4.05	self	3 yrs.
35	4.35	self	4 yrs.
4	4.5	son	indefinite
28	4.5	self	10 yrs.
6	5.66	brother	4 yrs.
12	6	self	10 yrs.
52	6.75	son	5 yrs.
15	9	self	indefinite
14	9.33	son	6 yrs.
42	11.66	son	3 yrs.
16	12	son	8 yrs.
8	13.33	self	indefinite
34	13.5	self	10 yrs.
40	13.5	son	5 yrs.
38	13.59	self	indefinite
3	15	son	20 yrs.
10	15	self	indefinite
36	15	self	10 yrs.
7	15.25	self	indefinite
1	16.5	self	indefinite
39	18.46	sister	indefinite
41	19	son	indefinite
49	27	self	indefinite
30	27	son	50 yrs.
21	30	slave	indefinite

Text	*Value of commodities*	*Person*	*Duration*
22	30	self	indefinite
23	30	son	indefinite
24	30	self	indefinite
25	30	son	10 yrs.
26	30	self	20 yrs.
27	30	two sons	indefinite
29	33	slave	10 yrs.
2	39	self, two sons	indefinite
51	31.33+	self	50 yrs.
18	45.99	son	—
5	48.33	brother	death of *tidennu*
9	51.16+	son	2 yrs.
20	60	self + household	death of *tidennu*
19	120	self	indefinite
44	180	self	indefinite
45	180	son	indefinite
46	180	self	indefinite
47	180	self	indefinite
48	180	son	indefinite

Statistical investigation of the twenty contracts which contain a definite duration clause (excluding the "death of *tidennu*" duration) shows that the median value of the commodities is 9.9 shekels of silver, and the median duration of the contract is 6 years. The resultant median split presents the following array of data:

		Duration		
		6 and below	7 and above	total
	9.9 and below	8	2	10
Value	10 and above	3	7	10
	total	11	9	20

The duration of the contract tends to be significantly longer as values of the commodities given by party C increases.[111]

111. On the basis of a chi square analysis, the likelihood of these findings occurring by chance, and not by virtue of the hypothesis—duration increases with increasing values of the received commodities—is less than 5 out of 100 ($\chi^2 = 5.06$, df = 1, p = <.05). For a discussion of the concept of chi square in determining statistical probability see John Peatman, *Introduction to Applied Statistics* (New York, Harper and Row, 1963), pp. 228 ff.

For the 44 contracts which contain either a definite (again excluding the "death of *tidennu*") or an indefinite duration clause, the median value of the received commodities is 15.9 shekels of silver. The resultant median split presents the following array of data:

		Duration		
		definite	indefinite	total
	15.9 and below	16	6	22
Value	16 and above	6	16	22
	total	22	22	44

The indefinite duration clause occurs more frequently as the values of the commodities given by Party C rise above the median, i.e. become higher.[112] Thus it is reasonable to assume that, as the commodities given by Party C increased in value, Party C deemed it unnecessary to stipulate a definite period of time during which he would be assured of the services of the person given by Party D, since the quick return of the commodities became less likely as their value increased.

This interpretation of the data argues against Mendelsohn who, on the basis of the definite and indefinite duration clauses, differentiated between two types of *tidennūtu* transactions.[113] He maintained that the first type, containing an indefinite duration clause, represented transactions in which the person given by Party D "was held merely as collateral security."[114] The second type, containing a definite duration clause, represented transactions in which "the services to be rendered by the *tidennu* was the most essential feature."[115] That the services to be rendered by the person given by Party D are an essential element in all personal *tidennūtu* arrangements, regardless of the type of duration clause contained in the contract, is evident from the prevalence of the delinquency clause. This clause occurs in contracts containing either type of duration clause. Thus the distinction between definite and indefinite duration does not appear to be a differentiation in type, but rather is a feature determined to a significant extent by the value of the commodities given by Party D.

There seems to be no evident relationship between the value of the commodities given by Party C and the number of people held by Party C. In the

112. On the basis of a chi square analysis, the likelihood of these findings occurring by chance and not by virtue of the hypothesis—as value of the received commodities increases, the frequency of indefinite duration increases—is less than 1 out of 100 ($\chi^2 = 10.18$, df = 1, p = <.01).

113. *SANE*, p. 31.

114. Ibid.

115. Ibid.

four transactions which involve more than one person, the values of the commodities are 3.6, 30, 39, and 60 shekels of silver. In the majority of cases, even those involving commodities of the highest value, only one person is given to Party C.

We may therefore conclude that the personal *tidennūtu* transactions were not subject to any specific regulations. The details of the transaction were decided by the contracting parties and thus varied in each case. The duration of the servitude of the person held by Party C, however, would normally depend to a large extent on the value of the commodities given by Party C.

Nature of the Transaction

Before discussing the nature of the personal *tidennūtu* transaction, the major issues regarding the interpretation of *tidennūtu* which were referred to in Chapter 1 should be recapitulated.

One interpretation views the institution of *tidennūtu* as a type of secured loan, with the individual contract representing either a rental, a conditional sale, or a mortgage. However, the transactions in which the contracting parties furnish each other with the services of persons present a problem to this interpretation. Koschaker questioned the logic of a debtor entering into the house of a creditor as a *tidennu* so that the debtor might obtain the services of a slave (text 22). For this reason, Speiser suggested that such contracts may extend the accepted formulation of *tidennūtu* contracts to transactions of a different type. The other interpretation of *tidennūtu*, proposed by H. Lewy, takes its departure precisely from these problematic transactions in which each party furnishes the other with the services of persons. Lewy regards the institution of *tidennūtu* as a mutual exchange, with no debtor–creditor relationship between the contracting parties.

Since the transactions involving a mutual exchange of persons[116] are a crucial issue in the interpretation of the institution of *tidennūtu*, they will be treated separately, after the other transactions have been discussed.

In the majority of the personal *tidennūtu*-contracts a person is transferred to Party C in exchange for certain commodities which may consist of metals, livestock, produce, implements, or cloth. The seeming symmetry of the exchange is heightened by the fact that the modifying phrase *ana tidennūti* "in *tidennu*-ship" may be used to describe either or both exchanges.[117] But a

116. In the present corpus, there are nine such transactions: texts 18–23 and 25–27.

117. It should be noted, however, that this phrase seems to originate with the transfer of the person given by Party D since in the entire corpus it occurs thirty-four times with reference to the assignment of the person and only fourteen times with the assignment of the commodities given by Party C. Furthermore, only the person given by Party D is referred to as *tidennu* in the texts.

closer examination of the details of the transaction indicates that the symmetry is only superficial.

First, the exchanged sets of values are neither similar in type nor equal in value. The commodities given by Party C represent definite capital to be exploited by Party D, while the value of the person given by Party D lies in the service performed by him; thus currency is exchanged for personal service. The value of the person's services has been approximated at fifty-four shekels of silver per year. Multiply this sum by the number of years that the person is to remain in the service of Party C—the definite duration clause indicating the minimum number of years—and it will be evident from the summary chart that the value of the person's services in contracts containing a definite duration clause far exceeds that of the commodities given by Party C.[118] As for those contracts which contain an indefinite duration clause, it should be noted that even in the transactions containing the highest value of the commodities given by Party C (180 shekels of silver), the value of services of the person held by Party C represents a 30% return on Party C's investment. Thus the transaction is always to the advantage of Party C; only dire need could have made Party D enter into such an economically unfavorable arrangement.

The decisive argument against the semblance of symmetry is that the contracting parties are not on an equal footing. This inequality is shown by the one-sidedness of the contract. First, the initiative to terminate the contract always rests with the party who has received the capital and has furnished the other with the services of a person. Only Party D's return of the received commodities to Party C determines when the arrangement will end. Secondly, only the interests of Party C appear to be protected. The clauses of the contract are concerned with the death or disappearance only of Party D; with the prior-encumbrance only of the person given by Party D; and even the penalty clause is often specifically directed only against Party D's breach of contract. If the *tidennūtu* transaction were a mutual exchange, one would expect a reciprocity in the clauses of its contract. However, neither those contracts entitled *ṭuppi tidennūti* of Party D nor those entitled *ṭuppi tidennūti* of Party C exhibit such reciprocity.

Since the relationship governing the contracting parties does not seem to be one of reciprocity, its nature must still be determined. A few contracts contribute substantially to the understanding of this relationship.

Text 4 states that Party D has received certain commodities from Party C *ana* ur$_5$-ra "on an interest-bearing loan," (and) now has given his son to

118. Even if the expense of Party C's support of the *tidennu* is deducted from this sum, the net value (49.5 shekels of silver) is extremely high in proportion to the value of the commodities received.

Party C in *tidennūtu* in lieu of these commodities. However, the text is not unambiguous. The clause describing the transfer of Party D's son to Party C is introduced (in line 4) by the adverb *inanna* "now" rather than by the usual conjunctive particle *u* "and." H. Lewy therefore interpreted the first clause as referring to a prior transaction, i.e. the loan of certain commodities to Party D. According to this interpretation, the contract records the transformation of an earlier loan into a *tidennūtu* transaction.[119] This text, Lewy argued, would exclude the interpretation of *tidennūtu* as a secured loan.[120] However, the use of the adverb *inanna* in the clause describing the transfer of Party D's son to Party C does not prove conclusively that the previous clause describing the transfer of the commodities to Party D on loan referred to an earlier transaction, especially since the verbs of both clauses are in the same tense. But, even if Lewy's interpretation of this contract is accepted, the only conclusion that can be drawn from it is that the institution of *tidennūtu* is somehow distinct from an ordinary loan transaction. A similar conclusion may be drawn from contract texts 46, 47 and 48. According to the delin quency clause of these contracts, the failure of the person given by Party D to work for Party C nullifies the *tidennūtu* transaction and it automatically becomes a regular interest-bearing loan.

These four texts show that the *tidennūtu* arrangement may, on occasion, convert or be converted into a loan. The *tidennūtu* transaction must therefore be similar to, but not identical with, an ordinary loan. What, precisely, is the difference?

Assuming that Party C stands for the creditor and Party D for the debtor, the most obvious difference between the *tidennūtu* transaction and an ordinary loan is Party D's transfer of a person to Party C. Is this person, then, an ordinary pledge, given to secure the loan? Lewy denied it on the basis of text 4:

> It is evident that the son was not given to the creditor as security for the former debt, for if the creditor had wanted a security, he would have asked for it immediately when the debt was contracted. Nor was he given in order to work off his father's debt, for in this case his release would have depended upon the return of the barley to his father's former creditor.[121]

The role of the person given by Party D, and one of the essential elements in the *tidennūtu* transaction, is the performance of services for Party C. This is indicated in the personal *tidennūtu* documents by the following:

119. *Or*, N.S. *10* (1941), 321.
120. Ibid., especially n. 3.
121. Ibid. Although the first section of Lewy's statement may be disputed, her statement will be accepted here for argument's sake.

1. The stipulation of the compensatory *uriḫul* payments to be made to Party C in the event of the person's failure to work. It cannot be inferred that the person's service is essential only in those contracts which record compensatory payments in case of his absence, since texts 12 and 27 do not contain this clause, yet specify that the work be performed by the person given by Party D.

2. The stipulation of a clear title clause. This clause is not usually found in security transactions, but rather occurs in sale contracts.[122] Its inclusion among the clauses of the *tidennūtu* contract underscores the importance of the person's services, since it protects Party C against the deprivation of these services by a third party.

3. The stipulation of a penalty clause whose concern is to protect Party C from the premature termination of the *tidennūtu* relationship. In this manner, Party C is assured the benefit of the person's service for a definite period of time.

Since the disproportionate value of the service of the person given by Party D relative to the worth of the commodities given by Party C rules out the notion of a fair exchange between two equal parties, the purpose for which the person's service was offered to Party C remains to be explained. This purpose is suggested in a clause appearing in only two contracts, text 47 (lines 8–9) and 48 (lines 9–10): guškin máš nu *išu u* PN *uriḫulša* nu *išu*, "The gold (exchanged commodity) does not bear interest and PN (person given by Party D) does not receive his hire." This statement indicates that the person's service is in lieu of interest, an arrangement known to classical law as antichresis.[123] Since there is no positive evidence against the antichretic nature of the person's service in the other personal *tidennūtu* contracts in which the commodities given by Party C represent definite capital, it may be assumed that this purpose was implicit in all of them.

If the service given by Party D is antichretic, it follows that Party C is the creditor who lends certain commodities, the borrowed capital, to Party D, the debtor. Thus it is clear why only Party D, the debtor, may terminate

122. Petschow, *Pfandrecht*, pp. 114–15.

123. See R. Leonhard, "Antichresis," *Paulys Realencyclopädie der classischen Altertumwissenschaft* (Stuttgart, Metzler), *1*/2, 2396. Cf. A. E. Samuel, "The Role of Paramone Clauses in Ancient Documents," *Journal of Juristic Papyrology*, *15* (1965), 301 ff. Antichresis in Mesopotamian law was first recognized by Revillout, "L'Antichrèse non-immobilière dans l'Égypte et dans l'Chaldée," *Proceedings of the Society of Biblical Archaeology*, *9* (1886–87), 178 f. and subsequently discussed by Koschaker, *Griech. Rechtsurk.*, pp. 9 ff. For a discussion of antichresis in Biblical Law, see Weil, "Gage et Cautionnement dans la Bible," *AHDO*, *2* (1938), 182, 186, 237; for Talmudic Law, see B. Cohen, "Antichresis in Jewish and Roman Law," *Alexander Marx Jubilee Volume* (New York, Jewish Theological Seminary, 1950), pp. 179 ff.

the *tidennūtu* arrangement by returning the received commodities. But the *tidennūtu* transaction is not an ordinary interest-bearing loan inasmuch as the debtor provides the creditor with a *tidennu* who is to render service in lieu of interest. That is why Party C is protected against the loss of the person's services. This interpretation also fits the contract text 4, even according to Lewy's understanding of it: the contract records the transformation of a regular interest-bearing loan into a loan with personal antichresis. The son functions neither as mere security, nor as a means of working off the father's debt; rather, he is the provider of services which are considered to be in lieu of interest.

In nine of the personal *tidennūtu* transactions[124] both contracting parties furnish each other with persons. These contracts are the mainstay of Lewy's interpretation of *tidennūtu* as a mutual exchange. They have been a crux to those who view *tidennūtu* as a secured loan, for the seeming symmetry of the *tidennūtu* exchange is here heightened by the fact that the exchanged sets of values are of the same kind (human beings). Therefore both Koschaker and Speiser understood *tidennūtu* in this type of contract in the same manner as H. Lewy, i.e. as a transaction in which the parties furnish each other with the services of persons. However, a closer examination of the details of these contracts will indicate that here, too, the symmetry of the transactions is only superficial.

Although the exchanged sets of values are of the same kind, there is a definite distinction between them. The exchanged person given by Party C is always the slave (or slaves) of Party C, while the exchanged person given by Party D, with the exception of text 21, always belongs to the immediate family of Party D or is Party D himself. Moreover, the inequality of the contracting parties noted in the other personal *tidennūtu* contracts is again apparent in these. First, only Party D may terminate the relationship by returning the person given by Party C and thus take back the member of his family. Secondly, the delinquency clause protects only Party C against the loss of the services of the person given by Party D, and some of the penalty clauses[125] are specifically directed only against Party D's breach of contract. Thus the relationship of the contracting parties in these transactions is also clearly non-reciprocal.

Text 21, which is exceptional in that the person given by Party D is a slave of Party D rather than a member of his family, explicitly states (in lines 2–3) that Party D is indebted to Party C for two slaves. In the contract, Party D gives one slave to Party C as a partial payment for the two slaves which he owes him; he also gives another person as a *tidennu* until the time when he can

124. Texts 18–23 and 25–27.

125. See the penalty clause of texts 19, 20, and 22.

deliver the second slave. In other words, Party D's transfer of the first slave to Party C is permanent while the transfer of the *tidennu* is only temporary. The antecedents of this contract may be understood by referring to the non-*tidennūtu* transaction recorded in *AASOR, 16*, No. 95. According to this text, Party A gave Party B the advance purchase price of a slave to be delivered at a specified date.[126] If the slave is not delivered on the specified day, Party B shall pay a daily fine of one mina of copper for each day of his non-delivery. Text 21 seems to presuppose a similar arrangement; in it Party D received the purchase price for two slaves to be delivered at a certain date. However, at the specified time Party D could deliver only one slave to Party C. Instead of paying the daily fine for the non-delivery of the other slave, Party D gave one of his own servants to Party C in *tidennūtu* until he could deliver a second slave.[127] That the services of the person given by Party D could be equated with the daily fine of one mina of copper is evident from the amounts of the compensatory payments in the delinquency clauses of the personal *tidennūtu* contracts. Thus the contract of text 21 is only a variation of one in which the relationship of Parties C and D is that of creditor and debtor, and the service of the slave given by Party D is antichretic in nature.

Since the relationship of the contracting parties in all the *tidennūtu* transactions in which persons are exchanged is clearly non-reciprocal, and since one of them (text 21) explicitly shows that Party D is a debtor to Party C, there is every reason to assume that in this type of transaction, too, Party C is the creditor and Party D the debtor. However, the problem posed by Koschaker and Speiser now must be faced: Why would a person enter into debt and remain in the house of the creditor as a self-*tidennu* just to obtain the services of a slave?

This problem arose because this type of personal *tidennūtu* arrangement has been understood as one in which both parties furnish each other with the services of persons. However, from the fact that the delinquency clause of these contracts only refers to the person given by Party D, it would seem that only that person's services are deemed essential. The person given by Party C is wanted not for rendering service, but for his intrinsic market value. Thus the person given by Party C, who is always a slave, represents definite capital, as is true of the commodities given by Party C in all the other personal *tidennūtu* transactions. This is evident from the lawsuit text 18 which is based on a personal *tidennūtu* transaction in which Party D received twelve sheep and one slave from Party C—sheep and slave on the same footing, as capital. Again, in *JEN, 2*, 111, based on a real estate *tidennūtu* transaction, Party D

126. For other contracts which record the loan of a purchase price, see Cuq, *Études*, pp. 192 ff.

127. Cf. the circumstances related to the contract in text 24, above, pp. 30 f.

gives a female slave to Party C, in lieu of the return of certain commodities given him by Party C (tin and sheep), and in lieu of the payment of a fine stipulated in terms of barley and straw. Thus by recognizing that the *tidennūtu* contracts put slaves, grains, metals, and livestock on a common chattel footing in transfers, the apparent non-conformity of the personal *tidennūtu* contracts in which the exchanged item given by Party C is a person, namely a slave, disappears.

Analysis of all the personal *tidennūtu* transactions indicates that the institution of *tidennūtu* is identical to antichresis. Party C is the creditor who provides Party D, the debtor, with capital, and the *tidennu* given by Party D provides Party C with antichretic service, corresponding to the interest on the capital. Thus the delinquency clause is a guarantee for the receipt of interest. That the services of the *tidennu* are only in lieu of interest and are not applicable to the amortization of the loan follows from the fact that Party D must always return the entire value of the commodities in order to free the *tidennu*.

Although the texts do not explicitly state that the *tidennu* also secures the loan, this seems to be a logical inference. Thus the *tidennu* is also the antichretic security. This inference is supported by the fact that the appointment of guarantors to secure the payment of the debt in case of the death or disappearance of the debtor is found only in the self-*tidennu* transactions. Since there the debtor is also the *tidennu*, a guarantor is needed to secure the loan; but in all of the other contracts, the *tidennu* secures the loan. The value of the borrowed capital can be determined for forty-eight contracts; in thirty-six of these it is within or below the range of thirty shekels of silver—the approximate market value of the *tidennu*. Of the twelve contracts in which the commodities given by Party C are of a higher value, two deal with more than one *tidennu*. Thus the creditor's loan is covered in full by the person of the *tidennu* in 80% of the transactions. Furthermore, the phrase *ina bīt(i) C wašābu/erēbu* "to stay in/enter the house of C" signifies that the *tidennu* enters into a subservient relationship by becoming part of the creditor's household, and, in all likelihood, by receiving his support from him. However, the antichretic clause guškin máš nu *īšu u* PN *uriḫulša* nu *īšu* "the gold does not bear interest and the *tidennu* does not receive his hire" seems to characterize the transfer of the *tidennu* to Party C as a contract of hire[128] in which the debtor hires out the pledge to the creditor.[129] The extent of the

128. For the use of the verbs *erēbu* "to come under the control of" and *waṣū* "to go free" in contracts of hire, see Oppenheim, "Untersuchungen zum babylonischen Mietrecht," *WZKM*, Beiheft *2* (1936), 11 ff.

129. Cf. *Ḫḫ 1*, 367 ff. (*MSL*, *5*, 40:2 ff.). This view accords well with Cuq's interpretation of the *tidennūtu* transaction as a rental contract. That the personal *tidennūtu* transaction does not represent a redeemable sale is evident from the fact that the debtor, not the creditor, is held responsible for the disappearance or death of the *tidennu*.

creditor's authority over the *tidennu* would then be limited to that of a hirer over a hireling.[130]

Comparative legal studies on the theory of pledge law have indicated that the primitive pledge did not represent security for a loan, but rather a substitute payment for the borrowed capital.[131] The creditor gained full possession of the pledge at the onset of the loan, and the one who borrowed the capital bore no obligation to return the capital but only possessed a right to redeem the pledge. Thus the debtor's personal liability ended with his delivery of the pledge. Koschaker attempted to show that this concept of the pledge as a substitute payment still governed the institution of *tidennūtu*.[132] This may seem probable from the fact that in the *tidennūtu* transaction the delivery of the pledge takes the form of an exchange: in lieu of borrowed capital, the *tidennu* is to stay in the house of Party C. Nevertheless, the fact that the debtor assumes the liability in case of the absence, death, or disappearance of the pledge, that certain contracts record guarantors for the return of the capital, that the heir of the debtor may be sued for the return of the capital (text 18), and that the right of the creditor over the pledge is not absolute, all indicate that the personal *tidennūtu* transaction recognized the personal obligation of the debtor even after the delivery of the pledge. Thus the institution of personal *tidennūtu* seems to be governed by a concept of personal debt liability, although it preserves the older contractual form of a substitute payment pledge.

If the *tidennūtu* contract represents an antichretic security transaction which is not governed by the concept of the pledge as a substitute payment, there should be a period of time after which the creditor may demand the return of his capital or else foreclose the security. The very fact that some self-*tidennu* contracts appoint guarantors indicates that the possibility of such a demand being made was quite real.[133] The definite duration clause of the personal *tidennūtu* contract may have served to delimit the period after which the debtor must return the borrowed capital or else forfeit

130. *Contra* Koschaker (*NRUA*, p. 136), who considers the borrowed capital to be the sale price of the pledge, so that the *tidennu* becomes the slave of the creditor until the time that the pledge is redeemed.

131. Petschow, *Pfandrecht*, p. 75.

132. *NRUA*, p. 113; Review of Pfeiffer and Speiser, *AASOR*, 16, in *OLZ*, *44* (1941), 460.

133. There is only one tablet (text 37) which seems to record the transition of a person from the status of a *tidennu* to one of more permanent servitude by being "cast into chains." This phrase is perhaps best interpreted as a symbolic renunciation of all possibilities of future liberation. For similar symbolic acts related to medieval serfdom, see R. W. Southern, *The Making of the Middle Ages* (New Haven, Yale University Press, 1953), 99–100.

his security,[134] but it should be kept in mind that 47% of the contracts (twenty-two out of forty-seven) contain an indefinite duration clause which merely states that, upon payment of borrowed capital, the debtor may free the *tidennu*. In these contracts, there is no indication of a time after which the creditor's authority over the *tidennu* becomes so absolute that the debtor loses his right to free him, and there is no reference to any recourse which the creditor may have to force the debtor's return of the borrowed capital. Similarly, the purpose of many of the definite duration clauses need not be the establishment of a deadline for the return of the borrowed capital. The definite duration clause may also be interpreted as specifying the period after which the debtor has the legal right, but not the obligation, to terminate the arrangement. The clause is then to be translated in the following manner: "When the specified time has elapsed, the debtor *may* return the borrowed capital and thus free the *tidennu*" i.e. the debtor's right to liberate the *tidennu begins* with the expiration of the specified time and continues indefinitely. By the definite duration clause, the creditor ensures for himself the services of the *tidennu* for a specific length of time. That the creditor often desires such protection is confirmed by some of the penalty clauses. In the contracts containing indefinite duration clauses, and perhaps even in some containing definite duration clauses, the creditor seems to be more interested in continuing the services of the *tidennu* than in securing the return of his money.

If this is so, the institution of personal *tidennūtu* represents not only an antichretic security transaction but also a type of indentured servitude.[135] As long as the debt remains unpaid, the *tidennu* loses his freedom of movement. He and his children and grandchildren are bound to the creditor by an obligation of service.[136] Thus by means of the personal *tidennūtu* contract, the Nuzi landlords could assure themselves of a long-term labor force on which to draw. Such service would be superior to that of a slave, since the creditor is always protected against the flight, disappearance or death of the *tidennu*. It is also possible that, since the main need for labor in an agricultural economy is seasonal,[137] the *tidennu* could practice his trade for himself, or even work his own fields, whenever his service was not needed by the creditor. During such periods of absence, the creditor would not be obligated to support him.

134. According to Middle Assyrian pledge law, the creditor gains full power over a forfeited pledge only after he has reimbursed the debtor for the difference between the market value of the pledge and the debt. Only then does the status of the security change from that of a pledge to that of a person sold for debt. Cf. J. Lewy, "The Biblical Institution of Deror in the Light of Akkadian Documents," *Eretz-Israel*, 5 (1958), 26 and n. 48.

135. Cf. Mendelsohn, *SANE*, pp. 118–19.

136. Cf. texts 17 and 45.

137. Cf. Southern, *The Making of the Middle Ages*, pp. 101–2.

Of course, a uniform interpretation of all personal *tidennūtu* transactions obscures the significant variations of the individual contracts. Those self-*tidennu* contracts which specify the appointment of guarantors for the return of the borrowed commodity indicate that the transaction is a loan in which the pledge covers the interest by his personal services. Those *tidennūtu* contracts which terminate with the death of the *tidennu* indicate that the arrangement is one of limited indentured servitude, concerned with securing the service of a particular person. And those *tidennūtu* contracts which obligate the succeeding generations to serve indicate that the arrangement is a means of securing a long-term source of labor. The common denominator of all of these contracts is the creation of an obligation for the performance of services by means of a loan with personal antichresis.

A deeper insight into the institution of personal *tidennūtu* could be attained if the social status, economic position, and other activities of the two contracting parties were better known. For example, that Teḫib-tilla son of Puḫi-šenni was one of the most economically influential people in Nuzi,[138] that he owned vast real estate,[139] that he was in need of obtaining the services of others,[140] strengthens the assumption that Teḫib-tilla utilized the institution of personal *tidennūtu* as a means of securing a long-term labor force by using the *tidennūtu* transaction to gain indentured servants. Especially instructive would be those occurrences in which the same parties appear together in other transactions. The groundwork for such an investigation has already been laid through the publication, by Gelb *et al.*, of *Nuzi Personal Names* which includes an index of the occurrences of the personal names in the Nuzi texts; but that study must first be brought up to date through the inclusion of all subsequently published Nuzi material. After that, analyses of the economic and social roles in which persons appear in the Nuzi documents would establish a prosopography of the Nuzi citizenry. The resultant work, a volume of "Who's Who in Nuzi," would be a great help in interpreting social and economic institutions in Nuzi. This is a formidable task if undertaken by a single scholar. It is therefore suggested that any future study of Nuzi documents should contain, whenever possible, a listing of the personal names mentioned, together with a description of the individual's economic and social role as reflected in the texts discussed. Such a listing for the *tidennūtu*-contracts is found in Appendix 2, below.

138. Lewy, *Or.*, N.S. *11* (1942), 9.

139. He is a prominent figure in sale-adoption contracts. See Cassin, *Adoption*, pp. 51 ff.

140. He is a prominent patron in the *ḫāpiru* documents. See Greenberg, *Ḫāb/piru*, p. 65.

Personal Tidennūtu and Nuzi Ḫāpiru Documents

Before leaving the sphere of Nuzi socio-legal institutions, it should be noted that the personal self-*tidennūtu* contract shares a certain similarity with the *ḫāpiru* documents from Nuzi.[141] Both types of document represent contracts in which free people voluntarily enter into a state of servitude without selling their person to the patron. However, this is the limit of their similarity. A comparative study of the contracts reveals that they reflect different institutions.[142]

The differences stem from the primary motivation of each of the transactions. The self-*tidennūtu* contract represents a loan transaction that an impoverished Nuzi citizen, in need of obtaining definite capital, is forced to make. Therefore the duration of the *tidennu*'s service depends on the return of the borrowed capital. As a rule the debtor must have looked to the time when he would again be independent. The *ḫāpiru* contract, however, represents a form of commendation[143] in which the indigent *ḫāpiru*, because of his status as an "outsider," is compelled to become a dependent of a patron in order to obtain the basic necessities of life. Since the *ḫāpiru* receives no capital upon his entrance into servitude, the duration of his service and the means of his redemption differ from that of a *tidennu*. The *ḫāpiru* obligates himself for the lifetime of the patron, and may only free himself by providing the patron with a substitute.

The self-*tidennūtu* and *ḫāpiru* transactions represent varying degrees of indentured servitude. While both reflect a status superior to that of ordinary slaves,[144] the status of a *tidennu* seems to have been decidedly higher than that of a *ḫāpiru*. This is borne out by the greater mobility accorded to the *tidennu*: he may temporarily absent himself from work by means of a monetary payment. This superior position is in keeping with the originally superior position of the impoverished Nuzi citizen vis-à-vis the indigent migrant outsider.

141. For a full treatment of the Nuzi *ḫāpiru* texts, see J. Bottéro, *Le Problème des Ḫabiru à la 4ᵉ Rencontre Assyriologique Internationale,* Cahiers de la Société Asiatique, 12 (Paris, Imprimerie Nationale, 1954), 43–70; and Greenberg, *The Ḫāb/piru*, pp. 23–32, 65–70.

142. Cf. the note of E. Cassin incorporated in Bottéro, *Le Problème des Ḫābiru*, pp. 65–69.

143. M. Greenberg, *The Ḫāb/piru*, p. 69 n. 40.

144. For those features which show the socio-legal position of the Nuzi *ḫāpiru* to be higher than that of the slave, see ibid., pp. 67 ff.

CHAPTER 3

Mesopotamian Analogues

Although unified by the basic premise from which its essential characteristics have developed,[1] Mesopotamian law is not monolithic. On the basis of language, legal formulation, and practice, various traditions within Mesopotamian law have been isolated.[2] The Mesopotamian legal documents of the first and second millennium B.C. may be divided into two main traditions: (1) the "core" tradition of central and southern Mesopotamia, formulated in Sumerian and closely related to the practices of the Ur III period; and (2) the "provincial" tradition of the fringe areas, formulated in Akkadian and closely related to the practices of the Old Akkadian period.[3]

The subjectively oriented Nuzi contracts are written primarily in Akkadian, and exhibit the imposition of monetary fines rather than oaths to ensure the incontestability of the transaction; this places the Nuzi documents within the "provincial" tradition of Mesopotamian law.[4] However, the term *tidennūtu* is unique to the Nuzi legal formulary. Thus the question arises whether the *tidennūtu* transaction reflects a Mesopotamian practice or whether it is distinctively Nuzian, perhaps rooted in Hurrian legal tradition. The purpose of this chapter is to investigate the Mesopotamian legal institutions of *mazzazānūtu*, *šapartu*, and *be'ūlātu*, which appear to have had much in common with that of Nuzi personal *tidennūtu*. If they were indeed analogous, the premise of a Mesopotamian background for the personal *tidennūtu*

1. Speiser summarized this premise in the following way: "Law is an aspect of the cosmic order and hence ultimately the gift of the forces of the universe. The human ruler is but a temporary trustee who is responsible to the gods for the implementation of the cosmic design. Because the king is thus answerable to powers outside himself, his subjects are automatically protected against autocracy, and the individual has the comfort and assurance of certain inalienable rights," *PAPS, 107* [1963], 537.

2. These traditions and their historical evaluation have been treated by Muffs, *Elephantine*, pp. 15 n. 3, 90 ff.

3. Ibid., p. 94. For a review of the scholarly opinion concerning the ultimate origins of these two traditions, see ibid., pp. 91 ff.

4. Ibid., p. 90 n. 5.

transaction would be strengthened and a broader perspective and deeper insight into this institution would be gained.

MAZZAZĀNŪTU

The institution of *mazzazānūtu*[5] appears in both the "core" and "provincial" traditions of Mesopotamian law; transactions are recorded in texts from central and southern Mesopotamia and the Diyala region, and they are attested as far west as Alalakh and as far east as Susa. Aside from its occurrence in legal contracts, the term *mazzazānu* appears in the *mīšarum*-edicts and in lexical lists. All specific references to the institution of *mazzazānūtu* date from the Old Babylonian period.

Since there has been no comprehensive treatment of the *mazzazānūtu* transactions,[6] a collection and investigation of all the relevant material is in order. The lexical sources will be considered first.

Lexical Series

The term *mazzazānu* occurs in the series *ana ittišu* and ḪAR-ra = *ḫubullu*.
a.i. 2 IV (*MSL*, *1*, 29)

21′. kù-ta-gub-ba	*ma-an-za-za-nu*		
22′. kù-ta-gub-ba-aš	*a-na*	"	
23′. kù-ta-gub-ba-aš mi-ni-in-gub	*a-na*	"	*uš-zi-iz*

(21′) *mazzazānu* (22′) as a *mazzazānu* (23′) he stationed as a *mazzazānu*.

a.i. 3 II 19 (*MSL*, *1*, 39)
Ḫḫ, I 345 (*MSL*, *5*, 36)

kù-ta-gub-ba *kasap man-za-zi*
capital involving *mazzazu*[7]

5. *Mazzazānūtu* is the abstract noun of the term *mazzazānu*. For the phonetic variants of both these terms see *AHw*, *1*, 638a.

6. The most important discussions of these transactions appear in Koschaker and Ungnad, *HG*, *6*, 21; Koschaker, *Griech. Rechtsurk.*, pp. 9–11, 94 n. 5, 106–09; Harris, "The Archive of the Sin Temple in Khafajah (Tutub)," *JCS*, *9* (1955), 60 f.; and Boyer, *ARMT*, *8*, pp. 218–20. J. Klíma's article, "Zu *manzazānum*-Garantien nach den altbabylonischen Urkunden," *ArOr*, *36* (1968), 551 ff. appeared while this manuscript was being prepared for publication.

7. This is the translation of the Akkadian entry. In order to reconcile the Sumerian with its Akkadian counterpart, a haplography for kù-kù-ta-gub-ba must be assumed (Landsberger, *MSL*, *1*, 139 n. 1).

For the term *mazzazu*, note Hirsch's recent identification of this term in an Old Assyrian letter ("Akkadische (altassyrisch) *mazzāzum* 'Pfand, Verpfändung',"

These lexical entries indicate that the Sumerian equivalent of *mazzazānu* is kù-ta-gub-ba "one who stands against the money." Thus both the Akkadian and Sumerian terms may be rendered as "stand-in" or "pledge." The corresponding verb, which describes the surrender of the pledge, is gub: *šuzuzzu* "to station."

a.i. 2 IV 27′–29′ (*MSL, 1,* 29)

mu-máš-kù-ga-a-ni-šè	*áš-šú ṣi-bat kas-pi-šu*
é a-šà kiri$_6$ sag-gèm-ìr	*bīta eqla kirā aštapīra*
kù-ta-gub-ba-aš mi-ni-in-gub	*a-na man-za-za-ni uš-zi-iz*

ibid., 39′–48′ (*MSL, 1,* 30 f.)

[u$_4$ kù]-babbar mu-un-tùm-da-aš	*i-nu kaspa ub-ba-lu*
é-a-ni-šè! ba-ab-ku$_4$-re	*a-na bīti-šu i-ru-ub*
u$_4$ kù-babbar mu-un-tùm-da-aš	*i-nu k*[*as*]*pa ub-ba-lu*
a-šà-ga-na ba-ab-gub-ba	[*i-na eq-li-šu*] *iz-za-az*
⸢u$_4$⸣ kù-babbar mu-un-tùm-da-aš	[*i-nu kaspa ub-b*]*a-lu*
[kiri$_6$]-ni bí-in-d[u$_8$-e?]	[*kirā-šu ir?-r*]*iš*
[u$_4$ kù-babbar mu-un-tùm-da-aš]	[*i-nu kaspa ub-ba*]*-lu*
ge[mé-ni]	[*a-mat-su i-t*]*a-bal*
u$_4$ kù-babbar [mu-un-tùm-da-aš]	[*i-n*]*u kaspa ub-ba-lu*
ìr-a-ni	[*a*]*rad-su i-tar-šú*

(27′–29′) Concerning the interest on his capital, he stationed house, field, orchard, (or) domestics as a *mazzazānu*-pledge.

(39′–48′) When he brings the capital, he may enter his house; when he brings the capital, he may stand in his field; when he brings the capital, he may claim (?) his orchard; when he brings the capital, he may take his slavegirl; when he brings the capital, his slave may return to him.

This entry attests to the antichretic nature of the *mazzazānu*-pledge. The *mazzazānu* not only secures the loan, but also serves as the interest on the capital. For this reason, the debtor redeems his pledge by returning only

---

WZKM, 62 [1969], 52 ff.). The text (*TCL, 20,* 91:10 ff.) states: 2 *ṭuppu ša* 10½ ma-na 5 gín kù-babbar *ša ḫubul ma!-za-zi-im* "Two documents concerning an interest-bearing *mazzazum* loan of ten and one-half minas, five shekels of silver." Hirsch (op. cit., p. 60) calls attention to the difficulty that the text, while designating the transaction as an interest-bearing loan (*ḫubullum*), specifies only the return of the principal sum (lines 14 ff.). This apparent difficulty can be resolved by assuming that the services rendered by the pledge are in lieu of interest. Hence this text indicates the antichretic nature of the Old Assyrian *mazzazu*-pledge which agrees with the interpretation of the nature of the Old Babylonian *mazzazānu*-pledge advanced here (cf. *ARM, 8,* 31, below).

the borrowed capital. The antichretic vs. the non-antichretic function of the pledge is also evident from *Ḫḫ* I 349–50 (*MSL*, *5*, 37):

[máš]-kù-babbar-bi-šè al-gub *a-na ṣi-bat kás-pi-šu iz-za-az*
[máš]-ku-babbar-bi-šè nu-al-gub ["] *ul iz-za-az*
(the pledge) stands for the interest on the (borrowed) capital.[8]
(the pledge) does not stand for the interest on the (borrowed) capital.

There are other lexical passages which contain clauses employed in antichretic pledge contracts.[9] But, as in the ḪAR-ra = *ḫubullu* references cited above, they do not specify the term *mazzazānu*. Nevertheless, these entries prove the existence of the institution of antichresis in the Old Babylonian period.[10]

In summary, the lexical evidence indicates that:

(1) the *mazzazānu* (Sumerian kù-ta-gub-ba) is a pledge;
(2) either real estate or persons may constitute a *mazzazānu*;
(3) the *mazzazānu* which secures the loan may also function as an antichretic pledge.

The evidence from legal records of actual *mazzazānūtu* transactions should support these findings. The discussion will be limited, however, to personal *mazzazānūtu* texts,[11] since their relationship to the institution of personal *tidennūtu* is our main concern.

8. The phrase "stands for the interest" is understood in the sense of "serves as the interest" rather than "guarantees the interest" (cf. Landsberger, *MSL*, *5*, 37). The usage of the clause in YBC 12191 (below, Simmons, *JCS*, *14* (1960), 121 No. 99) confirms this interpretation.

9. See *a.i.* 7 IV 13–22, with Landsberger's discussion in *MSL*, *1*, 247 ff; and *Ḫḫ* I 364–69.

10. Legal contracts attest the existence of personal and real estate antichresis in the Ur III period (see A. L. Oppenheim, *Catalogue of the Cuneiform Tablets of the Wilberforce Eames Babylonian Collection in the New York Public Library*, American Oriental Series, 32, pp. 133 f., 143; T. Fish, *Catalogue of the Sumerian Tablets in the John Rylands Library* [Manchester, Manchester University Press, 1932], p. 149 No. 688; and A. Pohl, *Rechts- und Verwaltungsurkunden der III. Dynastie von Ur*, Texte und Materialien der Frau Professor Hilprecht Collection, 1/2 [Leipzig, Hinrichs, 1937], No. 32). It is interesting to note, however, that there is no direct evidence that antichresis was connected with pledge law in these contracts (cf. A. Falkenstein, *Die neusumerischen Gerichtsurkunden*, *1* [München, Bayerische Akademie der Wissenschaften, 1956], p. 120 n. 5).

11. *Mazzazānūtu* transactions involving real estate are recorded in text Kh. 1935, 110 (Harris, *JCS*, 9 [1955], 60 No. 4) and YBC 11149 (Simmons, *JCS*, 14 [1960], 26 No. 54). Cf. *VAS*, *8*, No. 76:11–14.

Texts from Central and Southern Mesopotamia[12]

ARN, 105 (Ni 2977)

obv. 1. 13 gín kù-babbar na$_4$ ^{d}en!?-líl!?
2. máš nu-tuk
3. ki *A-li-dum* dumu *Ta-ri-bu-um*-ta
4. ^{I}*Ṣi-lí*-^{d}utu dumu ^{d}zuen-*ga-mil*-ke$_4$
5. šu ba-an-ti
6. 1 sag-mí ^{Id}*Ṣar-pa-an-ni-tum-li-wa-ir* mu-ni
7. á-ni nu-ub-tuk [gem]é *Ṣi-lí*-^{d}utu
8. ^{I}*Ṣi-lí*-^{d}utu [dumu ^{d}z]uen-*ga-mil*-e
9. ⸢^{I}*A-li-dum* dumu⸣ *Ta-ri-bu-um*-ra
10. kù-ta-[gub-b]a-aš í[b]-ta-an-gub
11. gemé á-ni [nu-u]b-tuk kù máš nu-ub-tuk
12. itu gan-gan-è [u$_4$] 29-kam

rev. 1. 13 gín kù-babbar [nu-mu-un-tú]m!?-ma
2. kù máš gá-[gá]-dam
3. igi *Il-ta-ni* [dumu] *I-bi*-^{d}nin-šubur
4. igi dingir-*šu* . . . . ì-du$_8$
5. igi *In-bi-ì-lí* dumu lú-ga-a
6. igi ^{d}utu-igi-kalam-ma kù-dím
7. igi *A-wi-li-ya* dumu *A-ḫi-ya-a*
8. itu šu-numun-a u$_4$ 1-kam
9. mu *Sa-am-su-i-lu-na* lugal
10. á-ág-gá ^{d}en-líl-lá-ta
11. nam-kù-zu nam-⸢á⸣-ág⸢x x⸣

u.e. 12. kišib *In-bi-ì-lí* sanga?

(1) Thirteen shekels of silver (according to) the weight-stone of Enlil(?)—bearing no interest—Ṣilli-šamaš, son of Sīn-gāmil received from Ālidum, son of Tarībum. (6) One female slave—Ṣarpānītum-līwa''ir by name, receiving no hire, the slavegirl of Ṣilli-šamaš—Ṣilli-šamaš, son of Sīn-gāmil stationed with Ālidum, son of Tarībum as a *mazzazānu*-pledge. (11) The slavegirl does not receive her hire; the capital does not bear interest. (rev. 1) Should he not return the thirteen shekels of silver by the twenty-

12. There are approximately twenty *mazzazānūtu* contracts in the corpus of texts found at Kisurra, near Nippur. They are being published by B. Kienast in his forthcoming book, *Die altbabylonischen Briefe und Urkunden aus Kisurra*. For the present see Kienast, "Zum altbabylonischen Pfandrecht," *SZ 83*/2 (1966), 334–38.

ninth day of the month Kissilimu the capital shall be placed on interest.

(3–7) five witnesses

(8) In the month Dumuzi, first day

(9) the year Samsu-iluna, the king, by the command of Enlil, wisdom (and) instruction (?) . . .

(12) one seal.

Notes

rev. 1. u$_4$ kù-babbar mu-un-túm = *ūmu kasapšu ubbal* (*MSL*, 5, 40:370).
rev. 2. gá-gá-dam = *iššakkan* (*MSL*, 1, 19:49; cf. *MSL*, *5*, 13:56).

This Nippur text, dated to the 28th year of Samsu-iluna, records a six-month loan of silver secured by a *mazzazānu*-pledge, the debtor's slavegirl. It specifies that the pledge is antichretic: she is to serve the creditor without wages in lieu of interest on the silver. However, if the debtor defaults at the expiration of the set term, the silver will begin to accrue additional interest. This interest will not be covered by the services of the *mazzazānu*-pledge.

PBS, *13*, 39 (CBS 14055)

obv. I	1.	II	1. . . . .
	2. . . . . šè		2. [tukumbi]
	3. ^{I}*Ša-at*-išdar sag-mí		3. ^{Id}. . . .
	4. gemé *I-pí-iq*-išdar		4. gá-la ba-a[n-dag]
	5. kù-ta-gub-ba-aš		5. u$_4$ 1-šè á-ni-šè
	6. íb-ta-gub		6. 1 bán-še-ta-àm
	7. tukumbi		7. al-ág-e
	8. gemé gá-la ba-an-dag		8. kù-babbar gur-da-bi
	9. [u$_4$]) (1-šè á-ni-šè		9. ìr-da-ni ba-an-tùm
	10. [x x x]-še-ta[-ám]		
	11. [al-ág-e]		

rest of col. I destroyed; only a few signs in each column are preserved on the reverse.

I (1) . . . he stationed Šāt-ištar, the female slave, the slavegirl of Ipiq-ištar, as a *mazzazānu*-pledge. (7) If the slavegirl stops working, [he shall measure out . . .] barley as her hire, per day.

II (1) . . . If PN stops working, he shall measure out per day one seah of barley as his hire. When the silver is returned, he may take back his slave.

Notes

I 2. This line may perhaps be restored as [máš-kù-babbar-bi]-šè "against the interest on the capital" (cf. *MSL*, *5*, 37:349).

I 7–10 and II 2–7. Cf. *MSL*, *5*, 40:366–369. Note, however, that traces of the sign before še on line I 10 do not seem to point to bán.

This Old Babylonian Nippur text is a register of contracts.[13] The first partially preserved contract records the giving of a slavegirl as a *mazzazānu*-pledge. It then stipulates a delinquency clause: if the pledge is absent from work, the debtor must pay a fine of . . . of barley per day to the creditor. This clause protects the creditor against the loss of the *mazzazānu*'s services and thus bespeaks the antichretic nature of the pledge.

In the other contract, two clauses are preserved, of which the second is an indefinite duration clause: whenever the debtor returns the silver, he may redeem his slave. This indicates that the contract represents a loan transaction secured by the debtor's slave. The first is a delinquency clause which proves the pledge to be antichretic. Both contracts thus confirm the interpretation of *mazzazānūtu* as an antichretic security transaction.

YOS, *8*, 78 (YBC 5694)[14]

obv. 1. 2 gín kù-babbar
2. ki *Ge-me-el-lum*
3. ^{I}*A-li-a-ḫu-ú-a*
4. šu ba-an-ti
5. ^{Id}utu-*li-w*[*a-ir* dumu-ni]
6. kù-ta ib-ta-an-gub
7. u_4 kù mu-un-tùm-ma
8. dumu-ni ba-an-túm-mu
rev. 9. igi ^{d}zuen-*ga-mil* mušen-dù
10. igi *Wa-ra-a-a* lú-geštin-na
11. igi *Li-pi-it*-išdar išib
12. igi ìr-^{d}nanna
13. igi *A-ḫu-ú-wa-aq-ru* ⌈x⌉
14. kišib-lú-inim-ma -⌈bi⌉-meš íb-r[a]
15. itu N[E.]NE-gar u_4 8-kam
16. mu inim!-an-^{d}en-líl-^{d}en-ki-ga-ta
17. ^{íd}ud-kib-nun-na ti-lim-da kù-ga ^{d}nanna-t[a]
18. sipa-zi *Ri-im*-^{d}zuen mu-ba-al
19. ki-unu^{ki}-ga zà a-ab-ba-šè x x x

13. The text, first copied by Legrain, was described by him as a fragment of a law code dealing with the wages of a slave (*Historical Fragments*, Publications of the Babylonian Section, 13 [Philadelphia, University Museum, 1922], 70). Poebel, in his review of the volume (*OLZ*, *27* (1924), 267), identified the text as a pledge transaction. See also Koschaker's treatment of this text in *Griech. Rechtsurk.*, p. 10.

I thank S. N. Kramer for permitting me to collate this tablet.

14. This text was first copied by E. Grant in his *Babylonian Business Documents of the Classical Period* (Philadelphia, 1919), No. 57. It was treated by Koschaker and Ungnad, *HG*, *6*, 25 No. 1474.

(1) Two shekels of silver Ālī-aḫūya received from Gimillum. (5) He placed his son, Šamaš-līwa''ir, against the money. (7) When he brings the money, he may take his son.

(9–13) five witnesses

(14) The seals of the witnesses were affixed.

(15) In the month Abu, the eighth day

(16–19) of the year Rīm-sīn, the faithful shepherd, by the command of An, Enlil, and Enki, dug the Euphrates, the holy *tilimdū*-vessel of Nanna, from Uruk to the sea. . . . .

This Larsa text, dated to the 23rd year of Rīm-sīn, describes a loan transaction secured by the debtor's son. It does not specify, however, that the pledge is antichretic, and thus raises an important methodological question. Under what circumstances may a pledge be considered antichretic? According to Koschaker,[15] any transaction involving a personal pledge held by the creditor to secure a loan which does not stipulate an interest charge may be considered antichretic. If this assumption is accepted, the above contract would represent an antichretic security transaction.[16]

Simmons, *JCS*, *14* (1960), 121, No. 99 (YBC 12191)

obv. 1. 6 gín kù-babbar
2. máš-bi-šè
3. *A-na-*^{d}zuen-*ták-la-*⌜*ku*⌝
4. dumu *Ì-lí-ša-am*
5. ib-ta-gub
6. ki *Ka-ti-tum*
7. *Ì-lí-ša-am*
8. dumu-mí *Za-ra-ma-a-nu-um*
9. kù šu ba-an-ti
10. itu NE.NE-gar
11. kù na-ab-sum-mu-dam
12. du[mu]-ni [na-an-d]u_8-e
several lines destroyed

u.e. 1′. mu ^{giš}⌜tukul⌝ . . . . ⌜x x⌝
2′. *Ma-na-na-a* mu-un-dím

(1) Six shekels of silver—Ana-sīn-taklāku, son of Ilišam, stands for its interest. (6) Ilišam, daughter of Zaramānum, has received the money from Katītum. (10) She shall give back the money in the month Abu and redeem her son.

(1′) The year Manana fashioned the weapon . . .

15. *Griech. Rechtsurk.*, p. 10.

16. For this reason, the self-pledge text *VAS*, *13*, 96 (Koschaker and Ungnad, *HG*, *6*, 28 No. 1481) may also be considered antichretic.

Notes

2–5. Cf. *MSL, 5,* 37:349; and Pohl, *TuM, 1/2,* 32:2–4.

11. For the affirmative particle na, see Falkenstein, "Untersuchungen zur sumerischen Grammatik," *ZA,* 47 (1942), 181 ff.
12. na-an-du$_8$-[e] = [*i-paṭ*]*-ṭar* (*MSL, 1,* 31:53′).

1′–2′. For a discussion of the date formula, see Simmons, *JCS, 14* (1960), 76, 79 ff.

This tablet of unknown provenience is dated to the early Old Babylonian period. The opening clause of the contract states that the services rendered by the debtor's son are antichretic. The final redemption clause indicates that the debtor's son also functions as a pledge. Thus, although the term kù-ta-gub-ba: *mazzazānu* is not employed, the contract records a loan transaction secured by an antichretic pledge.[17]

Texts from the Diyala Region

Harris, *JCS, 9* (1955), 70 No. 3 (Kh. 1935, 17)

obv. 1. 1 sag-ir
2. *Še-ri-a-a* mu-ni
3. ki *Ma-nu-u*[*m*]*-ki-*[*ì-lí*]*-a*
4. *a-na* 5! gín kù-babbar
5. *a-na ma-za-za-nu-tim*
6. *i-za-*˹*az*˺
7. *i-mu-*[*a*]*t*
8. *i-ḫa-li-iq-ma*
9. *i-nu-mi*

lo.e. 10. *i-pa-ra-ku-ú*
11. 1 bán še *i-ma-da-ad*

rev. 12. ki *Ku-a-a*
13. kù *e-le-qé*
14. igi *I-pí-iq*-išdar
15. dumu ^{d}*Še-ru-um-ba-ni*
16. igi *Bi-ni-tim*
17. dumu *Za-ri-ḫi-im*
18. igi *Ma-na-bi-iḫ-di-im*
19. igi *Ri-iš*-^{d}im
20. igi *I-din*-^{d}nin-˹x˺
21. igi en-^{d}im

17. See also *JCS, 14* (1960), 124 No. 107. Both of these texts were misinterpreted by Simmons (ibid.) who rendered the crucial line 5 ib-ta-gub as Akkadian *ip-ta-du.* I thank W. W. Hallo for permitting me to collate this tablet.

(1) One slave, Šeriya by name, stands under the authority of Mannum-kī-iliya for *mazzazānūtu* against five shekels of silver. (7) Should he die or disappear—(9) when he stops working, he (Kua) shall measure out the one seah of barley—then he (Mannum-kī-iliya) shall take back the money from Kua.

(14–21) six witnesses

Notes

3. The use of the preposition ki: *itti* "with," in this context of "standing with the creditor" seems to denote a subordination of the pledge to the creditor's authority.[18]

13. On the form *eleqqe* expressing the third person singular, see Harris, *JCS*, *9* (1955), 60.

In this *mazzazānūtu* text from Khafajah (ancient Tutub), Kua surrenders his slave as a *mazzazānu*-pledge to the creditor, Mannum-kī-iliya. This contract differs from the preceding texts in that it contains a permanent absence clause: if the slave dies or disappears, the creditor shall claim his money. Thus the permanent absence of the pledge immediately terminates the transaction, and the debtor must return the principal. The delinquency clause (lines 9–11), which applies to the temporary absence of the pledge, is inserted in the midst of the permanent absence clause and indicates that the pledge is antichretic, i.e. the service rendered by the slave is in lieu of interest on the loan of five shekels of silver.[19]

Harris, *JCS*, *9* (1955), 71 No. 5 (Kh. 1935, 120)

obv. 1. x x 1 gín kù-babbar
2. ki *Ma-nu-um-ki-ì-lí-a*
3. *Ba-ak-ši-šum*
4. šu ba-an-ti
5. *a-na ma-za-za-nu-tim*
6. *ma-ra-šu*
7. *iš-ku-*[*u*]*n*
8. *šum-*⌜*ma Ba-ak*⌝*-ši-šum*
9. *ma-ra-*[*šu*]

18. Cf. *AHw*, *1*, 405 sub *itti*, 8b). This usage appears to be analogous to the use of the Hebrew preposition *'im* in such passages as Gen. 32:5 and Lev. 25:35. See Speiser, "Leviticus and the Critics," *Yehezkel Kaufmann Jubilee Volume* (Jerusalem, Magnes Press, 1960), p. 38.

19. Harris appears to have misunderstood the formulation of an antichretic transaction in stating that "the five shekels of silver mentioned in line 4 is the interest on the debt which Kua owes Mannum-kī-iliya" (*JCS*, *9* [1955], 60). The five shekels of silver represent the principal sum borrowed and not the amount of interest due.

10. ....
11. kù-babbar *qá-[du-um]*
12. *ṣi-ib-ti-[šu]*
rev. 13. *i-ša-qá-[al]*
14. *i-mu-a[t]*
15. *i-ḫa-li-[iq-ma]*
16. ki *Ba-[ak]-ši-šum*
17. kù-babbar *e-le-qé*
18. igi *Ga-gu-um*
19. igi *Ḫu-ud-ḫu-du-um*
20. igi *Bi-bi-a-a*
21. igi *Ti-im-zu-na-a-*⌜*x*⌝
22. igi *Nu-uk-ra-nu-um*
23. ù [d]*en-šar-iš-mu* simug
le.e. 24. *Ì-lí-ma-da-nu-um*

(1) One x x shekel of silver, Bakšišum received from Mannum-kī-iliya; (5) (and) he placed his son for *mazzazānūtu.* (8) If Bakšišum . . . his son, he shall weigh out the silver together with its interest. (14) Should he (the son) die or disappear, then he (Mannum-kī-iliya) shall take back the silver from Bakšišum.

(18–24) seven witnesses

Notes

1. The first two signs may be read as 10 še "ten grains." However, since the grain of silver represents a smaller denomination of the shekel, it should appear after and not before the shekel specification.
7. The verb *iškun* reflects the Sumerian technical term for pledging, gar (cf. Falkenstein, *Gerichtsurkunden, 1,* 119)
10. Perhaps restore as **uš[parakka]*. Note, however, that Jacobsen's copy does not seem to support the reading *uš,* supplied by Harris in *JCS, 9* (1955), 61.
17. The form *eleqqe* has been noted in the preceding text, line 13.

This text, also found at Khafajah, records the giving of the debtor's son as a *mazzazānu*-pledge to the same creditor mentioned in the preceding text. In this contract, a new clause (lines 8–13) appears. The missing verb of the protasis prevents certainty, but it is clear from the apodosis that upon a certain action of the debtor with regard to the pledge, the debtor pays not only the principal sum but also the interest. This clause therefore argues for the original antichretic nature of the pledge. The new clause may deal with the temporary absence of the pledge, since the following clause (lines 14–18) considers his permanent absence. Accordingly, if the debtor causes his son to stop working, the *mazzazānūtu* arrangement is nullified and the transaction becomes a regular loan with interest.[20] But if the pledge should die or disappear (through no fault of the debtor), the *mazzazānūtu*-arrangement immediately terminates and the debtor must return the principal sum.

Texts from Mari

ARM, *8*, 31[21]

obv. 1. 5 gín kù-babbar u[r]$_5$-ra
2. *ṣa-ar-pu-um*
3. na$_4$ *Ma-ri*^{ki}
4. ki ^{d}utu-ta
5. *ù Ì-lí-i-din-nam*
6. ^{I}*Ya-ar-ip-é-a*
7. dumu ^{d}*Ba-bi-é-a*
8. itu *La-ḫi-im* u$_4$ 18-kam ba-zal-*ma*
9. kù-babbar šu ba-an-ti
10. ^{lf}*Ṭá-bu-ti-em-di*
11. *a-na ma-za-za-nu-tim*
lo.e. 12. *na-ad-na-*[*at*]
13. *u*$_4$*-um* kù-babbar *Ya-*[*ar-ip-é-a*]
rev. 14. *i-*⸢*ša*⸣*-qa-*[*lu*]
15. ^{lf}*Ṭá-bu-ti-*[*em-di*]
16. *i-ta-*[*ar*]
17. *i-ma-at i-ma-ra-aṣ!* [*i-ḫa-l*]*i-iq*
18. ^{I}*Ya-ri-ip-é-a*
19. kù-babbar *i-ša-qa-al*
20. igi *Ì-lí-tu-kúl-ti*
21. igi *Ak-ka* nagar
22. igi *I-din-ì-lí* ^{lú}⸢x⸣
23. igi *A-ḫu-ši-na* ^{lú}⸢x⸣
24. igi ^{d}zuen-*lu-ud-lu-ul*
u.e. 25. igi *Ya-aḫ-zi-ib* ^{lú}⸢x x⸣
26. igi *A-bi-ša-ki-im*
27. dub-sar

20. Cf. Nuzi *tidennūtu* texts *JEN*, *3*, 302, *JEN*, *5*, 489 and *JEN*, *6*, 609 (texts nos. 46–48 in the Appendix). The delinquency clause of these contracts does not stipulate the usual daily compensatory payments, but rather specifies that upon the *tidennu*'s absence from work, the borrowed capital accrues interest.

21. This text has been treated by Klíma in "Parerga Mariaca," *Ivra*, *16* (1965), 19. *ARM*, *8*, 72 seems to record the same transaction, with lines 1–5 corresponding to lines 10–14 of the present text, and lines rev. 1′–6′ corresponding to lines 15–20. If this be so, *ARM*, *8*, 72 rev. 1′ must read as ^{lf}*Ṭá-bu!-ti!-em-*[*di*].

(1) Five shekels of refined silver (according to) the weight stone of Mari, an interest-bearing loan. (4) Yar'ip-ea, son of Babi-ea, received the silver from Šamaš and Ilī-idinnam, in the month of Laḫḫum, the eighteenth day having passed. (10) Ṭābūti-emdī was given in *mazzazānūtu.* (13) When Yar'ip-ea weighs out the silver, Ṭābūti-emdī shall return. (17) If she dies, falls ill or disappears, Yar'ip-ea must weight out the silver.

(20–27) seven witnesses

Notes

1. As in Nuzi paleography, the GÍN sign seems to be identical with SU.
4. Note the position of the ablative postposition ta which should appear at the end of line 5 (Falkenstein, Review of *ARM, 7–8,* in *BiOr, 17* (1960), 178).
8. For the month name Laḫḫum, which also occurs in texts from Susa, see *ARMT,* 7, 207–08; *AHw, 1,* 528a.
17. Cf. *MSL, 1,* 103 lines 16, 19.

This Mari text, dated to the reign of Zimri-lim,[22] records a loan transaction in which a woman is surrendered as a *mazzazānu*-pledge. The sum of five shekels of silver is described as ur$_5$-ra "an interest bearing loan." Yet unlike the other ur$_5$-ra texts in Mari,[23] the interest rate is not specified. Furthermore, only the return of the principal is needed to redeem the woman; no mention is made of interest. This argues for the antichretic nature of the pledge; the services rendered by the woman for the creditor constitute the interest on his money.[24] The final clause of the contract (lines 17–19) specifies that the *mazzazānūtu* relationship terminates not only with the permanent absence (death, disappearance) but also the temporary absence (illness) of the pledge.

ARM 8, 52

obv. 1. 10 gín k[ù-babbar]
2. *it-ti* ^{d}im-*ma-lik* dumu *Me-qí-bi-im*
3. ^{I}*Ki-ri-ib-še-ri-*⸢*iš*⸣
4. dumu *Ya-am-ṣí-ḫa-at-nu-*⸢*ú*⸣
5. *a-na ma-za-za-nim*
6. kù-babbar šu ba-an-ti
7. u_4*!-um* mu 3-kam *ú-ma-la-ma*
8. kù-babbar *i-ša-qa-al-ma*
9. *it-ta-aṣ-ṣ*[*i*]
10. ⸢*in-na*⸣*-ab!-*[*bi-it*]

22. Boyer, *ARMT, 8,* 52 n. 2.
23. *ARM, 8,* 24, 31, 34, 40, 55–57.
24. Boyer, *ARMT, 8,* 219. Cf. the Nuzi *tidennūtu* text *HSS, 9,* 15 (text no. 4 in the Appendix).

lo.e. 11. *a-n[a qa-ta-ti-im]*
12. dam-*sú ka-le-et*
rev. 13. igi *Ḫi-im-di-ma-lik*
14. dumu *Ku-sa-bi-ya*
15. igi *E-te-el*-ka-^{d}utu
16. dumu *Ḫa-ni-ma-lik*
17. igi *I-la-ra-ḫe-e*
18. dumu *Bu-ṣí-ya*
19. igi *Ib-ni-*^{d}*ìr-ra*
20. dumu *Ì-lí-ú-ṣur-šu*
21. igi *Ṣú-ri-*^{d}im dub-sar
22. ⸢dumu ^{d}utu⸣*-na-ṣir*
23. itu *[T]ám-ḫi-ri-im*
u.e. 24. *li-mu A-ḫi-ya-a-ya*
25. [dumu] *Ta-ki-gi*

(1) Ten shekels of silver. (2) Kirib-šeriš son of Yamṣi-ḫatnu, as a *mazzazānu*, received the silver from Adad-mālik, son of Mēqibum. (7) When he fulfills three years, he may weight out the silver and go free. (10) Should he flee, his wife will be held as surety.

(13–22) five witnesses

(23–25) Month of Tamḫirum. Eponym: Aḫiyaya son of Takigi.

Notes

3. Kirib-šeriš is a Hurrian personal name (*NPN*, pp. 228, 256). The presence of Hurrians at Mari in the Old Babylonian period is attested from other personal names as well as from Hurrian religious texts unearthed at Mari.[25]

9. From the context, this reading seems preferable to *it-ta-az-z[a-az]* (Boyer, *ARMT*, *8*, 76). Cf. Nuzi contracts which employ the verb *waṣū* to indicate liberation from *tidennu* servitude (above, p. 20).

11. Cf. *ARM*, *8*, 53:5. For a comparative treatment of the role of the *qātātum* in Mari legal texts, see Boyer, *ARMT*, *8*, 222 ff.

23. The month name, Tamḫirum, also occurs in texts from Susa and Chagar-Bazar (Gadd, "Tablets from Chagar Bazar and Tall Brak, 1937–1938," *Iraq*, 7 (1940), 24).

24–25. As Boyer has noted, (*ARMT*, *8*, 78 n. 1) this eponym also appears in the Chagar-Bazar texts. (See *ARMT*, 7, 171 n. 1).

According to the proposed restoration, this text represents a self-*mazzazānu* transaction in which the debtor himself secures the loan of silver.[26] It contains a definite duration period of three years. After that time, the debtor may free

25. These texts have been published by Thureau-Dangin, "Tablettes hurrites provenant de Mari," *RA*, *36* (1939), 1–28.

26. Cf. Boyer's interpretation of this text (*ARMT*, *8*, 77 n. 3, 219).

himself by returning the principal sum. Since the pledge is in the possession of the creditor and there is no stipulated interest charge, it may be assumed that, in this case too, the pledge is antichretic. This contract, however, differs from all previous *mazzazānūtu* texts by specifying a clause concerning the flight of the debtor. In such an event, the debtor's wife may be seized as surety. This clause is appropriate in a self-pledge transaction, for only in such an arrangement does the flight of the debtor represent a loss of the pledge.

ARM, *8*, 71

obv. 1. *qa-ta-at Ya-an-ti-in-*⸢*e*⸣*-ra-aḫ*
2. *a-na* 6 1/2 gín kù-babbar
3. ^{I}*Ri-im-ši-ìl* dumu *Da-da*
4. *il-qé-e*
5. *a-na ma-za-za-ni* ^{f}*A-ḫa-sú-nu*
6. dam *Ya-an-ti-in-e-ra-aḫ*
7. *a-na Ri-im-ši-ìl*
8. *na-de-et*
lo.e. 9. *a-na* itu 2-kam
10. kù-babbar *ú-ul iš-qu-ul-ma*
11. ^{I}*A-ḫa-sú-nu*
rev. 12. dam *Ya-an-ti-in-e-*⸢*ra-aḫ*⸣
13. *a-na* kù-babbar *in-na-ad-di-in*
14. igi *I-din-*^{d}*di-ri-tim*
15. igi ^{d}zuen*-ib-ni*
16. igi *Ḫa-mu-ra-pí* ^{lú}uku-úš
17. igi ^{d}⸢zuen⸣*-i-din-nam*
18. igi *A-ku-na-tum*
19. igi *Ḫa-*⸢*ṣí*⸣*-ir-*^{d}utu
20. igi *Bi-in?-x-*AN
21. igi *Ib-ni-*^{d}zuen
u.e. 22. itu *Ú-ra-ḫi-im* u_4 4-kam
23. mu *Zi-im-ri-li-im*
le.e. 24. *Áš-la-ka-a*^{ki} *iṣ-ba-tu*

(1) Rīmši-il, son of Dada, assumed suretyship for Yantin-eraḫ, against six and one half shekels of silver. (5) Aḫassunu, wife of Yantin-eraḫ, has been committed to Rīmši-il, as *mazzazānu*. (9) Should he not weigh out the silver in two months, Aḫāssunu, wife of Yantin-eraḫ may be sold.

(14–21) eight witnesses

(22) In the month Uraḫim, the fourth day

(23–24) the year Zimri-lim captured Ašlakkā.

Notes

8. The term *nadēt* should not be viewed as simply an interchange with *nadnat*, i.e. the giving of the pledge (Falkenstein, *BiOr*, *17* (1960), 179). Its usage here should be compared with its occurrences in Nuzi lawsuits (e.g. *AASOR*, *16*, No. 38:34) where it expresses the committing by the court of the liable party into the hands of the injured party.

22. For the month Uraḫim, see *ARMT*, *7*, 207.

23–24. As noted by Boyer (*ARMT*, *8*, 104 n. 1), this is the date formula for the second year of Zimri-lim.

The antecedents to this text may be construed as follows: Yantin-eraḫ was indebted to a prior creditor for 6½ shekels of silver. Upon default of payment, Rīmši-il, who had assumed suretyship for Yantin-eraḫ, paid the creditor this sum. Thus a new creditor-debtor relationship was formed. The present contract was then drawn up in order to assure Rīmši-il of prompt compensation. Accordingly, Yantin-eraḫ is now indebted to Rīmši-il for six and a half shekels of silver, and his wife is committed to the new creditor as a *mazzazānu*-pledge. The term of the loan is set at two months. Upon default of payment, Rīmši-il may foreclose upon the pledge.[27]

There is no direct evidence as to the nature of the pledge. However, since the creditor is in possession of the pledge and there is no charge of interest, the pledge may be considered antichretic.

Texts from Alalakh

Wiseman, *Alalakh*, No. 27

obv. 1. 70 gín kù-babbar
2. ki *Am-mi-ta-qum* lugal
3. ^{I}*Kam-mu-ša* dam-a-ni *ù* dumu-meš-*šu*
4. *il-qú-ú*
5. [*a-na ma-az*]-*za-za-nim*
6. [*wa-aš-bu* itu . . .]
7. u_4 6-kam ba-zal
8. mu *Ya-ri-im-li-*⟨*im*⟩ lugal-e

rev. 9. igi *We-ri-ki-ba* $^{\mathrm{l\acute{u}}}$sukkal
10. igi *Ta!-al-ma-am-mu*
11. igi $^{\mathrm{l\acute{u}}}$sanga-^{d}išdar
12. igi *Ni-iq-mé-pa*
13. igi *A-ri-iš-lu-bar*

27. The Ur III text *ITT*, *3*, 6563:2–10 presupposes a similar sequence of events (cf. Falkenstein, *Gerichtsurkunden*, *1*, 117; 2, 317). For a different interpretation, see Boyer, *ARMT*, *8*, 220.

(1) Kam-muša, his wife and sons received seventy shekels of silver from Ammi-taqum, the king. (5) They are to stay as *mazzazānu.*

(6–7) In the month . . . , the sixth day having elapsed,

(8) the year, Yarim-lim became king.

(9–13) five witnesses

Notes

1. As in Nuzi and Mari paleography, the GÍN sign seems to be identical with SU.
8. The year formula records the accession of Yarim-lim III to the throne of Yamḫad. For the chronological relationship between the rulers of Alalakh and Yamḫad, see H. Klengel, *Geschichte Syriens im 2. Jahrtausend v.u. Z., 1: Nordsyrien,* Veröffentlichung der Deutschen Akademie der Wissenschaften zu Berlin, Institut für Orientforschung, 40, Berlin, Akademie Verlag, 1965, 203–18.

Wiseman, *Alalakh*, No. 36

obv. 1. 3 gín kù-babbar
2. 20 *pa-ri-si* zíz
3. *ša Ta-al-ma-am-mu*
4. ugu *Eḫ-li-a-du*
5. *ù* dumu-*šu! At-ri-a-du*
6. *ma-za-za-nim wa-ši-ib*
7. IGI *Pé-en-dì-li*
8. ^{lú}*ḫa-za-nim*

rev. 9. igi *Uš-ti-ni-*^{d}*x*
10. igi *Ḫe-er-še*
11. igi *A-na-a-na*
12. igi *Am-mu-uš-ki!-na!*

(1) Three shekels of silver (and) twenty *parīsu* of emmer belonging to Talm-ammu is charged to Eḫli-adu; (5) And his son, Atri-adu is to stay (as) *mazzazānu.*

(7–10) five witnesses

Notes

2. For references to the dry measure *parīsu,* often indicated by the abbreviation PA, see Wiseman, *Alalakh,* p. 14.
12. Cf. Wiseman, Alalakh, No. 39:10

Wiseman, *Alalakh*, No. 43 (*JCS*, 8 [1954], 6)

obv. 1. 10 *pa-ri-si* zíz ugu *Bi-*[x]*-ya*
2. *a-na ma-az-za-za-nim*
3. ^{I}*Ta-ak-ki* dumu-⸢*šu!?*⸣ ⸢*id!-di!-in*⸣
4. 15 pa zíz ugu *Ḫe-er-šu*

5. *a-na ma-az-za-za-nim-*[*m*]*a*
6. ^{I}dumu-*šu* ^{I}*Wa-an-di-lim*
7. *id-di-in*
8. 6 gín kù-babbar
9. ugu *Im-me-ni*
10. *ḫu-un-na*

rev. 11. *a-na ma-az-za-za-nim*
12. dumu-[*šu*] ki-^{d}im
13. *id-di-in*
14. *a-na* [gín] kù-babbar *ù* pa zíz
15. ^{I}⌜x x⌝ *ku mu-u*[*n-x*]

(1) Ten *parīsu* of emmer is charged to Bi-x-ya; (2) he gave his son, Takki, as *mazzazānu.* (4) Fifteen *parīsu* of emmer is charged to Ḫeršu; (5) likewise as *mazzazānu* he gave his son, Wandilim. (8) Six shekels of silver is charged to Immeni, *ḫunna*; (11) as *mazzazānu*, he gave his son, Itti-adad. (14) For the shekels of silver and *parīsu* of emmer . . .

Notes

3. According to the copy, the verb *iddin* appears at the end of line 4. Nevertheless, context and parallel formulation require the verb to be at the end of line 3. The scribe probably inserted the verb between the two lines.
6. The rendering of the entire line as a personal name ^{I}*I-šu-wa-an-di-lim* (Wiseman, *Alalakh*, 45) is not without difficulty since the personal name determinative also occurs before the *wa* sign. Context and parallel formulation seems to favor the above transliteration.
10. The meaning of the term *ḫunna*, considered to be Hurrian (Draffkorn, *Hurrians*, p. 173 sub *ḫuni*), is unknown. It may be descriptive of either the payment or the person.

Wiseman, *Alalakh*, No. 44 (*JCS*, 8 [1954], 6)

Aside from the names of witnesses, the month and the year formula, only the clause *ana mazzazāni*[*m*] *wašib* "he stays as *mazzazānu*" remains.

Wiseman, *Alalakh*, No. 25

obv. 1. $33\frac{1}{3}$ gín kù-babbar *ša šar-*[*ra-ak-ki*]
2. *ki-ma* $33\frac{1}{3}$ gín kù-babbar
3. *ša šar-ra-ak-ki*
4. ^{I}*Wa-an-di* dumu *Ku-uš-ḫa-dá-*[*al*]
5. *a-na* é *Am-mi-ta-qum* lugal
6. *a-na ma-az-za-az-za-nim*
7. *a-ši-ib*
8. igi *E-wa-ri-ki-ba* sukkal

9. igi *Sú-un-na*
10. igi *E-wa-ri-ba*
11. igi *Am-mu-ir-ba*

(1) Thirty-three and one-third shekels of silver, pertaining to the oblates.

(2) In lieu of the thirty-three and one-third shekels of silver pertaining to the oblates, Wandi, son of Kušuḫ-adal, is to stay in the house of Ammitaqum, the king, as *mazzazānu.*

(8–11) four witnesses

Notes

1. and 3. For the term *šarrāku* "oblate," cf. *ŠL* 115:182. The expression *ša šarrāki*, modifying a quantity of silver, also appears in Wiseman, *Alalakh*, No. 368:5–7: *kīma* kù-babbar *ša* lú-meš *šarrākī*. Another Old Babylonian reference to *šarrāku* occurs in the Mari text *ARM, 10*, 8:15 (cf. Moran, "New Evidence from Mari on the History of Prophecy," *Biblica, 50* [1969], 31). That these oblates lived in special settlements seems evident from the term *āl šarrākī* (cf. Gelb, *Glossary of Old Akkadian*, Materials for the Assyrian Dictionary, 3 [Chicago, University of Chicago Press, 1957], 284; Goetze, "The *šakkanakkus* of the Ur III Empire," *JCS, 17* [1963], 20; and possibly *ARM, 10*, 81:7), although little is known of their role in Mesopotamian society. It is questionable whether the Middle Babylonian occurrences of the term lú*šarrāk/qu* in Alalakh (Wiseman, *Alalakh*, Nos. 165, 180, and 228) describe a different category of person from the above designation (cf. Greenberg, *Ḫāb/piru*, p. 21).

Wiseman, *Alalakh*, No. 18

obv. 1. $\frac{1}{3}$ ma-na 1 gín kù-babbar
2. *ša Am-mi-ta-qum* lugal
3. ugu *Am-mi-ya-a-du* lúmušen-dù
4. I*A-ya-aš*-lugal *ù Bé-en-di-a-du*
5. dumu-meš *Am-mi-a-du*
6. *ki-ma* kù-babbar *an-ni-i-im*
7. *a-na ma-az-za-az-za-nu-tim*
8. *a-na* é *Am-mi-ta-qum-ma*
9. *wa-aš-b*[*u*]
10. [k]in! lú!mušen-dù ⸢x⸣ . . .
11. *e-li* lugal [*ip-pé-šu*]
12. *ša-ni-a-am-ma* . . .
13. *ša it-ta-* . . .

rev. 14. *ú-ul i-ba-* . . .
15. igi *E-wa-ri-ki!-ba*
16. igi *Ta-al-ma-am-mu*
17. igi *Im-me-ri*

(1) One-third mina and one shekel silver, belonging to Ammi-taqum, the king, is debited against Ammi-adu, the fowler. (4) Aya-šarrī and Pendi-adu, sons of Ammi-adu, are to stay in the house of Ammi-taqum in lieu of this silver, for *mazzazānūtu.* (10) They shall [perform the w]ork of a fowler . . . for the king.

(12–14) broken verbal forms do not permit translation

(15–17) three witnesses

Notes

8. Note the use of the preposition *ana* for *ina* (Aro, "Remarks on the Language of the Alalakh Texts," *AfO, 17* [1956], 364). A similar phenomenon occurs in the Nuzi texts (below, p. 114).
11. For the meaning of *eli* "on behalf of, for" see *AHw, 1,* 210, sub 5c.

Despite the brevity of these contracts, one may conclude that in Alalakh the *mazzazānūtu* arrangement results from a loan transaction secured by a member or members of the debtor's family who are designated as a *mazzazānu*-pledge. Wiseman, *Alalakh,* No. 25, stipulates that the pledge remains in the house of the creditor. Thus the pledge is in the possession of the creditor and subject to his authority. The assumption that the pledge performs services for the creditor during his detention is verified by Wiseman, *Alalakh,* No. 18, which specifies the type of service to be rendered by the *mazzazānu*-pledge.

Wiseman, *Alalakh,* No. 21 (*JCS,* 8 [1954], 5)

obv. 1. $\frac{1}{2}$ ma-na ⟨1⟩ gín kù-babbar
2. *ša Am-mi-ta-qum* lugal
3. ugu *Wa-an-dì-iš-ḫa!-ra* ^{lú}uš-bar
4. ^{I}*Wa-an-dì-iš-ḫa-ra*
5. *i-na* é ^{I}*Am-mi-ta-*[*qum*] lugal
6. *a-na ma-an-za-za-nu-tim*
7. *wa-aš-bu*
8. *ša qa-tá-ti*
9. ^{f}*We-ra-a-ni* dam
10. kù-babbar$^{\textit{pá-am}}$
11. *i-na* é lugal
rev. 12. *ú-ša-al-la-am-šu*
13. *a-ša-ar li-*
14. *ib-bi-i-šu*
15. *i-il-la-ak-ma*
16. igi *A-ri-ib-*[*ša-uš-ka*]
17. igi *Iš-me-g*[*a*]

18. igi *Ya-ri-im-li-im*
19. lú*ḫa-za-an-*[*nu*]
20. uru *Ir-ki-il-li*
21. mu-kam I*Ḫa-am-mu-ra-*[*pí*]
22. lugal *Ya-am-ḫa-ad*

(1) One half mina [and one] shekel of silver belonging to Ammi-taqum, the king, is charged to Wandi-išḫara, the weaver. (4) Wandi-išḫara is to stay in the house of Ammi-taqum, the king, for *mazzazānūtu.* (8) The surety is Werani, the wife. (10) (Whenever) he restores the silver to the house of the king, he may go wherever he pleases.

(16–20) three witnesses

(21–22) The year Ḫammu-rapi became king of Yamḫad.

Notes

1. Cf. Wiseman, *Alalakh*, No. 18:1.

10–15. Note that the circumstances of these clauses are not expressed conditionally but are set down as definite facts in an asyndetic construction. This is characteristic of the formulation of many clauses in Old Babylonian contracts from Alalakh.

11. The preposition *ina* is here used for *ana* (cf. Wiseman, *Alalakh*, No. 18:8).

16–17. Cf. Wiseman, *Alalakh*, No. 22:16–17.

21–22. The year formula records the accession of Ḫammu-rapi II to the throne of Yamḫad. Cf. Klengel, *Geschichte Syriens im 2. Jahrtausend v.u. Z., 1: Nordsyrien*, 161–62.

Wiseman, *Alalakh*, No. 22

obv. 1. 30 gín kù-babbar
2. *ša Am-mi-ta-qum* lugal
3. ugu *Na-aš-we* dumu *Ta-aḫ-e*
4. I*Na-aš-we a-na* é
5. I*Am-mi-ta-qum* lugal
6. *a-na ma-an-za-za-an-nu-tim*
7. *wa-a-aš-bu*
8. I*Ta-aḫ-e*
9. dumu *Ša-ma-ya*
10. *ša qa-tá-ti*

rev. 11. kù-babbar*pá-am*
12. *i-na* é lugal
13. *ú-ša-al-la-am*
14. *a-ša-ar li-ib-bi-šu*
15. *i-il-la-ak*
16. igi ⸢*A-ri*⸣*-ib-ša-uš-ga*
17. igi [*Iš-m*]*e-ga*

18. igi *Ya-ri-im-li-im*
19. lú*ḫa-za-an-nu*
20. uru *Ir-ki-il-li*
le.e. 21. mu *Ḫa-am-mu-ra-pí*
22. lugal *Ya-am-ḫa-ad*

(1) Thirty shekels of silver, belonging to Ammi-taqum, the king, is charged to Našwe, son of Taḫe. (4) Našwe is to stay in the house of Ammi-taqum the king, for *mazzazānūtu.* (8) The surety is Taḫe, son of Šamaya. (11) (Whenever) he restores the silver to the house of the king, he may go wherever he pleases.

(16–20) three witnesses

(21–22) The year Ḫammu-rapi became king of Yamḫad.

Wiseman, *Alalakh,* No. 24

obv. 1. 1 ma-na kù-babbar
2. *ša Am-mi-ta-qum-ma* lugal
3. ugu *Na-di-na* ù *Zi-ki-⸢il-da⸣*
4. lú.meš*ku-ut-tu-ru*
5. *ki-ma* 1 ma-na kù-babbar
6. *a-na ma-za-za-nim*
7. *i-na* é-gal*lim*
8. *ú-wa-aš-bu*
rev. 9. kù-babbar *i-ip-pa-lu!*
10. *a-šar lìb-bi-šu-nu*
11. *i-⸢la⸣-ku*
12. *ka-⸢at!⸣-tu-šu-nu*
13. *ni-ši-šu-un*

(1) One mina of silver, belonging to Ammi-taqum(ma), the king, is charged to Nādina and Zikilda, the *kutturu*-men. (5) In lieu of the one mina of silver they are to stay in the palace as *mazzazānu.* (9) (Whenever) they repay the silver, they may go wherever they please. (12) Their surety is their family.

Notes

4. The term *kutturu* may indicate an occupation, profession, or social class (cf. *AHw, 1,* 519).

12. The term *ka-at-tu-šu-nu* also appears in Wiseman, *Alalakh,* No. 23:12 as *ka-tu-šu-nu.* These occurrences are to be connected with the term for surety, *kattū* (from the Assyrian verb *katā'um, AHw, 1,* 465–66), and must be differentiated from the standard term in Alalakh for surety, *qātātu* (from the noun *qātu*). Cf. Ebeling, *Or,* N.S. *22* (1953), 356.

This group of Alalakh texts, which record self-*mazzazānu* transactions, stipulates an indefinite duration clause. The *mazzazānūtu* arrangement terminates whenever the debtor restores the capital to the creditor. Since the *mazzazānu*-pledge is freed by the return of the principal sum alone, it is reasonable to assume that the services rendered by the pledge are in lieu of interest. As is the usual practice in self-*mazzazānu* transactions, these contracts also appoint additional persons as surety. These designated people guarantee the loan in case the debtor who also serves as the *mazzazānu*-pledge is not present.

Wiseman, *Alalakh*, No. 20 (*JCS*, 8 [1954], 5)

obv. 1. . . . gín kù-babbar
2. ⌜*ša Am-mi-ta-qum-ma*
3. ugu *A-ra-am-mu*
4. ^{lú}uš-bar^{tum}
5. *qa-du-um* dam-ni-*šu*
6. *ù* dumu-meš-*šu*
7. *i-na* é^{ti}
8. *Am-mi-ta-qum-ma* lugal
9. *a-na ma-za-za-nim*
rev. 10. *wa-aš-bu-ú*
11. *ba-al-ṭu*$_4$*-um-ma*
12. kù-babbar *u-ša-lim*
13. igi *A-ri-ib-ša-uš-*[*ka*]
14. igi *Eḫ-li-a-du*
15. igi *Ab-tu*
16. igi $^{\text{lú!}}$sanga

(1) . . . shekels of silver, belonging to Ammi-taqum(ma) is charged to Arammu, the weaver. (5) Together with his wife and sons, they are to stay in the house of Ammi-taqum, the king, as *mazzazānu*. (11) He who survives shall restore the silver.

(13–16) four witnesses

Notes

4. The phonetic complement *tum* may have been used to indicate the plural form of *ušparu* i.e., *ušparātu* (*CAD*, I–J, p. 255). Since the debtor's sons, probably weavers by trade, were also involved in the transaction, the scribe mistakenly used the plural form.
11. The use of *ṭum* for *ṭu* indicates the decay of mimation in Old Babylonian Alalakh (Aro, *AfO*, *17* [1956], 361).
12. The preterite form *ušallim* appears for the expected present-future *ušallam*.

11–12. Cf. Wiseman, *Alalakh*, No. 42:7–9 *i-na be-ri-šu-nu ba-al-ṭú ú-ma-al-la* "Whosoever among them survives shall pay the full amount."

The last clause of this text (lines 11–12) has been interpreted as expressing a joint responsibility[28] rather than a date of maturity.[29] The legal concept of joint responsibility in cuneiform law was reconstructed by Koschaker.[30] He showed that in joint responsibility each co-debtor, although he owes only his share of the received money, guarantees the payment of the entire sum. The implications of this reconstruction are two-fold: the creditor has a right to bring suit against any one of the co-debtors for the entire sum; and the payment of the entire sum by one of the co-debtors frees the others from prosecution by the creditor.[31] If the interpretation of this clause is correct, this Alalakh text records a *mazzazānūtu* transaction in which the members of the family are co-debtors, all serving as self-*mazzazānu*-pledges.

Wiseman, *Alalakh*, No. 28

obv.
1. ^{I}*Aš-ma-⸢a⸣-du* dumu *Da(?)-ka-bi-ti*
2. ^{I}*Wi-i[k-ki]-en*
3. ^{I}⸢x x x x⸣
4. ^{I}*Ta-[a'-ú]-g[i]*
5. $^{\text{lú.meš}}$⸢*ús*⸣*-an-du*
6. *aš-šum* 30 kù-babbar sag-du
7. ^{I}*Kur-bi-ša-an* dumu *Ni-mi-na-šu*
8. *um-ma-ad-šu-nu-ti-ma*
9. ^{I}*Am-mi-ta-qum-ma*
10. *a-na* 30 kù-babbar
11. *it-ti* ^{I}*Kur-bi-ša-an*
12. *ip-ṭú-ur-šu-nu-ti*
13. ki 30 kù-babbar sag-du

rev.
14. ugu *Aš-ma-a-du*
15. ^{I}*Wi-ik-ki-en*
16. *ù Zu-uk-ra-šu!*
17. ^{I}*Ta-a'-ú-gi!*
18. *ù* ugu $^{\text{mí.meš}}$dam-ni-*šu*
19. dumu-meš-*šu-nu*
20. kù-babbar *ma-za-za-nim*

28. I.e., "He who survives will restore the silver" (A. L. Oppenheim, in his review of Wiseman, *The Alalakh Tablets*, in *JNES, 14* [1955], 198).

29. I.e., "He shall repay the money in his lifetime" (Mendelsohn, "On Slavery in Alalakh," *IEJ, 5* [1955], 67).

30. *Bürgschaftsrecht*, pp. 84–97.

31. Ibid., pp. 93–94.

21. *i-na bé-ri-šu-nu* kù-babbar
22. *ša Am-mi-ta-qum* lugal
23. ^{uru}*A-la-la-aḫ*^{ki}
24. *ú-ma-al-la-ma*

le.e. 25. [*i-la-*]*ak* gù *i-na pi-šu*
26. [*a*]*-bá-ra-am i-sa-pá-ku*

(1) Ašma-adu, son of Dakabiti, Wikki-en, PN (and) Ta'ugi, the fowlers. (6) Concerning the principal sum of thirty (shekels) of silver, Kurbi-šan, son of Niminašu, made them jointly responsible. (9) But Ammi-taqum(ma) redeemed them from Kurbi-šan for thirty (shekels) of silver. (13) Ašma-adu, Wikki-en, and Zukrašu,Ta'ugi, and their wives and sons are debited with thirty (shekels) of silver, the principal sum. (20) The *mazzazānu*-capital is their joint responsibility; (21) he who pays in full the silver belonging to Ammi-taqum, king of Alalakh, may then go (wherever he pleases). (25) He who raises a claim, shall have lead poured into his mouth.

Notes

3. Cf. line 16.
4. Cf. line 17; *NPN*, p. 144 sub Taiuki. This name was read as Taḫpazi by Draffkorn (*Hurrians*, p. 55).
8. The verb *emēdu* "to attach or associate oneself (with another)," in the legal sense of assuming joint responsibility, also occurs in the Laws of Ḫammurapi, §176. The clause *ištu innemdū* "since they were joined together" (CH XIII rev. 80) seems to refer to a legal association assuming joint responsibility for post-marital obligations (cf. CH §§ 151 and 152) rather than to a physical relationship (cf. *CAD*, E, p. 146).

20–21. Cf. the note to Wiseman, *Alalakh*, No. 20:11–12.

25. gù = *ragāmu* (*ŠL* 15:200)

26. This formula for securing the validity of the agreement also appears in Wiseman, *Alalakh*, Nos. 8:32, 61:18, 95 rev. 5, and 96 rev. 4. For other examples of the *š*/*s* interchange in the Alalakh texts, see Aro, *AfO*, *17* (1956), 362.

Wiseman, *Alalakh*, No. 26

obv. 1. . . . gí[n] kù-babbar sag-du
2. *ša Am-mi-ta-qum-ma*
3. lú ^{uru}*A-*[*l*]*a-la-aḫ*^{ki}
4. ugu ^{I}[*Sú-u*]*n-na* dumu *Mu-ti-ya*
5. ^{f}dam-a-[ni *ù* dum]u-meš
6. *ki-ma* [kù-babbar *a*]*n-ni-i-im*
7. *a-na* é [*A*]*m-mi-ta-qum-ma*
8. *a-*[*na ma-az*]*-za-az-za-nu-tim*
9. [*wa-aš-bu i-ḫa-l*]*i-iq*
10. . . . [*i-na-*]*bi-tu*

rev. 1′. . . . . ⌜x x⌝
2′. [*ú-ul uṣ-*]*ṣa-ab*
3′. [*ù ú-ul*] *it-ta!-*⟨*ra*⟩*-ar!*
4′. . . . ⌜x⌝ x
5′. igi *Ki*[-x-x]-*ra*-ᵈišdar?
6′. igi *W*[*a-an-di*]*-ša-uš-ka*
7′. igi *A-ri-ib-ša-uš-ka!*

(1) . . . . shekels of silver, the principal sum, belonging to Ammitaqum(ma), ruler of Alalakh, is charged to Sunna, son of Mūtiya. (5) His wife and sons, in lieu of this silver, are to stay in the house of Ammitaqum(ma) for *mazzazānūtu.* (9) He who disappears . . . or flees . . . (2′-3′) It bears [no interest, nor is it affected by] a remission of debts.

(5′–7′) three witnesses

Notes

10. On the basis of parallelism with *iḫalliq* of line 9, one would expect the singular rather than the plural form.

2′–3′. Cf. Wiseman, *Alalakh,* No. 29:9–11, 30:8–9. 31:8–9. For this formula, see Speiser, "The Alalakh Tablets," *JAOS, 74* (1954), 22.

Wiseman, *Alalakh,* No. 28 differs from the previous Alalakh contracts in that the *mazzazānūtu* arrangement does not arise from a loan transaction, but from a redemption transaction. The original indebtedness of the debtors is transferred to a new creditor who has redeemed them from a prior creditor by paying their debt.[32] This payment constitutes the principal sum owed to the new creditor. The released debtors, together with their families, now enter into the household of the new creditor as *mazzazānu*-pledges. When the principal sum is restored, they may go free. Thus the services of the pledges may be considered antichretic.

Wiseman, *Alalakh,* No. 26 records a *mazzazānūtu* arrangement which may also have arisen from a redemption transaction. The restored clause (lines 2′–3′)—"(The money) bears no interest nor is it affected by a remission of debts"—appears in contracts dealing with the redemption of debtors by a new creditor.[33] This clause, which describes the money charged to the debtors who were redeemed from a prior creditor, probably indicates that the released debtors serve as *mazzazānu*-pledges in the household of the new creditor. Hence the money bears no interest.

32. The Nuzi *tidennūtu* texts *JEN, 3,* 312 and SMN 2047 (nos. 20 and 50 in the Appendix) may also reflect a similar circumstance. See above, p. 14.

33. Wiseman, *Alalakh,* Nos. 29–31.

Wiseman, *Alalakh*, No. 41

obv. 1. 5 . . . gín ! kù-babbar
2. *ša* ⌜*Ir*⌝-*pa*-^{d}im
3. *ša* ugu *Am-ma-ra-du*
4. *i-šu-ú*
5. kù-babbar *a-na* ^{uru}*Ku-nu-we*
6. *a-na* ⌜*ma-az*⌝-*za-az-za-ni*-[*im*]
7. *na-d*[*i-in*]
8. ^{I}*Ya-ri-i*[*m-l*]*i*-[*im*]
9. lú *A-la-la-aḫ*
rev. 10. kù-babbar *a-na Ir-pa*-^{d}im
11. *i-p*[*u-u*]*l*
12. u_4*-ra še-ra*
13. ^{I}*Am-ma-ra-du*
14. *it-ti Ir-pa-da*
15. *ú-ul i-ra-ag-gum*
16. *ša i*-[*r*]*a-ag*-gu_5*-mu*
17. 1 li kù-babbar 1 me guškin
18. ì-lá-e

(1) Five . . . shekels of silver, belonging to Irpa-ada, which was charged to Ammar-adu; (5) the silver was given for the city, Kunuwe, for *mazzazānu.* (8) Yarim-lim, the ruler of Alalakh, paid the silver to Irpa-ada. (12) In the future, Ammar-adu shall not raise a claim against Irpa-ada. (16) He who raises a claim shall weigh out one thousand (shekels) of silver (and) one hundred (shekels) of gold.

Notes

3. Wiseman, *Alalakh*, No. 53 attests to the fact that Ammar-adu is the owner of the city Kunuwe. Also cf. Wiseman, *Alalakh*, No. 368.
12. The idiom *urra šēra*, lit. "day(and)dawn" (Speiser, *JAOS*, *74* [1954], 23), expresses the idea of "in the future, for all time." Cf. Kupper, in his review of Wiseman, *Alalakh* in *BiOr*, *11* (1954), 119.

This text also records a *mazzazānūtu* arrangement resulting from the transfer of an original indebtedness to a new creditor. The unique feature of this contract, however, is that a village constitutes the *mazzazānu*-pledge. The new creditor has paid the debt of the owner of the village. In return, he secures for himself the revenues and services of the village held as a *mazzazānu*-pledge. Since there is no stipulation of an interest charge, one may assume that these services and revenues are antichretic. It is interesting to note that Wiseman, *Alalakh*, No. 53 records the eventual purchase of this village from its owner by the new creditor.[34]

This entire corpus of Alalakh *mazzazānūtu* contracts indicates that creditors (including the rulers of Alalakh) acquired for themselves the services of individuals,[35] families,[36] and even villages[37] on the basis of a loan transaction. The loan, usually in silver or emmer, varies in value from over three shekels to seventy shekels of silver. The people who secured the loan were attached to the household of the creditor as *mazzazānu*-pledges.[38] They included fowlers,[39] weavers,[40] and *kutturu*-men,[41] who served the creditors in these capacities.[42] Their services may be considered antichretic since the loans do not stipulate an interest charge but state that the return of the principal sum alone redeems the pledge. In the case of a self-*mazzazānu* arrangement, the contracts specify additional surety[43]; in the case of co-debtors, the contracts specify their joint responsibility.[44]

All of these documents have been unearthed from Old Babylonian Alalakh (Level VII, 18th century B.C.). A dark age[45] separates this body of texts from those of Middle Babylonian Alalakh (Level IV, 15th century B.C.). Despite the great cultural and political changes which had been wrought in this time,[46] the legal tradition and formulary of the two levels are remarkably similar. Investigation of the Middle Babylonian legal material at Alalakh reveals the following two documents which record antichretic pledge transactions:

Wiseman, *Alalakh*, No. 47

u.e. na$_4$-kišib ^{I}*Niq-me-pa*

34. This seems to attest the Mesopotamian legal principle that the absolute acquisition of property depends upon payment of the full price; hence a creditor cannot obtain absolute title to a foreclosed pledge as long as its value is greater than the debt. (J. Lewy, *Eretz-Israel, 5* [1958], 26.) The purchase price paid by the creditor in Wiseman, *Alalakh*, No. 53 probably represented the value of the village minus the sum owed.

35. Wiseman, *Alalakh*, Nos. 21, 22, 24, 36, and 43.

36. Ibid., Nos. 20, and 26–28.

37. Ibid., No. 41.

38. This is distinct from being held as a *lîṭu* "hostage" (ibid., No. 23). Contract Wiseman, *Alalakh*, No. 19 may record a *liṭu* or a *mazzazānu* relationship.

39. Wiseman, *Alalakh*, Nos. 18, and 28.

40. Ibid., Nos. 20, and 21.

41. Ibid., No. 24.

42. Ibid., No. 18.

43. Ibid., Nos. 21, 22, and 24.

44. Ibid., Nos. 20, and 28.

45. Landsberger, "Assyrische Königsliste und 'Dunkles Zeitalter'," *JCS, 8* (1954), 51–61.

46. Speiser, "The Alalakh Tablets," *JAOS, 74* (1954), 19–23; and O'Callaghan, *Aram Naharaim*, 51–92.

obv. seal impression

1. *i-na pa-ni* ^{I}*Niq-me-pa* lugal
2. 60 gín *kás-pu*^{há}
3. ki ^{I}*I-lim-ìli-ma* dumu *Tu-ut-tu*
4. ^{I}*Aš-ta-bi-*lugal dumu *I-ri*
5. *il-qé-šu ù* ^{I}*Áš-ṭà-bi-šar*
6. *qa-du* dam*-šu-ma*
7. *a-na* é ^{I}*Ìli-ìli-ma*
8. *a-na* é ^{uru}*Al-la-la-aḫ*
9. *ḫi-mu-di aš-bu*

rev.

10. kù-babbar máš nu tuk *ši-na-ti*
11. *ig-ra* nu tuk*-ma*
12. *ma-*ti_4*-me-e* 60 gín^{há}
13. *i-ip!-pa-lu-ú-ši-na*
14. *ù a-šar lìb-bi-ši-na i-lak*
15. 60 gín^{há} *bal-ṭù-ma*
16. *i-ip-pá-al-ši-na*
17. igi *Ir-kab-tù* igi *A-*gi_5*-*^{d}im
18. igi *Ta-*gu_5*-ḫu-li* dumu *Uš-ta-a*
19. igi *A-*gi_5*-ya* dumu *Pár-ta*
20. igi *Ša-ru-we* dub-sar
21. igi *Zi-ti-*^{d}im

(1) In the presence of Niqm-epa, the king, Aštabi-šarra son of Iri received sixty shekels of silver from Ilimi-limma, son of Tuttu; (5) and Aštabi-šarra together with his wife are to stay *ḫimudi* in the house of Ilimi-limma, in the house at Alalakh. (10) The silver bears no interest and they receive no hire. (12) Whenever they pay the sixty shekels, they may go wherever they please. (15) He who is alive shall pay the sixty shekels.

(17–21) five witnesses

Notes

1. Niqm-epa was a contemporary and vassal of Sauššatar of Mitanni (Wiseman, *Alalakh,* Nos. 13 and 14)

7–8. These are other examples of the use of the preposition *ana* for *ina* (cf. Wiseman, *Alalakh,* Nos. 18:8 and 21:11).

8. Note the unusual writings of the city name with a double "l."

9. The term *ḫimudi* is of unknown origin. From the context, it seems to indicate a type of pledge (cf. *CAD, Ḫ,* 194; Draffkorn, *Hurrians,* p. 221.)

10–16. These clauses use feminine pronominal forms, perhaps to indicate a collective sense.

14. The singular form *illak* appears for the expected form *illakū.*

15–16. This clause which specifies joint responsibility indicates that the members of the debtor's family are considered as co-debtors. Cf. Wiseman, *Alalakh*, No. 20:11–12, above.

Wiseman, *Alalakh*, No. 49

obv. seal impression

1. *i-na pa-ni* ^{I}dingir^{lim}-dingir^{lim}-*ma* lugal
2. 30 gín kù-babbar *ṣar-pu*
3. ki ^{I}dingir^{lim}-dingir^{lim}-*ma* dumu *Tu-ut-t*[*u*]
4. ^{I}*Ku-ša-am-ma-dì*
5. dumu ^{uru}*Qu-uz-ya*
6. šu ba-an-ti
7. *ki-i-me-e* máš kù-babbar
8. *an-ni-im*

rev.

9. ^{I}*Ku-ša-am-ma-dì*
10. *a-na* é ^{I}*Ìli-mi-li*
11. *a-ši-ib* kù-babbar máš nu tuk
12. *ù* ^{I}XXX-*ma-di*
13. *ig-ra* nu tuk
14. *šum-ma in-na-bi-it*
15. *a-na* silim^{ma}-*ni* 1 me gín kù-babbar
16. *a-na* ^{I}*Ìli-mi-li*
17. *i-na-an-din*
18. šu-du$_8$-a a-šà-*šu*
19. é-*šu* ^{giš}geštin-*šu*
20. igi *Tag*$_4$-*ḫu-li*
21. igi *Té-ḫi-ya*
22. igi *Bi-ri-ya-aš*
23. ^{lú}dub-sar

(1) In the presence of Ilimi-limma, the king, Kušaḫ-madi, a citizen of the city Quzya, received thirty shekels of refined silver from Ilimi-limma, son of Tuttu. (7) In lieu of the interest on this silver, Kušaḫ-madi is to stay in the house of Ilimi-li(mma). (11) The silver bears no interest and Kušaḫ-madi receives no hire. (14) If he runs away, he shall pay one hundred shekels of silver to Ilimi-li(mma) as an extra payment. (18) His field, his house and his vineyard are surety.

(20–23) three witnesses

Notes

1. Ilimi-li(mma) II is the son of Niqm-epa and the great grandson of Ilimi-li(mma) I, father of Idrimi (Klengel, *Geschichte Syriens im 2. Jahrtausend v.u. Z., 1: Nordsyrien*, 236–38).
5. The city name may perhaps be read as *Qu-li-ya*.

10. Again note the use of the preposition *ana* for *ina* (cf. Wiseman, *Alalakh,* No. 47:7–8).
15. For the term *šulmānu* in general, see Finkelstein, "The Middle Assyrian Šulmānu Texts," *JAOS*, *72* (1952), 77 ff. Its occurrence in this context requires a slightly different nuance and has been translated as "extra payment."
18. According to the copy, the term is šu-du_8-a and not šu-zi-a.[47] šu-du_8-a is the technical term for surety, corresponding to the Akkadian *qātātu* (*MSL, 1,* 40:41; Falkenstein, *Gerichtsurkunden, 1,* 116 f.).

The similarity in formulary between these texts and the *mazzazānūtu* texts of Old Babylonian Alalakh is striking.[48] But it is interesting to note the absence of the term *mazzazānūtu* or *mazzazānu* on the one hand, and the appearance of the formula for personal antichresis—the money bears no interest; the pledge receives no hire—on the other. Unfortunately, the Middle Babylonian sampling is too meager to postulate any sound hypothesis. Nevertheless, it is tempting to assume that the institution of *mazzazānūtu* survived the upheavals of the age although the terms *mazzazānūtu* and *mazzazānu* were no longer in use.

Texts from Susa

Although no *mazzazānūtu* contracts have been discovered in Old Babylonian Susa,[49] the terms *mazzazānūtu* and *mazzazānu* occur in the following formula found in Susa sale contracts:

ul ipṭiru ul manzazānu šīmu gamru[50]
"It is not an *ipṭiru*; it is not a *manzazānu*; it is the full purchase price."

The meaning of this formula has been a subject of scholarly debate. Cuq[51] interpreted these clauses as stating that the property being sold is not encumbered either by a previous right of redemption (*ipṭiru*) or by having constituted a pledge (*mazzazānu*). Either of these encumbrances would

47. So Wiseman, *Alalakh*, 163. Although twice the copies indicate a *zi* (ibid., Nos. 48:1 and 84:4), the remaining five occurrences (ibid., Nos. 49:18; 70:15; 82:3, 8; and 83:6) contain the DU_8 sign. The first two occurrences should therefore also be read šu-du_8!-a.

48. Note, however, that the scribes of Level IV had a greater tendency to Sumerianize.

49. *MDP, 23,* 324 is a partially preserved litigation involving a real estate *mazzazānu.* Cf. Cuq's treatment of this text in "Le droit élamite d'après les actes juridiques de Suse", *RA, 29* (1932), 166.

50. *MDP, 22,* 50:16–19 *et passim.* In this formula, the term *mazzazānu* often alternates with *mazzazānūtu*; e.g. *MDP, 22,* 49:13–15. The expression *ul manzazānu* also occurs in a broken *ipṭiru* transaction (*MDP, 22,* 158).

51. E. Cuq, "Les actes juridiques susiens," *RA, 28* (1931), 60; *RA, 29* (1932), 166. This formula was recently interpreted in the same manner by Boyer (*ARMT, 8,* 219). He claims that, on the basis of this formula, the *mazzazānu* pledge in Susa must have been a hypothec, i.e. a security held by a creditor but not in his possession.

require an additional payment by the buyer in order to gain clear title to the property. For this reason, these clauses are juxtaposed with *šīmu gamru* "it is the full purchase price."[52] But this attractive interpretation has one major difficulty. As Koschaker pointed out,[53] this formula is usually preceded by the clause *ana baqrī u rāgimānī izzaz* "He (the seller) is responsible for any claim or contestation." The intent of this clause is to protect the buyer against any prior encumbrance on the property, so that Cuq's interpretation of the formula is redundant.

Koschaker then proposed a new interpretation of the formula, based upon the equation in a.i. 3 II 19 of kù-ta-gub-ba = *kasap manzazi* which he translated as "pledge ransom."[54] The formula thus would read "(Das Geld) ist kein Lösegeld, kein Pfandlösegeld, (sondern) ein voll bezahlter Kaufpreis."[55] Landsberger, however, has shown on the basis of parallel constructions that the term kù-ta-gub-ba can refer only to the "Pfandobjekt" and never to the "Pfandlösegeld."[56] He therefore translated the Susa formula as "es handelt sich nicht um Retrakt, nicht um Pfand, um Kauf,"[57] but unfortunately did not discuss the legal meaning of this formula. A possible explanation is that the formula protects the buyer against the contestation of the finality of the sale by the seller, while the prior encumbrance clause protects him against any outside claimants. Thus by stating *ul manzazānu* the seller can never claim that the sold property was only surrendered to the buyer in a pledge transaction and therefore never actually sold. Similarly by stating *ul ipṭiru* he can never claim that the sold property was only given to the buyer in an *ipṭiru* transaction. But this latter statement would be meaningful only if *ipṭiru* indicated a *redemptive* transaction, i.e. a sale with power of redemption.[58] However, the term *ipṭiru* seems to designate only a *redemption* transaction, i.e. the act of redeeming property or persons. This meaning is clearly attested by the formula *ul manzazānu ipṭiru gamrūtu kīma abum ana mārim ipṭuru īzibu* PN *ina kiden* DN *ana dārāti ipṭur* "it is not a pledge transaction but a final redemption transaction; PN redeemed (the property) forever under the legal protection(?) of DN, just as a father would redeem and bequeath it to a son."[59]

Since the legal implication of Landsberger's translation is not apparent,

52. Cuq, *RA*, *29* (1932), 166.
53. *Griech. Rechtsurk.*, p. 106.
54. Ibid., p. 107.
55. Ibid., p. 109. This interpretation is retained in the *CAD*'s translation of these quoted passages in *CAD*, I–J, p. 171, sub *ipṭiru*.
56. *MSL*, *1*, 139.
57. Ibid.; cf. Harris, *JCS*, *9* (1955), 60.
58. So Cuq, *RA*, *28* (1931), 69.
59. *MDP*, *18*, 229:2–8, which is transliterated and translated as *MDP*, *20*, 158:2–8.

the following interpretation of the Susa formula is proposed: "it is not a redemption transaction; it is not a *mazzazānu*-pledge transaction; (therefore) it is the complete purchase price." With the assumption that the value of the pledge is usually greater than the value of the secured loan, this formula attests to the fact that the money paid constitutes the full value of the property being bought.[60] Since the transaction is neither a redemption of property held as a pledge (i.e. the repayment of a loan on the part of the buyer), nor a pledging of property (i.e. the receiving of a loan on the part of the seller), the money constitutes the complete purchase price (i.e. the full value of the property in outright sale).

The Mīšarum Edicts

Akkadian *mīšarum* (Sumerian níg-si-sá) represents the concept of equity.[61] The *mīšarum* act consisted of specific ordinances which remitted certain types of financial obligations and indebtedness.[62] Its purpose was to restore an equitable balance in the economic sphere of society. The *mīšarum*-act was most probably an oral decree and must therefore be distinguished from the preserved texts of the *mīšarum*-edicts.[63] These written copies may either have served as administrative guides for enforcement of the *mīšarum*-act,[64] or may have been copied for their own sake as a type of literary genre.[65]

The term *mazzazānu* occurs in the following two ordinances of the Edict of Ammi-ṣaduqa and in a fragment from the Edict of Samsu-iluna. The formulation of the fragment is identical with that of paragraph 21 of Ammi-ṣaduqa's Edict.[66]

§ 20, A V 25–35 (Kraus, *Edikt*, pp. 40–41)

V 25. [*šum-ma* du]mu *nu-um-ḫi-a* dumu *e-mu-ut-ba-lu*[*m*^{ki}]

26. [dumu *i-da*]-*ma-ra-az*^{ki} dumu unu^{ki}

60. For the importance of the full purchase price in validating one's claim to property, see Muffs, *Elephantine*, pp. 47, 72 ff.

61. For the relationship of this term to *kittum* "truth" and its meaning in the phrase *kittum u mīšarum*, which represents the Mesopotamian concept of law, see Speiser, *PAPS*, *107* (1963), 537.

62. An extensive bibliography on this subject may be found in Petschow's article "Gesetze", *RlA 3*/4, 275.

63. F. R. Kraus, *Ein Edikt des Königs Ammi-ṣaduqa von Babylon*, Studia et Documenta ad Iura Orientis Antiqui Pertinentia, 5 (Leiden, Brill, 1958), 243 ff.

64. Ibid.

65. J. J. Finkelstein, "Ammiṣaduqa's Edict and the Babylonian 'Law Codes'," *JCS*, *15* (1961), 92.

66. A new numbering of the paragraphs of Ammiṣaduqa's Edict has been necessitated by J. J. Finkelstein's publication of "The Edict of Ammiṣaduqa: A New Text," *RA*, *63* (1969), 45–64. Thus § 18′ according to Kraus' numeration = 20, and § 19′ = 21.

27. [dumu ì-si-i]n-na^{ki} dumu ki-sur-ra^{ki}
28. [dumu murgu^{k}]^{i}*i- il-tum i-il-šu-ma*
29. *[pa-ga-a]r-šu aš-ša-az-zu*
30. *[ú-lu* dumu-meš-*š]u a-na* kù-babbar *a-na k[i-iš-š]a-tim*
31. *[ú-lu a-na ma-an-z]a-za-ni*
32. *[id-di-in aš-šum šar-ram mi]-ša-ra-am*
33. *[a-na ma-tim iš-k]u-nu*
34. *[uš-šu]-ur an-d[u-ra-a]r-šu*
35. *[ša]-ki-[i]n*

(25) If an obligation came due against a citizen of Numḫia, a citizen of Emut-balum, a citizen of Idamaraz, a citizen of Uruk, a citizen of Isin, a citizen of Kisurra, (or) a citizen of Malgium, and (29) he gave himself, his wife or his sons for money, for *kiššatum* or for a *mazzazānu*-pledge; (32) because the king has ordained equity for the land, he is to be released, his freedom is to be re-established.

Notes

28. The clause *i-il-tum i-il-šu* is paralleled by *eḫiltum iṣbassu* in CH § 117 (rev. III 55), and indicates the time when a creditor may exercise his right of foreclosure. Cf. Kraus, *Edikt*, pp. 168 ff.
30. For the restoration [*ulū* dumu-meš-š]u, see ibid., p. 168 n. 1.
32. For the restoration *iddin*, see ibid., p. 169.

§ 21, A V 36–VI 9 (Kraus, *Edikt*, pp. 40–41)[67]

V 36. [*šum-ma*] gemé ìr *wi-li-[i]d* é
37. [dumu *nu-u]m-ḫi-a* dumu *e-mu-ut-ba-lum*$^{k[i]}$
38. [dumu *i-d]a-ma-ra-az*^{ki} dumu unu^{ki}
39. [dumu ì]-si-in-na^{ki} dumu ki-sur-ra^{ki}
VI 1. dumu murgu^{k}[^{i} x x x x x x]
2. *š[a] ši-i[m]* x [x x x x]
3. [*a-na* k]ù-bab[bar] *in-n[a-di-in]*
4. *[ú-l]u a-[n]a [k]i-iš-ša-tim*
5. *[i]k-k[a]-ši-iš*
6. *[ú-l]u a-na m[a-an]-za-za-ni*
7. *[i]n-ne-[z]i-ib*
8. *[an]-du-ra-ar-[š]u*
9. *[ú-u]l iš-ša-a[k-k]a-an*

67. The fragment from Samsu-iluna's Edict (Si 507 rev. 1′–7′), published by Kraus, "Ein Edict Königs Samsu-iluna von Babylon," *Studies in Honor of Benno Landsberger*, Assyriological Studies, 16 (Chicago, Oriental Institute, 1965), 225–26, corresponds to lines 3–9. Kraus retranslated the entire paragraph in *AS, 16*, 226.

(36) If a female slave, a slave (or) a houseborn slave from Numḫia, from Emut-balum, from Idamaraz, from Uruk, from Isin, from Kisurra, (or) from Malgium . . . . was sold, handed over into *kiššatum*, or was surrendered as a *mazzazānu*-pledge, his freedom shall not be re-established.

Notes

36. For a discussion of the term *wilid bītim* see Kraus, *Edikt*, pp. 172–74. Cf. also Finkelstein, *JCS, 15* (1961), p. 99; Kraus, *AS, 16*, 226 n. 12.

Since Kraus has presented an extensive treatment of these paragraphs,[68] the following remarks will be limited to the present sphere of interest, that of *mazzazānu*.

These paragraphs are concerned with the consequences resulting from a debtor's inability to pay a private debt which has fallen due. Three possibilities are specified, of which the first two are also mentioned in CH § 117: the debtor or a member of his family may be sold, subjected to *kiššatum*, or surrendered as *mazzazānu*. *Mazzazānu* in this context is difficult, since all of the sources previously cited indicate that a *mazzazānu*-pledge is taken when the debt was first incurred. Furthermore, the term *nipūtu* "a distress" is employed in Old Babylonian legal usage for a pledge taken at the expiration of a loan in order to insure the satisfaction of a claim.[69] The difficulty may be resolved by assuming that the debtor surrenders himself or a member of his family as a *mazzazānu* to a third party. The third party agrees to satisfy the prior creditor and thus becomes the new creditor of the debtor. The debtor or a member of his family will then perform antichretic services for the new creditor as a *mazzazānu*-pledge. The *mazzazānūtu* transactions in Alalakh which resulted from a prior indebtedness support this interpretation by providing contractual proof of such a procedure.

The *mīšarum*-edict passages indicate that *mazzazānūtu* is to be differentiated from an outright sale and from *kiššatum*. The term *kiššatum* is based on the root *kšš* "to have power."[70] Hence it seems to denote a servant–master rather than a debtor–creditor relationship, and the term has therefore been translated as "bondage." It has, however, been impossible to define the exact nature of this institution because of the paucity of references and lack of documentation. Kraus[71] investigated all the known references[72] and

68. Kraus, *Edikt*, 167–75.

69. A. Goetze, *The Laws of Eshnunna*, pp. 69 ff. Cf. R. Yaron, *The Laws of Eshnunna*, (Jerusalem, Magnes Press, 1969), pp. 163f.

70. *AHw, 1*, 462.

71. *Edikt*, pp. 175–79.

72. Cf. B. Landsberger, "Neue Lesungen und Deutungen im Gesetzbuch von Ešnunna," *Symbolae Juridicae et Historicae Martino David Dedicatae, 1* (Leiden, Brill, 1968), 75 n. 4. Other new text references to *kiššatum* are the fragment from the

reviewed the scholarly literature but was unable to gain more than a superficial comprehension of this institution. The following speculative remark regarding the distinction between *mazzazānūtu* and *kiššatum* is therefore submitted with all due reserve.

In a *mazzazānūtu* transaction there is no indication that the services of the *mazzazānu*-pledge could ever amortize the debt. On the contrary, those texts which contain an antichretic clause specify the services to be only in lieu of interest. Furthermore, most of the contracts state that the redemption of the *mazzazānu* is dependent upon the return of the principal sum to the creditor. It is possible that, unlike a *mazzazānūtu* arrangement, the services of the person held in *kiššatum* are applied to the amortization of the debt.[73] If this be correct, the indigent debtor whose obligation is about to fall due has several alternatives: he can procure the needed money by selling a member of his family or by entering into a *mazzazānūtu* arrangement with a new creditor; or he may amortize the debt by surrendering a member of his family in *kiššatum* to the creditor.

A Comparison with Tidennūtu

All of the evidence adduced from the legal texts is in complete accord with the lexical evidence and indicates that the personal *mazzazānūtu* contracts represent a loan transaction secured by an antichretic *mazzazānu*-pledge. Thus both personal *tidennūtu* and *mazzazānūtu* transactions are based upon the institution of personal antichretic security.[74] An investigation of the Nuzi personal *tidennūtu* contracts has shown that they contain the following elements: (1) title; (2) transfer of borrowed capital; (3) transfer of personal pledge; (4) duration of arrangement; (5) statement of antichresis; (6) delinquency of pledge; (7) flight, disappearance, or death of pledge; (8) prior encumbrance of pledge; (9) support of pledge; (10) disappearance or death of debtor; (11) penalty for breach of contract; (12) *šūdūtu* clause. Since most

---

Edict of Samsu-iluna and *CT*, *45*, 14:6. For additional examples and literature on the *ḫ/k* interchange discussed by Kraus (*Edikt*, p. 175) see Bottéro, *Textes économiques et administratifs*, Archives Royales de Mari, Textes, 7 (Paris, Imprimerie Nationale, 1957), 212 n. 1; M. Held, "A Faithful Lover in an Old Babylonian Dialogue," *JCS*, *15* (1961), 12; L. Matouš, "Quelques remarques sur les récentes publications de textes cunéiformes économiques et juridiques," *ArOr*, *27* (1959), 439; E. A. Speiser, "The Syllabic Transcription of Ugaritic [ḫ] and [ḥ]," *BASOR*, *175* (1964), 44 ff.

73. This type of arrangement is usually designated as *Kapitalantichrese*, as distinct from *Zinsantichrese*, which is the type of antichretic arrangement that is found in the Nuzi personal *tidennūtu* texts, in which only the interest is covered by the services rendered.

74. The similarity between the Alalakh *mazzazānūtu* contracts and the Nuzi *tidennūtu* contracts was noted by Speiser, *Yehezkel Kaufmann Jubilee Volume*, p. 37.

of these elements find their counterparts in the Old Babylonian *mazzazānūtu* contracts,[75] it should prove interesting to compare their respective formularies.

Transfer of borrowed capital. The *mazzazānūtu* and *tidennūtu* contracts express this transfer in terms of the receipt of the borrowed capital by the debtor (šu ti: *leqū* "to receive").[76] In Nuzi, however, this transfer may also be expressed in terms of the delivery of the borrowed capital by the creditor (*nadānu* "to give"). Furthermore, the phrase *ana tidennūti* "for *tidennūtu*" is used occasionally to describe this transfer,[77] while the phrase *ana mazzazānūtim* "for *mazzazānūtu*," is never so used.

Transfer of personal pledge. In Nuzi, this transfer is expressed either by the surrender of the pledge to the creditor: *ana tidennūti nadānu* "to give for *tidennūtu*" or by the subjection of the pledge to the creditor's authority: *kīmū kaspī* PN *ana tidennūti ina bīt* PN_2 *ašib* "in lieu of the capital PN is to stay in the house of PN_2 (the creditor) for *tidennūtu.*"

The *mazzazānūtu* contracts from Nippur, Larsa, and the Diyala region exhibit the formulary known from the lexical series for the surrender of the pledge, kù-ta-gub-ba-aš íb-ta-gub: *ana mazzazānūtim izzaz/ušziz* "he stands/stations as a *mazzazānu*-pledge." The expression *ana mazzazānūtim nadānu* "to give for *mazzazānūtu*," however, occurs in both Mari and Alalakh. The transfer of the pledge in terms of his subjection to the creditor's authority is recorded only in the Alalakh contracts, where its formulation is identical with that of Nuzi: *kīma kaspī* PN *ana mazzazānūtim ina bīt* PN_2 *wašib* "in lieu of the capital PN is to stay in the house of PN_2 (the creditor) for *mazzazānūtu.*"[78]

Duration of the arrangement. Both the *tidennūtu* and *mazzazānūtu* contracts contain an indefinite duration clause stating that the arrangements terminate whenever the debtor returns the borrowed capital to the creditor and thus redeems his pledge. However, about half of the *tidennūtu* contracts contain a definite duration clause, specifying the time during which the arrangement is to remain operative: *enūma* x mu-mes*ti* *imtalā u* PN *kaspī ana* PN_2 *utārma u uṣṣi* "When the specified years have elapsed, PN may then return the borrowed capital to PN_2 and thus go free."[79] Such a definite duration clause

75. Elements 1, 8, 9, 11, and 12 are unique to the Nuzi *tidennūtu* contracts. Although Wiseman, *Alalakh*, No. 41 contains a penalty clause, this clause is directed against the debtor and prior creditor. Therefore it is not applicable to the *mazzazānūtu* arrangement established between the debtor and the new creditor.

76. In Alalakh, the *mazzazānūtu* contracts occasionally use the term ugu "against, charged to."

77. This usage seems to be a secondary development. See above, p. 37 n. 117.

78. In the Nuzi contracts, however, the verb, *erēbu* "to enter" sometimes alternates with the verb *wašābu* "to stay."

79. E.g., *HSS, 9,* 28:10–15 (Appendix, text 28).

appears also in a *mazzazānūtu* contract from Mari: *ūm* mu 3-kam *umallama* kù-babbar *išaqqalma ittaṣṣi* "When he fulfills three years, he shall weigh out the silver and thus go free."[80] The Mari and Nuzi clauses both employ the verb *malū*[81] to indicate the lapse of time and the verb *waṣū* to indicate the liberation of the pledge. Another of the expressions used in Nuzi to denote the freed status of the pledge is *ašar libbišu alāku* "to go wherever one pleases."[82] This expression is regularly employed in the Alalakh texts also.

Statement of antichresis. The occurrence of a specific statement of antichresis in either a *mazzazānūtu* or *tidennūtu* text is rare. It appears in only one *mazzazānūtu* contract and in two *tidennūtu* contracts. The *mazzazānūtu* text from Nippur states: gemé á-ni nu-ub-tuk kù máš nu-ub-tuk "The slavegirl does not receive her hire, the capital does not bear interest."[83] The two Nuzi texts state: guškin máš nu *īšu u* PN *uriḫulša* nu *īšu* "The gold does not bear interest and PN does not receive his hire."[84] The reason for the inclusion of this statement in these three contracts may perhaps be based on their unusual provisions. In this Nippur text, the services of the slavegirl are to be reckoned only in lieu of the initial interest. In the two Nuzi texts, the value of the borrowed capital is extremely high.

There are three other pledge contracts which record statements of antichresis but which do not employ the terms *mazzazānūtu* or *mazzazānu.* The formulation in two Alalakh texts from level IV is similar to those discussed above: kù-babbar máš nu-tuk PN *igra* nu-tuk "The silver bears no interest, PN (the pledge) receives no hire."[85] The Old Babylonian text YBC 12191, however, exhibits a different formulation: máš-bi-šè ib-ta-gub "He (the pledge) stands against its interest."[86]

Delinquency clause. A delinquency clause occurs in a Sumerian *mazzazānūtu* contract from Nippur[87] and in an Akkadian *mazzazānūtu* contract from the Diyala region.[88] The Sumerian formulation: tukumbi PN gá-la ba-an-dag u_4 1-šè á-ni-šè 1 bán-še-ta-àm al-ág-e "If PN stops working, he (the debtor) shall measure out one seah of barley for each day as his hire," and its abbreviated Akkadian equivalent: *inūma ipparakkū* 1 bán še *imaddad* "If he stops working, he shall measure out one seah of barley" are both

80. *ARM, 8,* 52:7–9.
81. The Nuzi text *AASOR, 16,* No. 63:9 (Appendix, text 26) employs in its definite duration clause the same verbal form *umalla* "he shall fulfill" as the Mari text.
82. SMN 2144:12 (Appendix, text 10).
83. *ARN,* 105:11.
84. *JEN, 5,* 489:9 f. and *JEN, 6,* 609:9 f. (Appendix, texts 47–48).
85. Wiseman, *Alalakh,* Nos. 47:10 f. and 49:11–13.
86. This formulation is attested in the lexical series *Ḫḫ* I 349.
87. *PBS, 13,* 39.
88. *JCS, 9* (1956), 70, No. 3.

closely related to the formulary appearing in the *Ḫḫ* lexical series. *Ḫḫ* I 367 ff. (*MSL*, *5*, 40:2 ff.) states: u_4 gán-ba-an-dag u_4 1-kam 1 bán-še-ta-àm á-bi ì-ág-gá = *u_4-mu ša ip-par-ku-ú u_4-mu-kal* 1 bán-ta-àm *še-im i-di-šu i-man-da-ad* "(For) the time when he (the pledged slave) has stopped working, he (the debtor) will measure out one seah of barley for each day as his hire."[89] This formulary is also reflected in the delinquency clause of the Nuzi *tidennūtu* contracts, e.g. *HSS*, *5*, 40:15–19: *šumma šipiršu ša* PN *ana* 1 *ūmi ezzib* 1 bán še *kīma uriḫulli ša ūmi u ūmi ana* PN *umalla* "If I (the pledge) shall leave the service of PN (the creditor) for a single day, I shall pay one seah of barley[90] to PN as the daily hire."

It is significant to note that the penalty incurred for delinquency in both the *mazzazānūtu* and *tidennūtu* contract is one seah (or 10 *qa*) of barley,[91] which is described as the daily rate of hire. According to the lexical entry *a.i.* 6 III 11, the daily wage for a hired man is specified at 1 seah of barley. This corresponds to the rate of hire in the Laws of Eshnunna. LE § 11 sets the monthly wages of a hired man at 1 shekel of silver, and according to the tariff in the same laws,[92] 1 shekel of silver purchases 1 kor (or 300 *qa*) of barley. The lexical entry *a.i.* 6 III 21 specifies the yearly wages of a hired man as 10 shekels of silver. At Eshnunna, based on LE § 11, the yearly hire would be 12 shekels of silver.[93] These yearly rates of hire amount to 300–360 times the daily hire, based on the ratio of silver to barley mentioned above. However, according to the Nuzi ratio of silver to barley,[94] the yearly rate of hire at Nuzi based upon a daily hire of 10 *qa* of barley would be 45–54 shekels

89. Cf. *a.i.* 7 IV 13–22 and Landsberger's discussion in *MSL*, *1*, 247 ff.

90. The more common penalty at Nuzi is one mina of copper which has been shown to be equal in value to one seah of barley on the basis of independent references; above, p. 24.

91. This is also the penalty for delinquency in an Ur III hire contract (T. Fish, "A Nippur Tablet of Ur III," *JAOS*, *56* [1936], 494). Another Ur III hire contract stipulates a penalty of 7 *qa* of barley (Pohl, *TuM*, *1/2*, 24). Cf. Falkenstein, *Gerichtsurkunden*, *1*, 120 n. 6.

The delinquency clauses in the Neo-Babylonian antichretic security contracts also specify compensatory *mandattu* payments (Petschow, *Pfandrecht*, pp. 108–09). However, unlike the Nuzi *uriḫul* payments, the rate of the *mandattu* payments was not uniform but amounted to 15–33% annual interest on the borrowed capital (ibid., p. 109 n. 336).

92. LE § 1. This same ratio of silver to barley is attested in the lexical series *a.i.* (*MSL*, *1*, 106:15′–19′) and in the contracts of the Ur III period (Goetze, *Laws of Eshnunna*, p. 30 with nn. 21 and 22).

93. Cf. CH § 273. The Old Babylonian contracts indicate that the yearly wages ranged from 10–14 shekels of silver (G. R. Driver and J. C. Miles, *The Babylonian Laws*, *1* [Oxford, Clarendon Press, 1952], 477).

94. 1 homer (or 100 *qa*) of barley ~ 1.5 shekels of silver.

of silver.[95] This is an extremely high rate of hire, especially since the purchase price of a slave at Nuzi is only 30 shekels of silver. It may be explained by assuming that the penalty of 10 *qa* of barley at Nuzi no longer reflected an economic reality, but rather represented a fine based upon a fossilized legal formulary.[96] If this be so, it would be a strong indication of the influence of Old Babylonian legal practice upon the institution of personal *tidennūtu.*

Flight, disappearance, or death of the pledge. In certain Nuzi contracts the flight, disappearance, or death of the pledge results in the termination of the *tidennūtu* arrangement, since under such circumstances the debtor is required to return the principal sum immediately; e.g. *AASOR, 16,* No. 61:33–35 *šumma* PN *ittābit u iḫalliq u* PN_2 *umalla* "If PN (pledge) runs away or disappears, then PN_2 (the debtor) shall make full payment."[97]

Such a provision is recorded in three *mazzazānūtu* contracts also. At Mari the formula is: *imāt imarraṣ iḫalliq* PN kù-babbar *išaqqal* "if she dies, falls ill, or disappears, PN (the debtor) must weigh out the silver."[98] At Khafajah the clause is in both instances: *imūat iḫalliqma* ki PN kù-babbar *eleqqe* "Should he (the pledge) die or disappear, then he (creditor) shall take back the silver from PN (the debtor)."[99]

Disappearance or death of the debtor. There are four Nuzi self-*tidennu* contracts[100] which specify the appointment of additional security in case of the death or disappearance of the debtor-pledge. The term for this surety is *māḫiṣ pūti*, and usually applies to persons.[101]

Some contracts from Mari[102] and Alalakh[103] also designate persons as additional surety, using the terms *qātātu* and *kattū.* Like the Nuzi contracts, these texts record self-indenture transactions; and like the *māḫiṣ pūti*, the *qātātu* and *kattū* secure the loan in the event of the death or disappearance of the debtor-pledge.

This comparative survey of the personal *mazzazānūtu* and *tidennūtu* clauses indicates that these contracts are not only based on the same principle of personal antichretic security, but also exhibit a striking similarity in form-

95. These sums represent 300–360 times the daily hire.

96. Cf. Landsberger, *MSL, 1,* 252.

97. Cf. *JEN, 3,* 295:30 f. and SMN 3857:12–17 (Appendix, texts 15, and 5).

98. *ARM, 8,* 31:17–19.

99. *JCS, 9* (1955), 71 No. 5:14–17; cf. ibid., 70 No. 3:7–13.

100. *TCL, 9,* 10; SMN 1598; *AASOR, 16,* No. 60; and SMN 2102 (Appendix, texts 32–35).

101. In SMN 1598 (text 33), the debtor designates real estate as his *māḫiṣ pūti.*

102. *ARM, 8,* 52.

103. Wiseman, *Alalakh,* Nos. 21, 22, and 24. Note that in ibid., No. 49 real estate is designated as additional surety.

ulary. The formulation of the Nuzi texts is most closely related to those of Mari and Alalakh.

ŠAPARTU

In the Assyrian legal tradition the technical term for pledge is *šapartu.*[104] An investigation of the *šapartu* contracts from the Middle Assyrian period is warranted by both their geographical and chronological proximity to the Nuzi documents. Since the Middle Assyrian *šapartu* texts have been fully treated by Koschaker,[105] remarks here will be limited to the relationship between these texts and those of Nuzi personal *tidennūtu.* Before any comparison can be undertaken, however, two basic issues must be brought to mind.

The first issue concerns the matter of interest in the Middle Assyrian loan documents. The rate of interest is never stated in the contract. Furthermore, whenever interest is mentioned, the reference is only to interest accrued upon default of payment; for example, *edannu ētiqma* an-na *ana* máš gin "Should the term expire, interest will be charged on the tin." The question arises whether the Middle Assyrian loans were interest free until the expiration of the term. Doubting the reality of such an arrangement in common business transactions, Koschaker marshalled inferred evidence for the existence of initial interest.[106] This interest, probably charged at a fixed rate, he assumed to have been deducted from the borrowed sum at the onset of the loan period. Thus the debtor did not receive the entire principal stipulated in the contract.[107]

The second issue concerns the physical possession of the pledge. Certain Middle Assyrian contracts contain clauses which indicate that the pledge is in the possession of the creditor for the duration of the loan,[108] that is, the pledge

104. Koschaker, *NRUA*, p. 96.

105. Ibid., pp. 96–131. The major corpus of Middle Assyrian pledge documents has been published by E. Ebeling, *Keilschrifttexte aus Assur juristischen Inhalts*, Wissenschaftliche Veröffentlichungen der Deutschen Orientgesellschaft, 50 (Leipzig, Hinrichs, 1927). A selection of these contracts was transliterated and translated by M. David and E. Ebeling, "Assyrische Rechtsurkunden," *Zeitschrift für vergleichende Rechtswissenschaft*, *44* (1929), 305–81. The Tell Billa material published by J. J. Finkelstein ("Cuneiform Texts from Tell Billa," *JCS*, 7 [1953], 111 ff.) also contains some Middle Assyrian pledge texts. The corpus of documents includes both real estate and personal pledge contracts. However, as in Nuzi, the great majority of texts deals with the pledging of lands and not people.

106. *NRUA*, p. 95.

107. A similar assumption has been made by E. Bilgiç with reference to the *ḫubuttātum* loans (Simmons, *JCS*, *13* [1959], 84 ff.).

108. E.g. *ki šaparti*. . . šu-nigin 9 gán a-šà. . . PN *ukāl ētannarraš* (*KAJ* 13:10–25) "As a pledge, PN holds and cultivates . . . a total of nine *iku* fields." Since the creditor is to utilize these fields they must be in his possession.

is possessory (*Besitzpfand*); other contracts contain clauses which indicate that the pledge is not in the possession of the creditor for the duration of the loan,[109] that is, the pledge is hypothecary. The examples cited in the footnotes show that both clauses contain the verb *ukāl* in their respective formulary. In the former case the verb is to be translated as "he holds"; in the latter case, as "he shall hold." However, the most common statement of pledging in the Middle Assyrian contracts is simply *kī šapartu* object PN *ukāl* "PN (the creditor) holds/shall hold the object (real estate/person) as a pledge." Does this common formulary refer to the surrender of the pledge ("he holds") or rather to the designation of the pledge to be surrendered at a future date, probably upon default of payment ("he shall hold")? This problem concerning the possessory vs. the hypothecary nature of the Middle Assyrian *šapartu* cannot be satisfactorily resolved in many of the contracts.[110]

Koschaker's penetrating analysis of the Middle Assyrian *šapartu* contracts has revealed three types of *šapartu* pledges:

1. the *Verfallspfand*, which the debtor forfeits upon his default of payment at the expiration of the set term[111];
2. the *Lösungspfand*, which the debtor retains a right to redeem even after the expiration of the set term[112];
3. and the *Nutzungspfand*, which the creditor has a specified right to use.[113]

Since the Nuzi personal *tidennūtu* transactions involve a redeemable pledge whose services are at the disposal of the creditor, the last two categories of *šapartu* texts will be discussed in greater detail.

Lösungspfand

The four personal pledge contracts[114] found in the Middle Assyrian corpus

109. E.g. *kī šaparti mimmūšu zakua ukāl* (*KAJ* 29:16 f.) "As a pledge, he shall hold any of his unencumbered property." Cf. *KAJ* 66:17–22 which specifies that the creditor may hold either the field, houses, threshing floor, wells or children of the debtors. This lack of specification seems to indicate that the creditor does not take the pledge at the onset of the loan.

110. Koschaker, *NRUA*, p. 99 n. 3.

111. Ibid., pp. 102 ff. At the expiration of the set term, the borrowed capital becomes the price paid by the creditor for the foreclosed pledge. Although only real estate pledge contracts of this type have been found, Koschaker (ibid., p. 104) believed that the principle could be applied to personal pledges as well. Cf. *KAJ* 66.

112. Koschaker, *NRUA*, pp. 106–07.

113. Ibid., pp. 108 ff.

114. *KAJ* 17, 28, 60, and 70. Ibid., Nos. 31, 53, and 66, and TR 3021 (Wiseman, "The Tell Al Rimah Tablets, 1966." *Iraq*, *30* [1968], 183) record the pledging of real estate and persons. Cf. *KAJ* 61. The Middle Assyrian Laws, Tablet A §§ 39, 44, 49; Tablet C §§ 2 and 3 also deal with personal pledges dwelling in the house of their creditors.

specify that the pledges are redeemable. However, these Lösungspfand contracts may be further divided into two groups, of which the following texts are examples.

KAJ 60[115]

obv. 1. [ki]šib *La-qí-pi*
2. 2 anše 6 [? *qa*] *še-um*
3. *i-na* ^{giš}[bán *ša*] é *ḫi-bur-ni*
4. ki ^{I}*I-din-ku-bé* dumu ^{I}*Ri-iš*-^{d}nà
5. ^{I}*La-qí-pu* dumu *Ṣíl-lí-ku-bé*
6. dumu ud-man-kam
7. šu ba-an-ti *a-na* 7 itu^{ḫi}
8. sag-du *še-im*
9. ì-ág-e
10. *e-da-nu e-ti-iq-ma*
11. ⸢*še-um*⸣ *a-na* máš gin
lo.e. 12. *ki ša-pár-ti*
13. ^{f}*A-la-ni-tu*$_4$
14. dumu-mí *Ma-nu-gír*-dingir-⸢*šu*?⸣
rev. 15. dam-*sú* ^{I}*I-din-ku-bé*
16. *ú-ka-al i-na u*$_4$*-me*
17. *še-am ù* máš-meš-*šu*
18. *i-du-nu-ni*
19. dam-*sú i-pa-ṭar*
19a. kišib dingir-*ma-lik*
20. igi dingir-*ma-lik* dumu *I-din*-en
21. igi *Pu-ḫu-nu* dumu ìr-^{d}*Taš-me-ti*
22. kišib dub-sar
23. igi di-ku$_5$^{nu} dub-sar
24. dumu ^{d}im-^{d}utu^{ši}
25. itu *Ḫu-bur* u$_4$ 8-kam
26. *li-mu* ^{d}en-líl-^{mu}sig$_5$
27. dumu *A-sa-ni*
28. kišib *Pu-ḫi-ni*

(1) seal

(2) Two homers, six + ? *qa* of barley in the seah measure of the *ḫiburnu*-house, Lā-qīpu, son of Ṣillī-kube, son of Šamaš-šarra-ēriš, received from Idin-kube, son of Rīš-nabū. (7) At seven months he shall measure out the principal sum of barley. (10) Should the term expire, interest will be

115. The text appears as No. 48 in David and Ebeling, *Zeitschrift für vergleichende Rechtswissenschaft*, *44* (1929), 347.

charged on the barley. (12) As a pledge, Idin-kube holds his wife Alānītu, daughter of Mannu-gīr-ilišu. (16) Whenever he returns the barley and its interest, he redeems his wife.

(19a) seal
(20–21) two witnesses
(22) seal
(23–24) one witness
(25) The month Ḫubur, the eighth day
(26–27) Eponym: Enlil-mudammiq, son of Asānu
(28) seal

Notes

3. The term *ḫiburnu* refers to vessels used for the storage of barley (*AHw*, *1*, 334). The building é *ḫiburni* may be either part of the palace or temple (*CAD*, Ḫ, p. 182).

25. The Assyrian name for the tenth month of the year occurs more frequently as Ḫibur (*AHw*, *1*, 352).

26–27. The eponym year of Enlil-mudammiq, son of Asānu, dates to the reign of Aššur-uballiṭ I c. 1350 B.C. (*RlA*, *2*, 448).

With the exception of *KAJ* 17, this text is representative of the Middle Assyrian personal *Lösungspfand* contracts. The interpretation of this group of *šapartu* contracts is affected by the basic issues concerning an initial interest charge and the time when the pledge is taken. If one assumes that the pledge is surrendered upon default of payment, the pledge cannot be considered antichretic; for the redemption clause stipulates that the debtor must return the accrued interest as well as the principal sum in order to redeem his wife. If, however, one assumes that the pledge is surrendered at the onset of the loan and that there is an initial interest charge, the services of the pledge may perhaps be antichretic with regard to the initial but not the accrued interest. According to the latter interpretation, this type of personal pledge contract would be similar to the Nippur *mazzazānūtu* text *ARN* 105.[116]

Although both interpretations are possible, the plain sense of the text favors the first. The redemption clause of the contract envisions the redemption of the pledge only after the debtor has defaulted at the set term, since it refers to the necessity of the debtor's paying the accrued interest. Similarly, the contract makes no reference to the redemption of the pledge upon the repayment of the principal sum at the set term. This seems to indicate that the creditor may seize the designated pledge only upon default of payment at the expiration of the set term. And if this be so, the inclusion of

116. Above, p. 52.

the accrued interest in the redemption clause shows that the pledge is not antichretic.

KAJ 17[117]

obv. 1. kišib ^{I}en-sum-*a-ḫi*
2. 1 gun an-na
3. *ṭí-ri* ⸢na$_4$⸣ é *a-lim*
4. ki ^{I}*Ki-din*-^{d}im dumu ^{I}*I-din-ku-be*
5. ^{I}en-[sum]-šeš-meš dumu en-ur-sag
6. dumu ìr-*ku*-[*be š*]*a* uru *ša . . . ni*
7. šu⸢ba⸣-an-ti *i-na u$_4$*-⸢*mi*⸣
8. *e-re-šu-šu-ni*
9. sag-du an-na *i-ḫi-aṭ*
10. *ki ša-pár-ti*
11. ^{I}*Ya-a-ku*-⸢zalág⸣^{er} dumu-*šu*
12. ^{I}*Ki-din*-^{d}im
rev. 13. *ú-ka-al i-na u$_4$-me*
14. an-na *i-ḫi-ṭu-ni*
15. dumu-*šu* [*i*]-*pa-aṭ-ṭar*
16. kišib dub-sar
17. igi é-an-na-zalág^{er} dumu en-sum-*a-ḫi*
18. igi *Bu-ni-ya* dumu *Ap-pa-pa*
19. igi *Ab-ši-ya* dumu *Ma-ni-ya*
20. igi ^{d}en-líl-^{mu}sig$_5$ dub-sar dumu *A-nu*-du$_{10}$^{bi}
21. kišib ^{I}*Bu-ni-ya*
22. itu *Ḫu-bur* u$_4$ 19- kam
23. *li-mu* ^{Id}*A-šur*-mu-*ú-ṣu*[*r*]
24. dumu ^{d}im-^{mu}kar
25. kišib ⸢x x⸣ kišib *Ab-ši-ya*

(1) Seal

(2) One talent of tin, measured(?) by the weight stone of the "city-house", Bēl-nādin-aḫḫē, son of Bēl-qarrād, son of Arad-kube of the city Ša . . . . . ni received from Kidin-adad son of Idin-kube. (7) Whenever he requests it, he shall weigh out the principal sum of tin. (10) As a pledge, Kidin-adad holds his son, Ayakku-limmir. (14) Whenever he weighs out the tin, he shall redeem his son.

(16) seal

(17–20) four witnesses

117. This text appears as No. 13 in David and Ebeling, *Zeitschrift für vergleichende Rechtswissenschaft*, *44* (1929), 316.

(21) seal
(22) The month Ḫubur, the nineteenth day
(23–24) Eponym: Aššur-šuma-uṣur, son of Adad-mušēzib
(25) two seals

Notes

3. The term *ṭiri* seems to refer to the weight stone standard rather than to the quality of the tin.[118] For the building *bīt āli*, see *CAD*, A, p. 389.

7–9. The clause specifying that the loan is payable on notice also occurs in Old Babylonian documents. See *CAD*, E, pp. 281 f. *sub* 3′ and 5′ for text citations.

22. The eponym year of Aššur-šuma-uṣur, son of Adad-mušēzib, also dates to the reign of Aššur-uballiṭ I (*RlA*, *2*, 445).

This *šapartu* text differs from the other personal *Lösungspfand* contracts in that it does not stipulate an accrued interest charge upon default of payment. According to this text, which records a loan transaction payable on demand, the debtor may redeem his pledge at any time by repaying the principal sum alone. If one assumes that the pledge is surrendered at the onset of the loan rather than upon default of payment, and that no assumed initial interest is deducted from the principal sum, the following situation results: the pledge is in the possession of the creditor; it secures a loan transaction which does not stipulate an interest charge and it may be redeemed by returning the principal sum. This arrangement is similar to the Larsa text *YOS*, *8*, 78 which has been understood as an antichretic pledge transaction.[119] Thus *KAJ* 17 is the only personal Middle Assyrian *šapartu* text which seems to be antichretic.

Nutzungspfand

There are three *šapartu* contracts in the Middle Assyrian corpus which contain a redemption clause and also specify the creditor's right to use the pledge. All three involve the pledging of real estate and the creditor's right to cultivate the fields: for example, *kī šaparti* a-šà PN *ukāl ētanarraš* "as a pledge, PN (the creditor) holds and cultivates the field."[120] The texts *KAJ* 21 and 58 stipulate the charging of accrued interest upon the expiration of the set term; and despite the creditor's cultivation of the held field, their redemption clause requires the paying of the accrued interest as well as the principal sum. Thus these two texts are similar to the first group of personal *Lösungspfand* texts and their plain sense seems to indicate that here, too, the pledges are not antichretic.

118. The term, transliterated as *ḫi-ri*, is translated by David and Ebeling as "auserlesenes" (ibid.) and by Wiseman as "available" (*Iraq*, *30* (1968), 184).

119. Above, p. 54.

120. *KAJ* 13:25, 21:22, and 58:18. The last text was collated for Koschaker (*NRUA*, p. 108 n. 3).

Text *KAJ* 13 is also a real estate *Nutzungspfand*[121] contract. It records a six-year loan transaction, secured by fields which are to be cultivated by the creditor. Unlike the other texts, however, it contains no accrued interest charge and its redemption clause requires the paying of the principal sum alone. Furthermore, it contains a specific statement of antichresis: an-na máš nu-tuk *ù* a-šà GA.RI nu-tuk "the tin bears no interest and the field bears no rent(?)." This contract thus records an explicit antichretic pledge transaction,[122] which proves that the principle of antichretic security was recognized in the Middle Assyrian legal tradition. It also strengthens the supposition that text *KAJ* 17 may indeed be a personal antichretic pledge transaction.

The principle of personal antichresis, however, seems to operate more frequently in the Middle Assyrian legal tradition outside the sphere of pledge law. There are three Middle Assyrian loan contracts which obligate the debtor to perform antichretic services for the creditor. Text *KAJ* 52, which records a five-month loan transaction, specifies the following obligations incumbent upon the co-debtors (lines 10–18): *kīmū* máš an-na *annē bilat* 5 gán a-šà *ina adri še'am u tibna ana* PN *inaddi*[*nū*] *edannu ētiqma kī pānītišunuma* a-šà *erru*[*šū*] "In lieu of the interest on this (borrowed) tin, they shall deliver the yield of a five-*iku* field, the barley and straw, on the threshing floor (at threshing time) to PN (the creditor); should the set term expire (without repaying the loan), they shall, as previously, seed the field." Thus the initial interest is covered by the harvesting of the field and the accrued interest is covered by the seeding of the field. Similarly, the other two loan contracts specify that in lieu of interest the debtor is to harvest a field (*KAJ* 50:9–13) and to perform a certain task with clothing (*KAJ* 77:8–13).

As Koschaker noted,[123] none of these documents mention the term *šapartu*. Furthermore, the lack of a redemption or foreclosure clause strengthens the assumption that the one who performs the antichretic services does not also secure the loan. Thus these contracts are not to be associated with pledge law.[124] They seem rather to be related to those loan documents in which the debtor is obligated to provide a certain number of harvesters for

121. This contract has been transliterated and translated by Koschaker, *NRUA*, pp. 160–61 and by David and Ebeling, *Zeitschrift für vergleichende Rechtswissenschaft*, *44* (1929), 337, No. 38.

122. A partially preserved antichretic real estate pledge transaction also appears in the Tell Billa material, *JCS*, 7 (1953), 150, No. 5. For Neo-Assyrian antichretic pledge contracts, see Koschaker, *Griech. Rechtsurk.*, p. 12.

123. *NRUA*, p. 108.

124. For antichretic contracts operating outside the sphere of pledge law in the Neo-Babylonian period, see Petschow, *Pfandrecht*, 116 f. See above, p. 51 n. 10.

the creditor at harvest time, in addition to repaying the loan.[125] According to Koschaker,[126] the service of the harvesters was most probably in lieu of the initial interest charge and may therefore be considered antichretic.

It therefore appears that personal antichresis in the Middle Assyrian contracts was not bound to the sphere of pledge law, but operated independently in loan transactions as an accessory obligation of the debtor. This type of separation between personal antichresis and pledge security does not seem to exist in the Nuzi *tidennūtu* transactions.

BE'ŪLĀTU

Another Assyrian legal institution which merits attention as a possible Mesopotamian analogue to the Nuzi institution of personal *tidennūtu* is that of *be'ūlātu*.[127] The *be'ūlātu* transaction is documented in the Old Assyrian legal texts and in commercial correspondence from Asia Minor. These transactions represent a system of "working-capital" in which an employer places capital at the disposal of his employee. The employee, while in the service of his employer, is free to utilize this capital in the hope of realizing a profit from it. The right to dispose of the capital, which must be returned at the termination of his service, and the profit realized from its use constitute the wages of the employee.[128]

The *Be'ūlātu* Contract

The contracts regulating the *be'ūlātu* transaction exhibit strong affinities to the personal *tidennūtu* contracts. This can be demonstrated best by isolating the various clauses of the *be'ūlātu* contracts, typical of which is text *ICK*, *2*, 107A.

1. 1/3 ma-na kù-babbar *ṣa-ru-pu-um*
2. *be-ú-lá-at*
3. *En-um-a-šùr* dumu *A-nu-né-e-ì*

125. E.g. *KAJ* 11, 29, 62, and 81, and TR 3015 (*Iraq*, *30* [1968], 182). For a discussion of this type of contract, see Koschaker, *NRUA*, pp. 109–10; *Griech. Rechtsurk.*, p. 12; and J. G. Lautner, *Personenmiete*, 22–26.

126. *NRUA*, p. 110.

127. A similarity between the two institutions was first noted by H. Lewy, *Or*, N.S. *10* (1941), 322 f.

128. G. Eisser and J. Lewy, "Die altassyrischen Rechtsurkunden vom Kültepe," *MVAG*, *33* (1930), 127 ff., 146 ff. Lewy's interpretation has formed the basis for all subsequent studies (cf. P. Garelli, *Les Assyriens en Cappadoce*, Bibliothèque archéologique et historique de l'Institut français d'Archéologie d'Istanbul, 19 [Paris, Maisonneuve, 1963], 249; and M. T. Larsen, *Old Babylonian Caravan Procedures*, Uitgaven van het Nederlands Historisch-Archeologisch Instituut te Istanbul, 22 [Istanbul, Nederlands historisch-archeologisch Instituut in het Nabije Oosten, 1967], 41).

4. *iš-ti Púzur-a-šùr*
5. dumu *Ku-bi₄-a il₅-qé*
6. *En-um-a-šur*
7. ki kù-babbar ⌜*uk*⌝-*ta-al*
8. *i-nu-mì* k[ù]-babbar
9. *ú-ta-ru-ú*
10. *ù a-šar*
11. *li-bí-šu*
12. *i-la-ak*
13. igi *Aḫ-ša-lim*
14. igi *A-mur-a-šur*

(1) One-third mina of refined silver, the *be'ūlātu* of Enum-aššur, son of Anunei, he received from Puzur-aššur, son of Kubiya. (6) Enum-aššur is bound by the silver. (8) When he returns the silver, he may then go wherever he pleases.

(13–14) two witnesses

Transfer of Capital. The first clause of this contract records the transfer of a sum of money from an employer to an employee.[129] This sum is designated as *be'ūlātu*, i.e. capital which is placed at the disposal of another party.[130] The term is occasionally used in the phrase *ana be'ūlātim* "for *be'ūlātu*"[131] to describe the transfer of the capital; but most often it appears in construct with a personal name: *be'ūlāt* PN. As in this contract, the personal name usually is that of the employee. At times, however, the personal name may be the employer.[132] Thus the designation *be'ūlāt* PN describes the capital which is either received or given by the specified person. The verbs which describe the transfer of the capital are *nadānu* "to give," *laqā'u* "to receive," and *ka''ulu* "to hold, to utilize."[133]

The transfer of the *be'ūlātu* capital establishes a debtor–creditor relationship between the parties. The indebtedness of the party who received the

129. *EL*, 127 ff. In a few contracts, the received capital is not retained by the employee but rather is transferred to a member of his family. For example, in texts *EL*, Nos. 159–161, the sum is transferred to his father; in *TCL, 21*, 246, to his mother. Note that in all of these contracts the capital is still described as the *be'ūlātu* of the employee.

130. The term *be'ūlātu* (*būlātu*) stems from the verb *be'ālu* "to have power of disposition over money and goods."

131. E.g. *ICK, 1*, 10; *ICK, 2*, 105 and 108; *BIN, 6*, 240; and Gelb, *Inscriptions from Alishar and Vicinity*, Oriental Institute Publications, 27 (Chicago, University of Chicago Press, 1935), No. 16.

132. E.g. *TCL, 21*, 246; *WO, 5* (1969), 32; *ICK, 1*, 126; and *EL*, No. 226.

133. E.g. *nadānu*: *EL*, No 159; *BIN, 6*, 240; *ICK, 1*, 10, 131; *ICK, 2*, 109; *laqā'u*: *EL*, Nos. 160–162; *ICK, 2*, 107, 109; and *ka''ulu*: *TCL, 21*, 246; *ICK, 1*, 126.

capital is evident from his obligation to return the capital. This is confirmed by lawsuits in which the creditor sues for the return of the *be'ūlātu*, as well as by *be'ūlātu*-quittance documents.[134]

Obligation of Service. The second clause of this contract records an obligation which is created by the acceptance of the *be'ūlātu*-capital. According to J. Lewy, this clause constitutes an obligation to remain in the employment of the creditor.[135] As is the case here, the obligation is usually incumbent upon the recipient of the *be'ūlātu*-capital. In those contracts in which the capital has been transferred to a member of the recipient's family,[136] the original recipient is bound in service. In only one case (*ICK*, *1*, 10) is the obligation to serve incumbent upon the slave of the recipient of the *be'ūlātu*-capital.

Most of the *be'ūlātu* contracts do not stipulate the nature of the services to be performed. However, text *EL*, No. 163 states that the recipient of the *be'ūlātu*-capital is to undertake a three-month business trip at the completion of which the capital is to be repaid. More specifically, text *EL*, No. 159 states that the person is to serve as a *sāridu* "caravan driver."[137] Additional information about the nature of the services rendered by the recipients of *be'ūlātu*-capital may be gleaned from the commercial correspondence. Larsen's study of the Old Assyrian caravan procedures reveals that members of caravan staffs were often paid with the right to utilize *be'ūlātu*-capital loaned to them by their employers. This was especially common with respect to the *kaṣṣāru* "harnesser" who seems to have been entrusted with the care of the animals and goods en route.[138]

Duration of Arrangement. The final clause of the contract under discussion states that the obligation to serve terminates with the repayment of the *be'ūlātu*-capital. The clause does not stipulate a time limit for the repayment of the capital, and hence implies that the arrangement is of indefinite duration. This seems to be the more prevalent situation, since only a few *be'ūlātu*

134. E.g. lawsuits, *EL*, Nos. 260, and 263; and quittances, *EL*, No. 144, and 170. Also note declarations of indebtedness with regard to *be'ūlātu*-capital (B. Kienast, *Die altassyrischen Texte des Orientalischen Seminars der Universität Heidelberg und der Sammlung Erlenmeyer-Basel*, *ZA*, Ergänzungsband, 1 (Berlin, de Gruyter, 1960), No. 9, and the occurrences of *be'ūlātu* contracts in Sammelurkunden together with other loan transactions (e.g. Gelb, *OIP*, *27*, No. 59; Kienast, *ATHE*, No. 55; and *EL*, No. 226).

135. *EL*, 128a. This interpretation is confirmed by the inclusion of a delinquency clause in some *be'ūlātu* contracts.

136. Above, p. 96 n. 129.

137. Also see the partially preserved text *OIP*, *27*, No. 50 which is probably a *be'ūlātu* contract. For references concerning the task of a *sāridu*, see Larsen, *Old Assyrian Caravan Procedures*, p. 79.

138. Ibid., p. 41.

contracts contain definite duration clauses.[139] Nevertheless, it is possible that those *be'ūlātu* arrangements which do not contain definite duration clauses but involve caravan personnel may have implicitly been understood to terminate with the completion of the business trip.

The terms employed in the duration clauses to denote liberation from service are *ašar libbišu alāku* "to go where one pleases" (*ICK*, *2*, 107) and *waṣā'u* "to go out" (*ICK*, *2*, 109). When a member of the employee's family frees him by returning the capital, the verb *tarā'u* "to fetch" (*EL*, No. 161) is used.[140]

Delinquency. Some *be'ūlātu* contracts contain a delinquency clause which protects the creditor against the loss of services resulting from the absence of his indebted employee. This clause stipulates: *šumma* PN *ayēma udapper agram eggarma igrī agrim umalla* "if PN (the recipient of the *be'ūlātu*-capital) goes somewhere else, I (the creditor) shall take on a hireling, but he shall pay the wages of the hireling."[141] Thus the *be'ūlātu*-creditor is to receive payments equivalent to the wages of a hireling from the debtor in order to compensate for the resultant loss of service.[142]

Breach of Contract. Penalty clauses concerning breach of contract are found in only a few *be'ūlātu* contracts. In two of these contracts, the aim of the penalty clause is to ensure the prompt repayment of the *be'ūlātu*-capital. According to text *EL*, No. 163, the debtor is fined an additional payment of one-half mina of silver if the capital is not repaid at the end of the designated term. Similarly, text *ICK*, *1*, 10 stipulates that the borrowed capital will accrue interest if it is not returned on the specified date.

The penalty clause in text *EL*, No. 159, entailing a fine of two minas of silver, is directed against a different breach of contract.[143] This text specifies a term of five years for the duration of the *be'ūlātu* transaction and its penalty

139. E.g. text *EL*, No. 163 specifies a term of three months; text *EL*, No. 159, a term of five years; and text *ICK*, *1*, 10 specifies the date upon which the capital is to be returned.

140. The personal *tidennūtu* contracts also employ the terms *ašar libbišu alāku* and *waṣū*, while the Nuzi reflex of *tarā'u* is *leqū*.

141. *ICK*, *1*, 126:6–10. Cf. *TCL*, *21*, 246:6–10; *EL*, No. 161:9–14; and *OIP*, *27*, 50:2′–7′.

142. The Nuzi reflexes of *duppuru* and *igrī agrim* are *reqū* and *uriḫul*. Note the use of *puzram ṣabātu* in a commercial letter dealing with a debt of *be'ūlātu* published by H. M. Kümmel, "Ein altassyrischer Geschäftsbrief," *WO*, *5* (1969), 32 ff.; and in text *EL*, No. 97. The term *puzram aḫāzu* occurs in text *ICK*, *1*, 83. Both of these latter texts may involve *be'ūlātu* transactions. The Nuzi reflex of *puzram ṣabātu*/*aḫāzu* is *ḫesū*.

143. The verb denoting breach of contract is *šamāḫu*. Cf. its occurrences in *WO*, *5* (1969), 32, 38.

clause is designed to protect the creditor against the premature termination of the arrangement.[144]

The Be'ūlātu and Tidennūtu Transactions

It is evident from this brief survey that the *be'ūlātu* contract, like the Nuzi personal *tidennūtu* contract, creates an obligation for the performance of services by means of a loan transaction. Although none of the *be'ūlātu* contracts contain a specific statement of antichresis, there is some evidence that the services rendered were in lieu of interest on the borrowed capital. First, a commercial letter equates the *be'ūlātu* transaction with an interest-bearing loan, even though an interest charge is never mentioned in any of the *be'ūlātu* documents. This letter (*KTS*, No. 12:30–34) states: kù-babbar *aḫum lušēbilamma ul ṣibtam kīma aḫum ana [a]ḫim iddunu laddin ul be'ūlātim lū ḫabbulākušum* "Let an associate send me the capital and I shall either pay interest (at the same rate) as one associate should give another or else be indebted to him on the basis of *be'ūlātu*-capital." Secondly, contract *ICK*, *1*, 10 stipulates that if the *be'ūlātu*-capital is not repaid at the specified date the borrowed capital begins to accrue interest. Hence at the end of the specified period, presumably at a time when the services of the person are no longer needed by the creditor, the *be'ūlātu* transaction converts into an interest-bearing loan. It seems, therefore, reasonable to assume that the services rendered by the recipient of the *be'ūlātu*-capital were considered to be in lieu of interest on the capital.

It is less easy to ascertain whether the *be'ūlātu* transaction also represents a pledge transaction, as is the case with the personal *tidennūtu* transaction. Koschaker thought that the clause *išti kaspim uktāl* "He is bound by the silver" referred to a type of pledging.[145] However, J. Lewy has shown that this clause is an obligation of service whereby the recipient of the capital is bound to serve his creditor.[146] Thus there is no positive evidence for assuming that the employee also served to secure the loan. Furthermore, since the Assyrian pledge term, *šapartu*, does not appear in any of the *be'ūlātu* contracts, and since the employee does not usually stay in the immediate vicinity of the creditor,[147] it may be assumed that the *be'ūlātu* arrangement does not involve a pledge transaction. The difference in outlook between the *be'ūlātu* and

144. For a similar breach of contract in the personal *tidennūtu* contracts, see above, p. 30.

145. *Griech. Rechtsurk.*, p. 11 n. 2.

146. *EL*, 128, 147, 149.

147. According to the commercial letters, the employee usually embarks upon a business trip on behalf of the employer. Note that in the text *WO*, *5* (1969), 32, the goods of the *be'ūlātu*-debtor rather than his person, are to be seized.

personal *tidennūtu* transactions is evident from their titulary: the term *be'ūlātu* refers to the borrowed capital, while the term *tidennu* refers to the antichretic pledge.

It is certain that both the *be'ūlātu* and personal *tidennūtu* contracts represent loan transactions with personal antichresis. However, the socio-economic background of these transactions is quite different. The Old Assyrian documents reveal that the *be'ūlātu* transaction usually involved loans made by business firms who placed the *be'ūlātu*-capital at the disposal of travelling merchants or caravan personnel. This capital would be utilized by its recipients to finance their own commercial enterprises with the hope of realizing profits from the borrowed capital.[148] Thus the institution of *be'ūlātu* is basically a commercial transaction which is in keeping with the "capitalist" spirit pervading Old Assyrian trade.[149] On the other hand, the Nuzi documents reveal that the personal *tidennūtu* transactions usually involved loans made by wealthy landowners who thereby secured the agricultural and domestic services of the debtor and his family. The fact that the persons rendering service were also held as pledges and that self-*tidennu* contracts often specified guarantors, seems to underscore the impoverished status of the Nuzi debtor who entered into such an arrangement. Thus the institution of personal *tidennūtu* is basically a pledge transaction, representing a type of indentured servitude.

This investigation has shown that the institution of personal antichresis, already attested in the Ur III period,[150] was an integral component of Old Babylonian pledge law in both the "core" and "provincial" traditions. The lexical evidence and all of the personal *mazzazānūtu* contracts support the thesis that the personal *mazzazānu*-pledge not only secured the loan but also served the creditor in lieu of interest. Thus the personal *mazzazānūtu* contract and the personal *tidennūtu* contract are both antichretic pledge transactions. A detailed comparison of their clauses also reveals a striking similarity in formulary, which supports the supposition of a Mesopotamian background for the Nuzi institution of personal *tidennūtu*.[151]

148. There is a group of texts which exhibit great similarities to the *be'ūlātu* documents, but which do not mention the term (e.g. *EL*, No. 97; *ICK*, *1*, 83, 137; and *ICK*, *2*, 73, 74). One of these documents (*ICK*, *1*, 83) stipulates that the creditor is to receive two-thirds of the profits realized from the borrowed capital.

149. Larsen, *Old Assyrian Caravan Procedures*, p. 38.

150. Above, p. 51 n. 10.

151. Both the *mazzazānūtu* and *tidennūtu* contracts specify an identical sum, which serves as compensatory payment for the pledge's failure to work. The dependence of personal *tidennūtu* upon Old Babylonian legal practice would be heightened if this sum, described as the daily hire of a man, does not reflect an economic reality in Nuzi. See above, pp. 86 f.

The Mesopotamian institution of personal *mazzazānūtu* also provides a deeper insight into the institution of personal *tidennūtu*. The utilization by Nuzi landlords of the personal *tidennūtu* arrangement to provide for themselves a long-term source of labor is paralleled by the *mazzazānūtu* contracts from Alalakh. The rulers of Alalakh, using the *mazzazānūtu* contract, assured for themselves the services of individual craftsmen, families, and even villages. Thus both the personal *mazzazānūtu* and *tidennūtu* transactions represent not only a secured loan but a type of indentured servitude.

If the institutions of personal *mazzazānūtu* and *tidennūtu* are indeed analogous, and perhaps even identical, the difference in nomenclature must be explained. The term *mazzazānūtu* is attested only in the Old Babylonian period and subsequently appears to have fallen into disuse. The Alalakh contracts seem to verify this point. The pledge contracts from the Old Babylonian level of Alalakh use the term *mazzazānūtu*. But the antichretic pledge contracts from the Middle Babylonian level of Alalakh, which are almost identical in formulary with their Old Babylonian counterparts, do not mention the term *mazzazānūtu*: in Wiseman, *Alalakh*, No. 48, *mazzazānūtu* is replaced by the term *ḫimudi*. Thus, although the institution survived, the name *mazzazānūtu* was apparently no longer current. Since the Nuzi texts fall within the Middle Babylonian period, one may similarly assume that this institution was practiced in Nuzi although it was described there by the term *tidennūtu*.

The institution of personal antichresis also existed in the Assyrian legal tradition. However, the documentation of its practice during the Middle Assyrian period in connection with pledge law is far less extensive than in Nuzi. More common is its existence outside the sphere of pledge law, where it is an accessory obligation of the debtor to render antichretic service to the creditor. As such, it is attested in certain Middle Assyrian loan transactions as well as in the Old Assyrian *be'ūlātu* transactions.

CHAPTER 4

Etymology

One of the main difficulties in determining a possible etymology for the term *tidennūtu* arises from the inconsistent orthography of the Nuzi texts. This inconsistency stems from the use by the Nuzi Hurrian scribes of a syllabary whose main characteristics may be traced back to Old Akkadian times.[1] One important characteristic of this syllabary is its failure to differentiate between voiced and voiceless stops. The resultant graphic confusion of stops is evident in the transcription of both Akkadian words and Hurrian personal names.[2] The term *tidennūtu* is a prime example of this confusion, for its first two syllables have been written in five different ways. Most common by far are the spellings *ti-te* (*JEN*, *3*, 309:1) and *di-te* (*JEN*, *3*, 309:4)[3]; *ti-de* (Gadd, *RA*, *23* [1926], No. 2:1), and *di-ti* (*JEN*, *2*, 111:4) occur occasionally, and *te-te* appears only once (SMN 825:1). The term was twice written by Ṭāb-milk-abi, who was an early Akkadian scribe at Nuzi; his orthography should therefore be meaningful.[4] But he was also inconsistent. *JEN*, *3*, 298:5 reads *ti-te-nu-ti* while *JEN*, *6*, 568:7 reads *ti-de-nu-ti*. Although the second dental is represented once as *t* and once as *d*, the initial dental is voiceless in both cases. This initial voiceless dental seems to indicate that the term is either

1. E. A. Speiser, *Introduction to Ḫurrian*, Annual of the American Schools of Oriental Research, 20 (New Haven, American Schools of Oriental Research, 1941), p. 13.

2. Purves, *AJSL*, *57* (1940), 185.

3. Neither of these two spellings can muster a decisive majority of occurrences in the entire corpus of *tidennūtu* transactions. Note that both spellings occur in the same tablet, *JEN*, *3*, 309:1 and 4.

4. Some of the first generation scribes at Nuzi employed principles of orthography closely related to the Old Babylonian syllabary, which did distinguish between voiced and voiceless stops (see P. M. Purves, "Early Scribes at Nuzi," *AJSL*, *57* (1940), 171 ff.; and Speiser, *Introduction to Ḫurrian*, p. 12). It seems that these early scribes were Akkadians schooled in the Old Babylonian scribal tradition, while the later scribes were local Hurrians trained in a basically un-Semitic system of writing (Purvis, *AJSL*. *57* (1940), 171).

derived from an Akkadian base with an initial *t* radical, or is represented by the scribe as a Hurrian word.[5]

Koschaker was the first to propose a Hurrian origin for the term *tidennūtu*. Its formulation, he suggested, is analogous to the Nuzi Hurrian term *artartennūtu*[6]; and its meaning, on the basis of context, is "usufruct."[7] Speiser's main objection to this translation was the inappropriateness of the phrase *ana tidennūti* "for usufruct," when it refers to the giving of the capital to the debtor.[8] Subsequently H. Lewy, in accord with her interpretation of *tidennūtu* as a mutual exchange, proposed an etymology based on the Hurrian root *tad* "to be friendly."[9] However, besides the linguistic difficulties presented by such an etymology,[10] it is dependent upon an interpretation which has not been upheld in the present investigation of personal *tidennūtu*. Thus if one accepts a Hurrian origin for the term, the exact meaning and etymology of *tidennūtu* must remain obscure.

With regard to an Akkadian etymology, several possibilities have been suggested. The earliest proposal was that of Scheil[11] and Gadd,[12] who posited a derivation from *nadānu* or its byform *tadānu* "to give."[13] Speiser rejected this etymology "for semantic and grammatical reasons."[14] But since

5. If the term *tidennūtu* was considered to be Hurrian, Ṭāb-milk-abi's transcription should consistently have been *ti-de-nu-ti*; for the rule is *t* in initial and *d* in post-vocalic medial positions, unless the dental is doubled (Speiser, *Introduction to Hurrian*, p. 40). His spelling *ti-te-nu-ti* may perhaps be regarded as another example of his sporadic inconsistencies, which chiefly involve initial and post-vocalic dentals (Purves, *AJSL*, *57* [1940], 182). Note that in the *tidennūtu* contract *JEN*, *6*, 568 he writes the Hurrian name Edeya once with *de* (line 3) and once with *te* (line 11). A similar irregularity in the treatment of dentals has also been noted in Ugaritic Hurrian (Purves, *AJSL*, *57* [1940], 183).

6. *Griech. Rechtsurk.*, p. 87 n. 1; and E. A. Speiser, "New Kirkuk Documents Relating to Security Transactions," *JAOS*, *52* (1932), 357.

7. *Griech. Rechtsurk.*, p. 87.

8. *JAOS*, *52* (1932), 355 n. 22.

9. "The Titennūtu Texts from Nuzi," *Or*, N.S. *10* (1941), 323 n. 1. According to Speiser (*Introduction to Hurrian*, p. 83) *tad* means "love." As for the personal name Titena-Adad, cited by Lewy (*Or*, N.S. *10* [1941], 323 n. 1), it is to be read as di-temen.na-^{d}im = Šalim-pāliḫ-Adad (Gelb et al., *NPN*, p. 123).

10. Steele (*Real Estate*, p. 45 n. 14) questions the change from *tad* > *tid* and the function of *-en*(*n*). The latter objection does not detract from a possible Hurrian etymology in view of the admittedly Hurrian origin of the term *artartennūtu*.

11. *RA*, *15* (1918), 66 n. 1.

12. *RA*, *23* (1926), 55.

13. Koschaker at first accepted this derivation (*NRUA*, p. 131), but later rejected it (*Griech. Rechtsurk.*, p. 87).

14. He did not, however, specify his objections; see *AASOR*, *10* (1928–29), 12 n. 22 or *JAOS*, *52* (1932), 357. Semantically, a derivation from the verb "to give" is too general to characterize a specific type of transaction. For the morphologic difficulties, see below.

the overwhelming majority of abstract *-ūtu* nouns in Nuzi is Akkadian in origin, he sought another Akkadian etymology, proposing the reflexive stem of the Akkadian verb *danānu* "to become strong."[15] He later abandoned this derivation in favor of a connection with *dinānu* "a substitute."[16] Finally, Dossin tried to identify the term with the noun *kidinnu* "protection" by assuming a phonetic alternation of *d/k*.[17] But this suggestion is greatly weakened by the lack of evidence for such an alternation.

The initial *t* in Ṭāb-milk-abi's transcription of the term *tidennūtu* might seem to preclude all of the proposed Akkadian derivations except *tadānu*. Steele argued, on the basis of this scribe's inconsistent spelling of the term, that *tidennūtu* was a "Hurrianized but not fully naturalized" term derived from an uncommon Akkadian base.[18] But it is not necessary to resort to such a hypothesis in order to justify the possibility of a derivation from an Akkadian base *dnn*; metathesis of an initial *d* radical and an infixed *t* of the non-prefixed Gt and Gtn forms often takes place.[19] The choice of a possible Akkadian etymology between *tdn* or *dnn* must therefore be based on semantic and morphologic considerations.

A derivation from the reflexive stem of *tadānu* "to give" or *danānu* "to become strong" is morphologically difficult.[20] In addition both cases are semantically inadequate. However, the marked similarity between the institutions of personal *mazzazānūtu* and *tidennūtu* underscores the semantically faultless combination of *tidennūtu* with *dinānu*. The term *mazzazānūtu* literally means "stand-in-ship" which is identical with the proposed meaning of *tidennūtu* as "substitute-ship." Although Speiser stated that "the morphologic conditions are by no means impeccable,"[21] the semantic appropriateness of this etymology warrants the consideration of the following morphologic reconstruction:

One must first posit a verbal base *danānu* as a counterpart to the nominal form *dinānu*, and its occurrence in the durative Gtn stem with the meaning "to serve as a substitute."[22] The addition of an abstract ending to the Gtn

15. *JAOS*, *52* (1932), 359 ff.

16. "YDWN, Gen. 6:3," *JBL*, *75* (1956), 129.

17. In his review of Steele, *Real Estate*, in *BiOr*, *6* (1949), 145.

18. *Real Estate*, pp. 46–47. But see Purves, *JNES*, *4* (1945), 79 n. 43.

19. von Soden, *GAG*, p. 35 § 36a.

20. The suggested morphological development, based upon the abstraction of a Gt infinitive pattern (Koschaker, *NRUA*, p. 131 n. 4; Speiser, *JAOS*, *52* [1932], 359), should begin with an original **titdunūtu* or **ditnunūtu* form, respectively. Neither form could plausibly yield the term *tidennūtu*.

21. *JBL*, *75* (1956), 129.

22. Cf. *AHw*, *1*, 160 sub *dananu* III, which has been attested only in the D-R stem, and Speiser, *JBL*, *75* (1956), 127. For the durative force of the *tan* form, see Speiser, *JAOS*, *75* (1955), 119–20. Also note the occurrence of the term *dinānu* in the Nuzi text (Pfeiffer and Speiser, *AASOR*, *16*, 10:4).

infinitive would yield **ditannunūtu* > **tidannunūtu* by metathesis. Then an assumed haplology[23] would lead to the form **tidannūtu* > *tidennūtu.* Despite the admitted difficulties of this reconstruction, the connection of *tidennūtu* with *dinānu* remains the most attractive suggestion for a possible Akkadian etymology.

Regardless of the origin of the term *tidennūtu,*[24] its meaning in context must be the prime consideration. The use of the term in the personal *tidennūtu* contracts indicates that it represents an antichretic pledge transaction.[25] Such an arrangement is not unique to the Nuzi legal tradition, but finds a close parallel, both in principle and in formulary, in the Old Babylonian personal *mazzazānūtu* contracts and the Middle Babylonian pledge documents from Alalakh.

23. For other examples of haplology in Akkadian, see C. Brockelmann, *Grundriss der vergleichenden Grammatik der semitischen Sprachen, 1* (Berlin, Reuther and Reichard, 1908), 266.

24. This orthography of the term is required on the basis of Akkadian phonology and is also the proper transcription of the term if it were of Hurrian origin.

25. Nevertheless, the term has been left untranslated, since the phrase *ana tidennūti* "for *tidennu*-ship" modifies not only the transfer of the pledge but the transfer of the borrowed capital as well. Hence the translation of *tidennūtu* as "pledge" or "security" seems inappropriate. However, it should be noted that the application of this term to the borrowed capital may be a secondary development (above, p. 37 n. 117). The expression *ana tidennūti* may have then only indicated that the capital was given in a *tidennūtu* or pledge arrangement.

APPENDIX 1

Personal Tidennūtu Texts

Translations of the Nuzi personal *tidennūtu* texts are presented below with pertinent textual notes.

The grouping of these texts is based on clausal and contextual similarities. References to the publication history of the individual text and its previous treatment will be furnished at the beginning of the translation. An attempt has been made to transliterate Hurrian personal names in accordance with the phonetic values established in Speiser's *Introduction to Hurrian.* However, certain inconsistencies may appear as a result of either imperfect knowledge, or a desire to avoid undue confusion.

The following table shows the correspondence between the text numbers in this appendix and the original place of publication.[1]

NUMBER	PUBLICATION	PUBLICATION	NUMBER
1	*AASOR*, *16*, No. 26	Gadd, *RA*, *23*(1926), No. 32	41
2	*JEN*, *3*, 301	*TCL*, *9*, 10	32
3	*AASOR*, *16*, No. 28	*JEN*, *2*, 192	21
4	*HSS*, *9*, 15	*JEN*, *3*, 290	29
5	SMN 3587	*JEN*, *3*, 293	16
6	SMN 2013	*JEN*, *3*, 295	15
7	*JEN*, *3*, 316	*JEN*, *3*, 299	30
8	*JEN*, *3*, 308	*JEN*, *3*, 301	2
9	SMN 1592	*JEN*, *3*, 302	46
10	SMN 2144	*JEN*, *3*, 303	45
11	SMN 2803	*JEN*, *3*, 304	12
12	*JEN*, *3*, 304	*JEN*, *3*, 305	22
13	SMN 2493	*JEN*, *3*, 306	36
14	SMN 3719	*JEN*, *3*, 308	8

1. The SMN numbers refer to texts which will be published in a forthcoming volume of the Harvard Semitic Series (Cambridge, Harvard University Press) by E. R. Lacheman, *Excavations at Nuzi*, *9*.

NUMBER	PUBLICATION	PUBLICATION	NUMBER
15	*JEN*, *3*, 295	*JEN*, *3*, 309	19
16	*JEN*, *3*, 293	*JEN*, *3*, 312	20
17	*JEN*, *4*, 387	*JEN*, *3*, 316	7
18	*AASOR*, *16*, No. 38	*JEN*, *3*, 317	24
19	*JEN*, *3*, 309	*JEN*, *3*, 319	44
20	*JEN*, *3*, 312	*JEN*, *4*, 387	17
21	*JEN*, *2*, 192	*JEN*, *5*, 489	47
22	*JEN*, *3*, 305	*JEN*, *6*, 607	23
23	*JEN*, *6*, 607	*JEN*, *6*, 609	48
24	*JEN*, *3*, 317	*AASOR*, *16*, No. 24	25
25	*AASOR*, *16*, No. 24	*AASOR*, *16*, No. 25	51
26	*AASOR*, *16*, No. 63	*AASOR*, *16*, No. 26	1
27	*HSS*, *9*, 13	*AASOR*, *16*, No. 27	43
28	*HSS*, *9*, 28	*AASOR*, *16*, No. 28	3
29	*JEN*, *3*, 290	*AASOR*, *16*, No. 29	37
30	*JEN*, *3*, 299	*AASOR*, *16*, No. 38	18
31	*HSS*, *5*, 40	*AASOR*, *16*, No. 60	34
32	*TCL*, *9*, 10	*AASOR*, *16*, No. 61	40
33	SMN 1598	*AASOR*, *16*, No. 62	52
34	*AASOR*, *16*, No. 60	*AASOR*, *16*, No. 63	26
35	SMN 2102	*HSS*, *5*, 40	31
36	*JEN*, *3*, 306	*HSS*, *5*, 82	42
37	*AASOR*, *16*, No. 29	*HSS*, *9*, 13	27
38	SMN 1067	*HSS*, *9*, 15	4
39	*HSS*, *13*, 418	*HSS*, *9*, 28	28
40	*AASOR*, *16*, No. 61	*HSS*, *13*, 418	39
41	Gadd, *RA*, *23* (1926), No. 32	SMN 2803	11
42	*HSS*, *5*, 82	SMN 1418	49
43	*AASOR*, *16*, No. 27	SMN 1592	9
44	*JEN*, *3*, 319	SMN 2047	50
45	*JEN*, *3*, 303	SMN 2102	35
46	*JEN*, *3*, 302	SMN 2144	10
47	*JEN*, *5*, 489	SMN 2493	13
48	*JEN*, *6*, 609	SMN 3587	5
49	SMN 1418	SMN 1067	38
50	SMN 2047	SMN 2013	6
51	*AASOR*, *16*, No. 25	SMN 3719	14
52	*AASOR*, *16*, No. 62	SMN 1598	33
53	JENu 118	JENu 118	53
54	JENu 627	JENu 627	54

1. *AASOR*, *16*, No. 26

Pfeiffer and Speiser, *AASOR*, *16* (1936), 87

(1) Document of *tidennūtu*[a] of Puḫi-šenni, son of Wardu-kēnu. Accordingly, he caused himself to enter into the house of Tulbun-naya in *tidennūtu*; (5) and Tulbun-naya gave to Puḫi-šenni eleven homers of barley (according to) the *sūtu*-measure of u r$_5$-r a[b] in *tidennūtu.* (9) Whenever Puḫi-šenni returns the eleven homers of barley to Tulbun-naya, he then frees himself.

(13–25) thirteen witnesses[c] including scribe Šeršiya.

(26–33) eight seals

a. The etymology and possible meanings of this term have been discussed above, pp. 103 ff.

b. The different types of *sūtu*-measures in Nuzi have been discussed by Cross (*Property*, p. 14) and Oppenheim (in his review of Cross, *Property*, in *JA*, *230* [1938], 653). Cross maintains that there existed in Nuzi a large *sūtu*-measure of 10 *qa* and a small one of 8 *qa*. When the capacity of the measure is not specified, the *sūtu*-measure is assumed to contain 10 *qa*. For a different view, see R. T. Hallock, "The Nuzi Measure of Capacity," *JNES*, *16* (1957), 204–06.

c. Read the witness name on line 13 as *Ki-bá!-ar-ra-áp-ḫe* (*NPN*, p. 87a).

2. *JEN*, *3*, 301

(1) Document of *tidennūtu* [of] Mušeya, son of Ḫašiya, and of Tiwirra, son of [Ede]-ya. (4) Tiwirra has received four talents (and) twenty minas[a] of copper in *tidennūtu*; and in lieu of the copper, Tiwirra, himself, is to stay in the house of Mušeya, together with his sons,[b] Ḫanaya and Ilī-abī. (9) Whenever Tiwirra returns [the copper] to Mušeya, Tiwirra may take his sons (and) go free.

(13–24) eleven witnesses[c] including the wife of Tiwirra and scribe Kib-talli

(25–27) five seals

a. Oppenheim has argued for the presence in Nuzi of a system of weights whose shekel-mina ratio was 1:100; accordingly, this system coexisted with the more prevalent sexagesimal system whose ratio was 1:60 ("Šeqel, Mine und Talent in Nuzi," *OLZ*, *41* [1938], 485 f). However, since the Nuzi scribes did not seem to distinguish between types of minas as they did between different types of *sūtu*-measures (Cross, *Property*, p. 14; Oppenheim, *JA*, *230* [1938], 653), it is assumed that the reference in the text is to the more common sexagesimal mina.

b. Note the absence of the plural sign MEŠ after the logogram d u m u in line 7; but cf. lines 9, 11, where d u m u - m e š occurs. For other examples of such a capricious use of the MEŠ sign, see Berkooz, *Nuzi Dialect*, p. 19.

c. For the reading of the witness name in lines 22 f, as *Tup-pí-ya* and not *Um-pí-ya* (*NPN*, pp. 271 f.), see Draffkorn, *Hurrians*, p. 110. Also read the patronymic as *Ar-nu-ur-ḫe!* (*NPN*, p. 31a).

3. *AASOR, 16,* No. 28

Pfeiffer and Speiser, *AASOR, 16* (1936), 87

(1) Ten homers of barley belonging to Tulbun-naya daughter of Šeldun-naya, she gave to Taya, son of Ar-tamuzi; (4) and Taya gave his son, Ar-tirwe in *tidennūtu* to Tulbun-naya, for twenty years. (7) When the twenty years have elapsed, Taya shall return the ten homers of barley to Tulbun-naya and take back his son. (10) And now, after the four *urubātu*[a] m[en] of the walled-pre[cinct (?)][b] of the Storm-god of the cities were present, this document[c] was written. (13) This document was written after a [pro]clamation[d] before the gate of the city Temtena.[e]

(15–26) twelve witnesses including scribe Sīn-iqīša

(29–36) ten seals

a. The term *urubatu* is probably to be connected with the festival (*CAD*, E, p. 327 sub *erubatu*) or ritual (*ŠL* 567:25) rather than with *urpātu* "clouds" (Pfeiffer and Speiser, *AASOR, 16* [1936], 88). Gordon (*Or*, N.S. 7 [1938], 54) considers the term to be Hurrian.

b. *ké-er-*[*ḫi*]. For the meaning of the term *kerḫu* "rampart, walled enclosure," and its occurrences in other Nuzi texts, see *AHw, 1*, 467. It is questionable whether the phrase [d]im *ša* uru-meš should be emended to [d]im *ša* uru ⟨dingir⟩-meš.

c. *ṭuppa*/*ṭuppu*. In the Nuzi tablets, case endings are often used incorrectly (Gordon, *Or*, N.S. 7 [1938], 47 f.).

d. The various theories concerning the nature and purpose of the proclamation have been presented above, pp. 32–34.

e. For the location of this city, see H. Lewy, "A Contribution to the Historical Geography of the Nuzi Texts," *JAOS, 88* (1968) [= *Essays in Memory of E. A. Speiser*, American Oriental Series, 53 (New Haven, American Oriental Society, 1968)], 159 f.

4. *HSS, 9,* 15

Lewy, *Or*, N.S. *10* (1941), 332

(1) The tongue of Enna-madi, son of . . . –he has declared before witnesses:

(2) "I have received, on loan,[a] three homers of barley from Šilwa-tešub, son of the king.[b] (4) Now in lieu of the three homers of barley, I have given Ḫudiya, my son, to Šilwa-tešub in *tidennūtu*. (7) When I return the three homers of barley to Šilwa-tešub, I may then take back my son, Ḫudiya.

(9–14) five witnesses including scribe Elḫib-tilla, son of Wurrukunni

(15–20) six seals

a. In Nuzi, the term ur$_5$-ra:*ḫubullu* may designate either an interest-bearing loan or the interest itself (*CAD, Ḫ*, pp. 217–18).

b. For the Ancient Near Eastern usage of "the son of the king" as the title of a functionary of the king, see G. Brin, "On the Title Ben Hammelek," *Lēšonénu, 31* (1966), 5–20, 85–96; and A. F. Rainey, "'The King's Son' at Ugarit and among the Hittites," *33* (1969) 304–08. Cf. Speiser, *JBL, 74* (1955), 253 n. 5.

5. SMN 3587

(1) Document of *tidennūtu* [of] Iluya and of Ḫašše, sons of Adad-ēriš. They gave[a] Kaniya, son of Adad-ēriš, in *tid*[*enn*]*ūtu* to Kirib-šeri, son of Ḫu[d-tešub]. (6) And K[iri]b-šeri gave to Iluya and Ḫašše sixteen homers of barley, twenty min[as of ti]n, five ewes,[b] five rams, (and) one cloth[b]—four *kuduktu*[c] *šeḫtuni*[d] in [we]ight, fifteen cubits in length (and) five cubits in breadth. (12) If Kaniya dies, they shall return to Kirib-šeri the fifteen homers of barley, the twenty minas of tin, the five [ew]es, the five rams, (and) one cloth—four *kuduktu šeḫ*[*tun*]*i*, fifteen cubits in length (and) five cubits in breadth; (18) and Kaniya is taken.[e]

(19) one seal
(20–28) nine witnesses
(29–34) ten seals
(35) Utḫab-tae, the scribe[f]

a. *iddin*/*iddinū*. In the Nuzi tablets, singular and plural verbal forms are often confused. At times, number and person are confused simultaneously (Gordon, *Or*, N.S. 7 [1938], 220 f.).

b. Note the scribal caprice in the placement of the plural sign MEŠ: line 7, 5 udu-sal and line 8, 1 túg-meš (Berkooz, p. 19).

c. The *kuduktu* is a unit of measure used with wool and cloth (Cross, *Property*, p. 15 *contra* Gordon, *Babyloniaca*, *16* [1936], 81). Cross maintained that the measure represented the amount of wool obtained from a single plucking (*Property*, p. 15). This interpretation is unlikely since the variability of the amount of wool obtained from each plucking would seem to preclude its establishment as a standard measure of weight. Oppenheim equates *kuduktu* with the mina (*JA*, *230* [1938], 653), since it may be subdivided into shekels (*HSS*, *5*, 97:1). It should be noted that cloth, usually measured by the *kuduktu*, may also be measured by the mina (*HSS*, *5*, 82:11). This may argue for or against Oppenheim's interpretation.

d. The meaning of the term *šeḫtuni*, which probably modifies the *kuduktu*-measure is unknown. The copy does not seem to allow the rendering of *še-eḫ-tu-ni* as 40 *ḫe-et!-ni* which would then indicate an additional weight measurement (*AHw*, *1*, 342b).

e. *illeqqe*. This clause is subject to two interpretations. It may be an independent statement referring to the delivery of Kaniya to Kirib-šeri: Kaniya is (now) taken (cf. *JEN*, *3*, 317:20). On the other hand, it may be connected to the preceding sentence and thus be dependent upon the death of Kaniya and the subsequent return of the given commodities: Kaniya may (then) be taken. Cf. SMN 2372 (referred to by Liebesny in *JAOS*, *61* [1941], 134 n. 35), which states that the debtor's corpse is released only after the responsibility to pay his debt is assumed by another.

f. šu PN *ṭup-šar*-RUM. Goetze (*Language*, *14* [1938], 139 f.) has suggested that the RUM (= *rù*) sign is used in Nuzi with undetermined vowel. Hence all three grammatical cases appear to be identical. Cf. *JEN*, *3*, 303:30 and 319:15.

6. SMN 2013

(1) Document of *tidennūtu* of Minaš-šuk, son of Keliya, and of Unuš-kiaše, wife of Keliya. (6) Accordingly, they have given[a] Appuzizi, son of Keliya, to Šeḫal-tešub, son of Teḫub-šenni, in *tidennūtu* for four years. (10) And [Šeḫa]l-tešub has given ten minas of tin (and) two sound ewes to Minaš-šuk [and to] Unuš-k[iaše). (15) When the four years have elap[sed], Minaš-šuk and Unuš-kiaše shall [return] the ten minas of [tin and the two] ewes [to] Šeḫal-teš[ub], [and may then take back Appuzizi.][b]

rest of obverse destroyed

beginning of reverse destroyed

(24) Whoever [violates the agreement] shall pay a fine of one ox. [This document was written] in the city of Nuzi.

(27–35) nine seals[c]

a. *nittadin/ittadnū.* The first person plural form of the verb is illogical and reflects the apparent difficulty with which the Hurrian scribes handled the pronomial verbal prefixes (Gordon, *Or*, N.S. 7 [1938], 220; E. A. Speiser, "A Significant New Will from Nuzi," *JCS*, *17* [1963], 66).

b. Such a supplied reading is assured by parallel formulations of the *tidennūtu* contracts. Cf. *HSS*, *13*, 418:25–27; and *AASOR*, *16*, No. 27: 9–10 (texts 39 and 43).

c. Restore line 32 as [dumu]-meš since Šadam-mušni and Ḫāirānu are attested elsewhere as the sons of Unaya (*NPN*, p. 50a).

7. *JEN*, *3*, 316

(1) One sound, excellent four year old cow (and) three homers, five seah of barley belonging to Kel-tešub, son of Ḫudiya; (5) Ar-šanta, son of Anneya,[a] received them in *tidennūtu*. (8) When Ar-šanta returns one sound, excellent cow (and) [three] homers, five seah of barley [to] Kel-tešub, (13) he then fre[es himself fro]m the house of Kel-tešub. (16) But if Ar-šanta [hides from work,[b] Ar-šanta] must pay t[o Kel]-tešub his hire[c] (for a replacement) per day.

(23–30) eight witnesses[d]

(31) one seal

a. For the reading of the patronymic as *An-né-e!-a*, see *NPN*, p. 216.

b. Line 17 is to be restored as [*iš-tu* kin *i-ḫe-es*]-*sí*. Cf. SMN 2102:19–21 (text 35).

c. *uriḫulša/uriḫulšu.* The occurrence of the suffix -*ša* for -*šu* is very rare, since it is the masculine third person pronominal suffix which usually serves for the feminine in the Nuzi dialect (Gordon, *AJSL*, *51* [1934–35], 4 f.). For the translation of *uriḫul* "hire, wages" see above, pp. 22–24.

d. The name of the witness on line 23 is *Sí!-il-te-šub* (*NPN*, pp. 83a and 179b). The name of the witness on line 28 is *Ku-bar-ša!* dumu! *U*[*r-ku-ti*] (*NPN*, p. 91a).

8. *JEN*, *3*, 308

(1) Document of *tidennūtu* of Elḫib-tilla, son of Ibšaya; he, himself, has entered into *tidennūtu* to Takku, son of Enna-madi, in li[eu] of sheep.

(6) The tongue of Elḫib-tilla—he has declared before witnesses: "I have received five rams, twice plucked (and) five ewes, twice plucked, from[a] Takku, son of Enna-madi."

(11) Accordingly, whenever he returns the ten sheep specified in this document, Elḫib-tilla may [then] go wherever [he pleases].[b] (15) If [El]ḫib-tilla neglects the work of Takku and [hid]es,[c] he shall pay the hire (of a replacement)—[one mina of copper][d]—per day.

(21–28) eight witnesses[e] including scribe Kinniya, son of Ar-teššа[f]

(29) This document was written after a proclamation in the gate of Turša.[g]

(31–35) nine seals

a. The use of the preposition *ašar* "from, with" is characteristic of the Nuzi dialect (Goetze, *Language*, *14* [1938], 142; Gordon *Or*, N.S. 7 [1938], 224–25).
b. For the restoration [*ḫa-a-du*]-*ú*, see *JEN*, *3*, 309:9 (text 19).
c. The construction of this clause is similar to SMN 1592:14–15 (text 9). The partial restoration [*iḫ*]*essi* is based upon SMN 2102:21 (text 35).
d. [1 ma-na urudu]-meš. Cf. *JEN*, *3*, 295:16, 317:17, and *AASOR*, *16*, No. 60:21 (texts 15, 24, and 34). The occurrence of the MEŠ sign in these cases may indicate the final long vowel of the Akkadian *erā* "copper" (Berkooz, *Nuzi Dialect*, p. 19).
e. The personal name in line 27 is to be read as *Zi!-in-ni-ya* (*NPN*, p. 62b).
f. For the reading of the patronymic as *Ar-te!-eš-še*, see *NPN*, p. 32b.
g. The location of the city Turša is discussed by H. Lewy, *JAOS*, *88* (1968) [= AOS, 53], 150 ff.

9. SMN 1592

(1) [Document of *tidennūtu* of] Zi[rra, son of . . .; accordingly, he g]ave Pal-[tešub, his son] in *tidennūtu* to [Pai-tešub,] the agent(?)[a] [of] Šilwa-tešub. (7) And Pai-tešub gave one new(!)[b] set of wheels, (and) eight sound asses to Zirra. (9) Two years having elapsed, Zir[ra] shall return one set of wheels (and) eight asses to Pai-tešub and thus free his son, Pal-tešub. (13) If Pal-tešub neglects the work of Pai-tešub and does not do (it), Zirra [shall pay] one mina of copper—his hire (for a replacement) per day to Pai-tešub. (18) Whoever violates the agreement within the two contractual years shall pay a fine of one sound ox.

(22–29) eight witnesses including scribe, Ḫašib-. . ., son of . . . .-enni

(30–32) four seals

(33) This document was written after a proclamation in the Tiššae gate of the city of Nuzi.

a. The meaning of the term *še-el-li-in-ta-nu* is uncertain. It occurs most frequently in apposition to personal names, as the designation of a person or his occupation (*HSS*, *9*, 29, 68; *13*, 418; *14*, 11; and *TCL*, *9*, 10). However, it occurs also in the stative form *šellentānāku* "I am a *šellentānu*" (*HSS*, *13*, 24:5) with regard to a specified amount of barley which he had received (cf. *HSS*, *14*, 531:5). The term has been associated with the Semitic base *šlṭ*, normalized as *šeliṭānu* and translated as "plenipotentiary" (Saarisalo, *Slaves*, p. 27; Koschaker, *ZA*, *43* (1936), 196 n. 1; Gordon, *Babyloniaca*, *16* (1936), 130; Cassin, *Adoption*, p. 247 n. 4). Another possibility is that the term may be based upon the Hurrian root *šell* (*NPN*, p. 254b) whose meaning is unknown. It is interesting to note that Pai-tesub, who is also designated as a *še-el-li-(in-)ta-nu* in *HSS*, *9*, 29 and 68 (with *NPN*, p. 110a), is known from other texts as the *ardu* "slave" of Šilwa-tešub (*HSS*, *9*, 19, 20, and 22) or as his *šaknu* "representative" (*HSS*, *9*, 150).

b. Although positionally the adjective *eššu* "new" should modify the noun "asses," usage requires that it modify the preceding noun, "one set of wheels."

10. SMN 2144

(1) [Fifty minas of tin] belonging to [Tešub]-madi, son of Šerta-mailu, was received by Akkul-enni,[a] son of Tuniya in *tidennūtu*. (4) In lieu of the fifty minas of tin, Akkul-enni is to stay[b] in the house of Tešub-madi, likewise in *tidennūtu*. (8) Whenever Akkul-enni returns the fifty minas of tin to Tešub-madi, he may go wherever he pleases. (13) If Akkul-en⟨ni⟩ neglects the work of Tešub-madi for a single day, [Akku]l-enni shall pa[y a f]ine[c] of one mina of copper—his [dai]ly hire (for a replacement).

(20–25) six witnesses

(26) Iriri, the scribe

(27) This document was written after a proclamation in[d] front of the gate of the city of Ḫurazina-TUR.[e]

(31–33) three seals

a. It is clear from the context that Akkul-enni received the tin since he is obligated to return it to Tešub-madi. However, the Akkadian literally states, "He received to Akkul-enni." The scribe may have mistakenly written the verb *leqū* "to receive" for *nadānu* "to give." But the identical formulation occurs in *JEN*, *3*, 312:3, SMN 2047:4–5 and cf. *JEN*, *3*, 317:5 (texts 20, 50, and 24). Perhaps this formulation, influenced by the Hurrian passival orientation, is an attempt to render the receipt passively: "It was received by Akkul-enni."

b. *ašbu*/*ašib*

c. [*u-ma*]-*al-la*^{lá}. The last sign often serves as a phonetic complement when the verb *umalla* is written logographically (cf. SMN 1598:15 [text 33]). Hence scribal habit may be responsible for its inclusion even when the verb is written syllabically. It is less likely that the sign represents a logogram for the verb *išaqqal* "he shall weigh out," since the two verbs, *umalla išaqqal*, do not usually occur together in the Nuzi texts.

d. *ana/ina*. The occasional confusion on the part of the Nuzi scribes in their use of these two prepositions has been noted by Oppenheim (*Or*, N.S. 7 [1938], 376).
e. The name of this city and its location is discussed by A. L. Oppenheim, "Étude sur la topographie de Nuzi," *RA*, *35* (1938), 151–52. Cf. Wilhelm, *Untersuchungen zum Ḫurro-Akkadischen von Nuzi*, p. 4 n. 3.

11. SMN 2803

[Thus (declares) Agib-tašenni, son of . . .:][a] (1) "I [have caused my]self to enter into the house of [Mu]š-abu, son of Burna-z[ini] in *t*[*idennūtu* for three] years."

And [Muš-a]bu has given twenty minas of wrought copper[b] [and two homers] five seah of barley in *tidenn*[*ūtu* to Agib-]tašenni. (8) When three years have elapsed, Agib-tašenni shall then return the twenty minas of wrought copper and the two homers five seah of barley to Muš-abu and thus free himself. (13) If Agib-tašenni negle[cts the wo]rk of Muš-abu for a single da[y, Agib-taš]enni shall pay to Muš-abu [one mina] of wrought copper, his hire (for a replacement) per day.

(19) Thus (declares) Agib-tašenni:
a few remaining signs
the rest destroyed

a. The occurrence of *ramāniya* "myself" indicates that the beginning of the contract took the form of a personal declaration. Hence the opening lines of the document contained either the *lišānu* or its abbreviated *umma* formulation. Cf. line 19.
b. For the term urudu dù: *erū epšu* "wrought (or cast) copper," cf. H. Limet, *Le travail du métal au pays de Sumer au temps de la IIIe Dynastie d'Ur* (Bibliothèque de la Faculté de Philosophie et Lettres de l'Université de Liège, 155) [Paris: 1960], p. 128. The term may also appear in *LE* No. 1, if the rendering of obv. I line 17 as urudu *ep!-šum* is correct. Cf. *CAD*, *4*, p. 247.

12. *JEN*, *3*, 304

(1) Document of *tidennūtu* of Itḫin-nawar, son of Ar-šanta. He received twenty minas of tin from Enna-madi, son of Teḫib-tilla (6) and he, himself, entered the house of Enna-madi for *tidennūtu*. (9) For ten years, Itḫin-nawar shall serve[a] Enna-madi. (12) When the ten years have elapsed, Itḫin-nawar shall return the twenty minas of tin to Enna-madi and then he, himself, may go free. (17) [If] Itḫin-nawar [neglects the work] of Enna-madi. . . .

several lines destroyed
(19–21) three witnesses including scribe Sunzu
(22–23) four seals

a. In Nuzi, the verb *palāḫu* appears most frequently in real adoption clauses, denoting an obligation incumbent upon the adopted son with regard to his adoptive parent. The occurrences of the term in this text, and in the *ḫāpiru*-document *JEN*, *5*, 456:15, indicate that it refers to the performance of duties and not merely to an attitude of reverence (cf. Cassin, *Adoption*, p. 37 n. 1). Note that the text *HSS*, *19*, 11:22–23, glosses the term *palāḫu* with an obligation to feed and clothe the person. In the same context, *HSS*, *9*, 22:13, replaces the term with the verb *nadānu* "to give, provide." For a discussion of the legal usage of *palāḫu*, with full bibliographical citations, see Petschow, *Pfandrecht*, p. 111 n. 346.

13. SMN 2493

(1) The tongue of [Ay-abāš, son of . . .,—he has declared] in the presence of witnesses [as follows: "I gave [my son, Wa[ndiš-še,][a] in *tidennūtu* to Tarmiya, son of . . ."

(7) And Tarmiya has given one . . . to Ay-abāš in *tidennūtu* [for . . . years.] (10) When [the . . . years] have elapsed, Ay-abāš shall return one . . . to [Tarmiya] and then [take back his son,] Wandiš-[še.] (15) If Wa[ndiš-še] neglects the work of Tarmiya, Ay-abāš shall pay one mina of copper—his hire (for a replacement)— per day to [Tarmiya.] (21) Whoever violates the agreement shall pay a fine of two oxen. (24) This document was written[b] after a proclamation before the gate of the city of Nuzi.

(28–35) eight witnesses

(36–42) eight seals

a. The personal name may be restored either as Wandiš-še or as Wandiš-šenni (cf. *NPN*, p. 171b).

b. *saṭir*/*šaṭir*. For the *š*/*s* interchange in Nuzi, see Berkooz, *Nuzi Dialect*, p. 63.

14. SMN 3719

(1) Iluya, [son of Adad-ēriš, ga]ve his son Un-[teya] in *tidennūtu* to Ki[rib-šeri], son of Ḫud-tešub for six years. (6) And Kirib-šeri gave to Iluya son of Adad-ēriš, one ewe, twice plucked, two homers of barley (and) one cloth weighing four *kuduktu*.[a] (11) When the six years have elapsed, Iluya shall return the money specified in this document and take back his son.

(15) The tongue o[f Ilu]ya has decla[red: "I am satisf]ied." I[f Un]-teya . . .

beginning of reverse destroyed

(19-22) four witnesses[b]

(23–26) four seals

a. For a discussion of the *kuduktu* unit of measure, see above, text 5, note c.

b. For the rendering of the personal name in line 20 BE-*ti*-⟨*a?*⟩, see *NPN*, pp. 114a and 245a.

15. *JEN*, *3*, 295

Mendelsohn, *SANE*, p. 29

(1) Document of *tidennūtu* of Sīn-uballiṭ, son of Šamaš-ummāni. (4) Sīn-uballiṭ received one talent of copper in *tidennūtu* and in lieu of the copper, he is to stay[a] in the estate of Teḫib-tilla, son of Puḫi-šenni. (8) When Sīn-uballiṭ returns one talent of copper to Teḫib-tilla, he thus frees himself.[b] (13) But if Sīn-uballiṭ is not present[a] for a single day, he must pay one mina of copper per day.

(17–19) three witnesses

(20) The three witnesses of the delivered copper.[c]

(22–26) five witnesses including scribe, Šugriya

(27–29) five seals

(30) If Sīn-uballiṭ dies, then his sons must return the copper in full.

a. *ašbu/ašib*

b. *ušeuṣṣi/ušeṣṣi*

c. This is an alternate formulation of the designation of certain witnesses as official *nādinānu*-witnesses. See text 16, note c.

16. *JEN*, *3*, 293

H. Lewy, *Or*, N.S. *10* (1941), 330.

(1) [Document of *ti*]*dennūtu* of [Teḫ]ib-tilla, son of Puḫi-šenni. Ḫalu-šenni, [son of] Šadu-kewi received [eight] homers of barley; (5) and in lieu of the barley, his son, Ar-tidi, is to stay eight years in the house of Teḫib-tilla. (7) When the eight years have elapsed Ḫalu-šenni may return the eight homers of barley and then take back his son. (11) If he departs from the work of Teḫib-tilla for a single day, [he shall pay] one mina of copper per day. (13) If Ar-tidi dies, then [he shall take] another[a] son of Ḫalu-[šenni.] (16) If Ḫalu-šenni violates the agreement,[b] he shall pay a fine of one mina of silver.

(18–27) ten witnesses including scribe Itḫ-abiḫe

(28) These are [the deliver]ers[c] of [the barley.]

(29–32) four seals

a. *šanū/šanā*. Goetze (*Language, 14* [1938], 140) has observed that wherever the object precedes the subject—sometimes contained in the verbal form—both forms are in the nominative case. Cf. *HSS*, *9*, 13:5.

b. *ibbalkat/ibbalakkat*. The third person singular form of the verb *nabalkutu* in the present tense is subject to much variation in the Nuzi texts (Kramer, *AASOR*, *11* (1929–30), 97).

c. In Nuzi, the term *nādinānu* designates an official witness to the delivery and receipt of the given commodity (Koschaker, *NRUA*, pp. 67 ff.). Liebesny has suggested the translation "teller" (*JAOS*, *61* [1941], 132 n. 14) for this term. Cf. Hayden, *Court Procedure at Nuzu*, p. 19.

17. *JEN*, *4*, 387

H. Lewy, *Or*, N.S. *10* (1941), 331.

(1) Šurgi-tilla, son of [Teḫib-tilla], with Ar-[tidi], son of Ḫalu-šenni [appeared] before the judges [in a lawsuit.][a] (5) And the [tongue] of [Ar-tidi—he has declared be]fore the judges:

"[Ḫalu-šenni, my father,] has received[b] eight [homers of barley;] (8) and in lieu [of the barley], I am to stay in the house of Te[ḫib]-tilla. (11) But if I depart from the work of Teḫib-[tilla] for a single day I am to pay one mina of copper. (14) And now I have been absent[c] from work since the month of Ulūlu."[d]

(16) In accordance with his declaration, Ar-tidi was committed to Teḫib-[tilla] for the hire (of a replacement) of three [months] (and) twenty days—one talent, fifty minas of copper.

rest destroyed

a. This lawsuit is based on the *tidennūtu* arrangement recorded in contract *JEN*, *3*, 293 (text 16).

b. *nilteqe/ilteqe*. See text 6, note a.

c. The verb *rēqu* "to distance oneself" here denotes the absenting of oneself from service. For a similar Old Assyrian usage of *ruāqu*, see J. Lewy, "Grammatical and Lexical Studies," *Or*, N.S. *29* (1960), 26 n. 8. In Nuzi *rēqu* is also employed in the freeing of a person from a servile condition (cf. *AASOR*, *16*, No. 25:12 [text 51]).

d. Gordon and Lacheman ("Nuzi Menology," *ArOr*, *10* [1938], 54) equated the month-name *Ulūlu* with the more frequently occurring Hurrian month-name *Arkabinnu* (cf. *AHw 1*, 69a). Earlier studies on Nuzi menology include: C. H. Gordon, "The Names of the Month in the Nuzi Calendar," *RSO*, *15* (1935), 253–57; A. L. Oppenheim, "Die nichtsemitischen Monatsnamen der Nuzitexte," *ArOr*, *8* (1936), 290–305.

18. *AASOR*, *16*, No. 38

Pfeiffer and Speiser, *AASOR*, *16* (1936), 93

(1) [Tulb]un-naya [with] Utḫab-še, son of Kaliya, appeared before the judges [in a lawsui]t.

(5) Th[us] (declared) Tulbun-naya: "[Ta]e, son of Akawa-til accordingly gave his [so]n, Bēlaya, to me in *tidennūtu* in lieu of one slave and in lieu of twelve sheep. (11) [But there]after, Tae died and Utḫab-še was appointed the *ewuru*[a]-heir."

(14) And the judges [ques]tioned Utḫab-še: "Did Tae [gi]ve his son, [Bēl]aya, in *tidennūtu* [to Tulb]un-naya [in lieu of one] slave, (and) in lieu of twelve sheep?"

(20) [And thus (declared) U]tḫab-še: "Tae [did give his son, Bē]laya, in *tidennūtu*." And Tulbun-naya produced her[b] [document] of Tae's

tidennūtu. (25) [Furthermore] the tongue of Utḫab-še spoke [before] the judges in court: "My brother,[c] Tae, appointed me the *ewuru*-heir."

(28) Tulbun-naya prevailed in the lawsuit. Thus the judges committed Utḫab-še, in accordance with her document and in accordance with his declaration, to Tulbun-naya for the one slave and the twelve sheep of Tae's *tidennūtu,* (34) since Utḫab-še has taken the fields and buildings [of] Tae.

(36–38) three seals

a. With reference to the entry of *CAD* (E, p. 415b), "*ewuru* (or *ewiru*)," note that the syllabic writing *e-wu-ur-šu ša PN* (*JEN, 4,* 333:73) precludes the reading *ewiru*, which was originally preferred by Speiser (*AASOR, 10* [1928–29], 8, n. 5). Gadd, *RA, 23* (1926), No. 5 designates both the *māru rabū* "chief heir," lit. "oldest son" and the other heirs as *ewuru,* thereby indicating that the term does not denote the rank of the heir. It is noteworthy that this Hurrian term seems to occur only in the contexts in which the person inherits not by his natural right but by extraordinary circumstances, of which adoption is the most common. In this text, a brother inherits the property of the deceased, despite the existence of the deceased's son (cf. *HSS, 19,* 62:24). Perhaps the term may therefore specify a "non-automatic" heir. The periphrastic construction *ewurumma epēšu* would then mean "to appoint or become an *ewuru*-heir."

b. *-šu/ša.* In the Nuzi dialect, the third masculine pronomial suffix also serves for the feminine (Gordon, *AJSL, 51* [1934–35], 4 f.).

c. As Speiser has noted (*AASOR, 16* [1936], 94) the two brothers seem to have different fathers (cf. lines 2 and 6).

19. *JEN, 3,* 309

Saarisalo, *Slaves*, p. 53.
Lewy, *Or*, N.S. *10* (1941), 328.

(1) Document of *tidennūtu* of Eniš-tae, son of Ikkiu; Teḫib-tilla gave two men and two women to Eniš-tae in *tidennūtu.* (5) And in lieu of the two men and the two women, Eniš-tae is to stay in the house of Teḫib-tilla. (7) When Eniš-tae has returned the two men and the two women to Teḫib-tilla, he may then go wherever he pleases. (10) If Eniš-tae violates the agreement, he shall give four men and four women to Teḫib-tilla.

(12–21) ten witnesses including scribe Taya
(22–24) three seals

20. *JEN, 3,* 312[a]

Saarisalo, *Slaves*, p. 54

(1) [One boy] (and) one girl belonging to Enna-madi, son of Teḫib-tilla, was received by Ḫanadu,[b] son of Ar-teya and he gave them to Zini.

(5) Thus (declares) Ḫanadu: "I caused myself to enter into the house of [Enna]-madi together with my sons and together with my household." (8) [As long as] Ḫanadu is alive, he will not go free from the house of Enna-madi. Whenever Ḫanadu dies, the sons of Ḫanadu may give one boy, two and one half cubits[c] (and) one girl of the same height to Enna-madi; then they, themselves, may go free. (15) If Ḫanadu violates the agreement by going free [from the house] of Enna-madi, he shall give [one mi]na of silver (and) one mina of gold to Enna-madi, (19) [If] Ḫanadu is absent from the work [of] Enna-madi for a single day, he must pay the [hire] of one ass.[d]

(22–29) eight witnesses[e] including scribe Sunzu, son of Indiya

(30–32) five seals

a. Although the term *tidennūtu* does not appear in this text, its relation to the corpus of *tidennūtu* contracts is evident from the content and phraseology of its clauses. The text may have originally contained the superscription *ṭuppi tidennūti*, but it is no longer preserved. Cf. *JEN*, *6*, 609 (text 48) which mentions the term *tidennūtu* only in its superscription.

b. For the difficult construction *leqū ana PN* "to receive to PN," see text 10, note a.

c. The word *ma-lu-ṭì* represents a contraction of *mala ūṭi* "one half-cubit" (Landsberger, "Einige unerkannt gebliebene oder verkannte Nomina des Akkadischen," *WZKM*, *56* [1960], 109–10). The age of children is also indicated in terms of height in the Neo-Assyrian documents. References are listed in *CAD*, Ṣ, p. 238a sub *ṣuḫurtu*.

d. The rendering of this line as *ša* 1 ⟨ìr⟩^{du_4} "of one slave" rather than "of one ass" has been recommended above, p. 25 with n. 80.

e. See *NPN*, p. 165b for the rendering of the personal name on line 24 as [Ú]-*ba-ri-*⟨*ya*⟩ dumu ⟨⟨i⟩⟩ níg-ba-ᵈnin-šubur.

21. *JEN*, *2*, 192

Saarisalo, *Slaves*, p. 47

(1) Thus (declares) Amqa, son of Ambi-zina: "I am indebted to Uznā [for] two men.[a] And now, I have given to Uz[nā] one man from the land of the Lullu[b] [as her sla]ve(?)."[c]

(6) If that[d] man becomes the object of a claim,[e] Amqa shall clear (him) for[f] Uznā. (9) In addition, to Uznā Amqa has given another man in *tidennūtu* to Uznā in place of the other man. (13) And (given the case that) Amqa shall give one sound man to Uznā, then he may take back his man. (16) But if that *tidennu*-man dies, disappears, or runs away, for Amqa he is dead, lost, or gone.

(21–28) eight witnesses including scribe Šamaš-damiq, son of Itḫ-abiḫe

(29–33) seven seals

a. In Nuzi, the term lú:*awīlu* may designate a slave as well as a free man (Oppenheim, review of Pfeiffer and Speiser, *AASOR*, *16*, *Or*, N.S. 7 [1938], 377). For the position of the slave in Nuzi society, see Saarisalo, *Slaves*.

b. Nullu = Lullu. The frequent *l/n* interchange is a distinctive feature of the Nuzi dialect (Berkooz, *Nuzi Dialect*, pp. 57 ff.). For the location of the land of the Lullians east of Kirkuk in the vicinity of Suleimania, see E. A. Speiser, *Mesopotamian Origins* (Philadelphia, University of Pennsylvania Press, 1930), pp. 88–89; Saarisalo, *Slaves*, pp. 65–66; and E. F. Weidner, "Das Reich Sargons von Akkad," *AfO*, *16* (1952), 12. Evidence that the Lullians constituted one of the major population elements designated by the term Subarian has been offered by Speiser (*JAOS*, *68* [1948], 8 ff.) and Finkelstein ("Subartu and Subarians in the Old Babylonian Sources," *JCS*, *9* [1955], 4–5). Since most of the Nuzi slaves came from this region, the ethnic term Lullu also developed into an appellative term, signifying a person of lower class status (cf. B. Landsberger, "Ḫabiru und Lulaḫḫu," *KlF*, *1* [1930], 321–34). This appellative usage is reflected in *HSS*, *5*, 67:20.

c. The restored reading [*ana ar*]*dušu* "as her slave" was suggested by Saarisalo, *Slaves*, p. 47. In Nuzi, the feeling for differences in gender is weak since Hurrian does not recognize gender (Speiser, *Introduction to Hurrian*, p. 199). Thus use of the possessive suffix -*šu* for -*ša* is acceptable. Although the use of the genitive case is rather consistent, the *u/i* interchange in Nuzi may cause some confusion between the nominative and genitive cases (Goetze, *Language*, *14* [1938], 139), so that *du* for *di* is not impossible.

d. *šāšu* "that" is the regular demonstrative pronoun in Nuzi, serving for any case or gender (Gordon, *Or*, N.S. 7 [1938], 42).

e. *pirqu* "an actionable claim" is formed by a metathesis of the base *b/paqāru* "to claim" (*AHw*, *1*, 104).

f. *zukkū-nadānu* was interpreted by Shaffer ("*kitru/kiterru*: New Documentation for a Nuzi Legal Term," *Studies Presented to A. Leo Oppenheim* [Chicago, Oriental Institute, 1964], p. 189) as a hendiadys, in agreement with Landsberger, "Bemerkungen zu San Nicolò und Ungnad, Neubabylonische Rechts-und Verwaltungsurkunden," *ZA*, *39* (1929–1930), 288–89.

22. *JEN*, *3*, 305

Chiera and Speiser, *JAOS*, *47* (1927), 46

(1) Document of *tidennūtu* of Mušuya, son of Eḫliya. Teḫib-tilla, son of Puḫi-šenni gave one slave to Mušuya in *tidennūtu*. (5) And in lieu of the one slave, Mušuya is to stay in the house of Teḫib-tilla. (7) If Mušuya neglects the work of Teḫib-tilla, then Mušuya shall pay whatever be the hire of a slave to Teḫib-tilla. (11) When Mušuya wishes to go free, he shall restore a slave to Teḫib-tilla and then go free. If he violates the agreement, he shall pay two minas of gold to Teḫib-tilla.

(15–26) twelve witnesses[a] including scribe Taya, son of Apil-sīn

(27–29) three seals

a. For the rendering of the personal name in line 16 as *Ḫa-šu!-ar*, see *NPN*, p. 52a.

23. *JEN*, *6*, 607

(1) [Doc]ument of *tidennūtu* of Teḫib-tilla, son of Puḫi-šenni; he gave one female slave to Zikaya, son of Kutukka. (4) And Zikaya gave [his] son, [Ta]ḫirišti, to Teḫib-tilla for *tidennūtu*, in lieu of the one female slave. (7) When Zikaya returns one sound female slave to Teḫib-tilla, he may then take back his son, Taḫirišti. (11) But if Taḫirišti is absent from the work of Teḫibtilla for a single day, Zikaya must pay his hire (for a replacement) per day—one mina of copper. (16) If Zikaya dies, then any one [of] the sons of Zikaya may give one sound female slave to Teḫib-tilla, and thus free T[aḫirišti].

(23–32) ten witnesses including scribe Sīn-nādin-šumi

(33) The[ese me]n are the [deliverers] of the female slave.

(35–37) five seals

24. *JEN*, *3*, 317[a]

Saarisalo, *Slaves*, p. 56

(1) [Document of *tid*]*en*[*nūti* of] Enna-madi, son of Teḫib-tilla; [accordingly] the purchase price for one slave belonging to [Enni]gi, son of Tae, he has received [from[b] Enna]-madi. (6) [And now] in lieu of [one] slave from the land of the Lullu, Ennigi is to stay in the house of Enna-madi in *tidennūtu.* (9) When Ennigi gives to Enna-madi one sound boy, two and one half cubits, from the land of the Lullu, he may then go free from the house of Enna-madi. (15) If Ennigi neglects the work of Enna-madi for a single day, he must pay his hire (for a replacement) per day to Enna-madi. (20) And now it is given.[c]

(21–29) nine witnesses[d] including scribe Sunzu

(30) And Ennigi has received this money in front of the gate.

(32–34) six seals

(35) If Ennigi violates the agreement by returning the money to Enna-madi, he shall pay a fine of two slaves.

(38) The document was written after a proclamation in front of the gate.

a. This *tidennūtu* contract is closely related to those transactions which record the advance payment of a purchase price. Cf. *AASOR*, 16, No. 95 and above, pp. 30 f.

b. It is evident from the context and from lines 30–31 that Ennigi is the recipient of the money designated as the purchase price for his slave, which was given to him by Enna-madi. However, line 5 states "Enna-madi has received (the purchase price)." Saarisalo overcomes this difficulty by inserting the preposition *ašar* "from" at the end of line 4 (*Slaves*, p. 56). The text thus states, "He has received ⟨from⟩ Enna-madi (the purchase price)." Another possibility is that the scribe mistakenly used the verb *leqū* "to receive" for *nadānu* "to give." Cf. *JEN*, *3*, 312:3 (text 20, which is written by the same scribe).

c. This probably refers to the delivery of the money by Enna-madi, corresponding to Ennigi's receipt of the money in lines 30–31.

d. See *NPN*, p. 25b for the reading of the patronymic in line 22 as *Ši-im-⟨šar⟩*.

25. *AASOR*, *16*, No. 24

Pfeiffer and Speiser, *AASOR*, *16* (1936), 85

(1) A *tidennu* document.[a] Ḫabil-damqa gave his son Ḫanadu,[b] in *tidennūtu* to Tulbun-naya, daughter of Šeldun-naya; (4) and Tulbun-naya, daughter of Šeldun-naya gave one slave to Ḫabil-damqa. She shall retain him for ten years. (7) When[c] he returns one slave to Tulbun-naya, he may then take back his son, Ḫanadu.

(9–25) 17 witnesses[d] including scribe Nabū-nāṣir

(26–32) seven seals

a. The superscription *ṭuppi tidennu* also occurs in *JEN*, *3*, 290:1 (text 29). Both cases may be explained as scribal errors of omitting the final *ti* syllable. For examples of such omissions, see Berkooz, *Nuzi Dialect*, p. 24. However, Gordon (*Or*, N.S. 7 [1938], 49) cites other passages in which nouns and their abstract derivatives are interchanged.

b. As Speiser has noted (*AASOR*, *16* [1936], 86), Ḫanadu and Tulbun-naya also appear together in another contract; ibid., No. 23.

c. The meaning of *undu* "when" is clearly established from the context of its occurrences in the Nuzi texts, e.g. Gadd, *RA*, 23 (1926), Nos. 9:14, 26:18; *JEN*, *1*, 31:37; and *HSS*, *5*, 43:38. The use of this temporal conjunction in the Amarna dialect of Akkadian has been noted by Gadd (*RA*, *23* [1926], 95). It is also attested in Ras Shamra Akkadian (*PRU*, *3*, RS 16.249 line 13 and RS 16.356 line 9). For its relation to the Hurrian particle *undu* "now then," see Speiser, *Introduction to Ḫurrian*, pp. 89–90, especially n. 63.

d. See *NPN*, p. 154b, sub *Teššuia* for the reading of the patronymic on line 16 as *Te-su-*[*y*]*a!*

26. *AASOR*, *16*, No. 63

Pfeiffer and Speiser, *AASOR*, *16* (1936), 112

(1) Document of *tidennūtu* of Šugriya, son of Ri. . . . Ar-teššе, son of Ḫanaya, himself has entered into the house of Šugriya in *tidennūtu* for twenty years in lieu of one slave of three cubits from the land[a] of the Lullu. (7) When Ar-teššе fulfills twenty years in the house of Šugriya, Ar-teššе shall return one sound slave of [three] cubits from the land of the Lullu to Šugriya, and thus free himself. (13) If Ar-teššе neglects[b] the work of Šugriya for a single day, he shall pay one mina of copper, [his] hire (for a replacement), to Šugriya.

(18–26) nine witnesses[c] including scribe Nanna-adaḫ[d]

(27–33) seven seals[e]

(34) The docu[ment] was written [afte]r a proclamation before the gate.
(36) one seal

a. The phonetic complement *at* indicates that the determinative kur:*mātu* "land" was pronounced in Nuzi. Evidence for the pronunciation of other determinatives in Nuzi have been offered by Oppenheim (*WZKM*, *35* [1938], 42). For a discussion of determinatives in the Nuzi orthography, see Berkooz *Nuzi Dialects*, pp. 16–17.
b. *ezzib/izzib*. In the Nuzi tablets personal elements prefixed to verbal forms are sometimes confused. The most common confusion is between third and first person singular. (Gordon, *Or*, N.S. 7 [1938], 220).
c. For the rendering of the patronymic on line 22 as *Ku!-duk-ka*$_4$ see *NPN*, p. 172a.
d. The orthography of the name (Na-an-na-dah) seems to indicate that it was actually pronounced as Sumerian (*NPN*, p. 317).
e. Note the comment in *NPN*, p. 12 *sub Akap-tae* with regard to the personal name on line 33.

27. *HSS*, *9*, 13

Saarisalo, *Slaves*, p. 10.

(1) The tongue of Algi-tilla and the tongue of Zunnaya, sons[a] of Kainnuya—they have declared before witnesses:

(5) "Our father, Kainnuya, has received a boy of two cubits—a slave—from the house of Šilwa-tešub, son of the king; (9) And now he has made us enter into the house of Šilwa-te[šub] in lieu[b] of the boy [for] *tidennūtu*."

(11) But when Algi-tilla and Zunnaya return a boy of two cubits to Šilwa-tešub, they shall then free themselves from the house of Šilwa-tešub. (17) They shall perform[c] their work, including that of Zunnaya, in the meadow.[d]

(20–29) ten witnesses including scribe Nikriya, son of Tarmu(?)-šarri.[e]

(30–37) eight seals

a. The logogram dumu is not followed by a plural indicator. Also note the use of the singular verbal forms in lines 5 and 15. Although such confusion in number is common in Nuzi, the explicit reference to Zunnaya (line 18) may perhaps indicate that the declaration was made by Algi-tilla on behalf of himself and his brother.
b. *kī/kīmū* or *kīma*.
c. ma-an-dù. Although the use of the logogram dù:*epēšu* is very common in the Nuzi texts, its occurrence in a Sumerian verbal complex is rare.
d. *ina la-aš-qi-im-⟨ma?⟩*. Note that mimation is normally preserved in Nuzi only when an enclitic particle is suffixed to the noun.
e. The reading *mu* in the personal name, Tarmu-šarri (line 25) is doubtful (*NPN*, p. 150a).

28. *HSS*, *9*, 28

(1) Kubi-šarri, son of Milkuya, has received three homers of barley belonging to Turar-tešub,[a] son of Agib-tašenni in *tidennūtu.* (6) In lieu of the three homers of barley, he will maintain[b] the orchards of the city of Palaya, belonging to Šilwa-tesub, son of the king, for ten years. (10) When the ten years have elapsed, Kubi-šarri shall then return the three homers of barley and thus go free. (16) If Kubi-šarri departs from the orchards for a single day, he shall pay one mina of copper, the hire (for a replacement) per day.

(21–28) eight witnesses[c]

(29) Ḫašiya, the scribe

(30–38) nine seals

a. In *JEN*, *5*, 495:1, Turar-tešub, son of Agib-tašenni is described as a [lú]e n - n u - u n g i š - t i r: *maṣṣār qišti* "forest ranger." Hence, his interest in securing help to maintain the orchards of Šilwa-tešub.

b. *ukallū*/*ukāl*. In the Nuzi texts, *kullu* "to hold" commonly denotes utilization of property; here it denotes maintenance. Cf. *Ahw*, *1*, 502–03 sub *kullu*(*m*) 5d) and 7a). Also note the use of *ṣabtu* in CH § 64.

c. The name Turari (line 25) is treated as Hurrian in *NPN*, p. 270. However, Speiser (*JCS*, *17* [1963], 66) is uncertain of the Hurrian origin of this name.

29. *JEN*, *3*, 290

Saarisalo, *Slaves*, p. 51

(1) A *tidennu* document[a] of Wur-tešub, son of Agib-tašenni; (3) accordingly, Wur-tešub has given his slave, Artašenni, a carpenter, for *tidennūtu* in lieu of thirty shekels[b] of *ḫašaḫušennu*[c] silver (and) two homers of barley to Ḫud-arrapḫe, son of Tišam-mušni, for ten years. (9) And Ḫud-arrapḫe has given thirty shekels of *ḫašaḫušennu* silver (and) two homers of barley to Wur-tešub. (12) If Artašenni, the slave of Wur-tešub, has a claimant, then Wur-tešub shall clear Artašenni, the carpenter, for Ḫud-ar[rapḫe]. (18) When the ten years (of) Artašenni in the house of Ḫud-arrapḫe have elapsed, (21) Wur-[tešub shall re]turn the thirty shekels of *ḫašaḫušennu* silver (and) the two homers of barley [of] this document; (25) and thus free [Ar]tašenni from the house [of] Ḫu[d-arrapḫe]. (28) If Artašenni ne[glec]ts the work of Ḫud-arrapḫe for a single day (32) Wur-tešub [shall p]ay one mina of copper, [his hi]re per day (for a replacement) to Ḫud-arrapḫe. (36) Whoever between them violates the agreement within the ten years, shall pay a fine of two slaves. (38) This document[d] was written after a proclamation—when[e] Pai-tilla, son of Kuari was appointed m[ayor][f] in the city of Nuzi, *kaḫaššinna*[g]—in [the gate of] the city of Nuzi.

(44–49) five witnesses and the scribe Tarmi-tešub, son of Itti-šarri.
(50–52) six seals

a. For the superscription *ṭuppi tidennu* see text 25, note a.
b. Lacheman has demonstrated that the SU sign is the logogram for *šiqlu* in Nuzi and not an abbreviated form of *zūzu* (*JAOS*, *57* [1937], 181 ff.). Thus it seems that in Nuzi paleography the SU sign was identical with the GÍN sign.
c. The meaning of the term *ḫašaḫušennu*, commonly used with payments of silver, is uncertain. It may be descriptive either of the silver (Koschaker *ZA*, *41* [1933], 32 n. 1—accepted by J. Lewy in *ArOr*, *18*/3 [1950], 383 n. 79), or of the transaction in which the silver is paid (cf. *CAD*, Ḫ, p. 136; *AHw*, *1*, 333). Lacheman, in an oral communication, connected the term with Akkadian *ḫašāḫu* "to desire"; accordingly the silver would be paid in equivalent values of any desired commodity (cf. *HSS*, *9*, 25:3–12 and *HSS*, *19*, 127:6–8).
d. *ṭuppi anni*/*ṭuppu annū*.
e. The apparent temporal usage of the conjunction *šumma* is highly irregular. Date formulae of this type in Nuzi are usually introduced by *undu*, *šuntu*, or *kīma* (see Speiser, *AASOR*, 16 [1936], 61).
f. *ana ḫa*[*zanni*] *ša īpuššunūti*. Pai-tilla is mentioned as a *ḫazannu* "mayor" in *JEN*, *3*, 292:37. Hence the restored reading in line 41 is assured. The occurrence of the relative particle *ša* is inexplicable. The form *īpuššunūti* is to be translated "he appointed them," although the context demands the meaning "they appointed him." This is an example of the confusion caused by the passival orientation of the Hurrian transitive verb, which would require the form "he was appointed by them." The Nuzi scribe mechanically transferred this Hurrian form into Akkadian, where the verbal contruction is active. Other such instances are cited by Speiser, in *AASOR*, 16 (1936), 137; and by Wilhelm, *Untersuchungen zum Ḫurro-Akkadischen von Nuzi*, pp. 61 ff.
g. The meaning of the term *kaḫaššinna* is unknown (*AHw*, *1*, 420; and *CAD*, K, p. 36).

30. *JEN*, *3*, 299

H. Lewy, *Or*, N.S. *10* (1941), 329
Mendelsohn, *SANE*, p. 30

(1) Unaya, son of Agib-šarri, gave his son, Enna-madi, a weaver, to Teḫib-tilla, son of Puḫi-šenni for *tidennūtu* in lieu of three talents of copper, for fifty years. (6) And when he has fulfilled the fifty years, he shall return the three talents of copper and thus go free. (9) If Unaya violates the agreement by returning the copper and demanding his son, (12) then he shall requisition[a] a weaver for the man.

(14–23) ten witnesses[b] including scribe Tiam-biri
(24–25) four seals

a. Gelb has presented a thorough discussion, with bibliography, of the verb *šadādu* ("Old Akkadian Inscriptions in Chicago Natural History Museum," *Fieldiana: Anthropology*, *44* [1955], 188–90). Its primary meaning is "to pull, drag," with a secondary meaning "to measure." In this Nuzi text, as well as in

JEN, *5*, 471:10–11, the verb refers to the drafting of a person into service as a replacement for another.

b. For this rendering of the personal name *Ta-an-ni-mu-⟨ša⟩* (line 21), see *NPN*, p. 147a.

31. *HSS*, *5*, 40

Speiser, *JAOS*, *53* (1933), 36

(1) Thus (declares) Sige, son of Tai-tilla[a]; in the presence of witnesses he has declared as follows:

(4) "I have received twelve minas of tin from Agawatil, son of Ellu[a]; and for *tidennūtu*, in lieu of those twelve minas of tin, I have caused myself to enter into the house of Agawatil for *tidennūtu* and perform his work. (11) When I have harvested for him, I shall then return the twelve minas of tin to Agawatil, and thus free myself from the house of Agawatil. (15) If I neglect the work of Agawatil for a single day, I shall pay one seah of barley to Agawatil as the daily hire (of a replacement). (20) He who violates the agreement shall pay a fine of one ox. The tablet was written in the city of Nuzi at the gate.

(22–28) seven seals[b] including the seal of Nirari, son of Taya, the scribe.

a. Both contracting parties also appear together in texts *HSS*, *5*, 19 and 102.

b. See *NPN*, p. 119 for reading the patronymic *Pu-ru!-sa* (line 27).

32. *TCL*, *9*, 10

Koschaker, *NRUA*, p. 175

(1) Ḫurbi[ya], son of Tauga, has rece[ived] thirty minas of copper from Nudumar, the age[nt(?)[a] in *ti*]*dennūtu*. (5) And in lieu of the thirty minas of copper, Ḫurbiya is to stay [in] the house of Nudu[mar][b] in *tidennūtu*, performing the harvest-work of Nudu[mar]. (9) When Ḫur[biya] has perfo[rmed the work] of Nudumar, he shall ret[urn the thirty mi]nas of copper, and thus [go free]. (13) But if Ḫurbiya [is absent fr]om the work of Nudumar [for a single day], he shall pay one mina of copper [per day]. [Kiba]ya,[c] son of Sate, is the [guaran]tor[d] of Ḫurbiya [and of the coppe]r. (19) Therefore, if [Ḫurbiy]a dies [or disappea]rs, then Nudumar may seize [Kibaya] and he sh[all pa]y the copper in full.

(24–30) seven witnesses[e] including the scribe Ḫudiya, son of Utamansi[f]

(31–36) six seals

a. For the term *šellintānu* "agent(?)," see text 9, note a.

b. Read [*i-na*] É! [I]*Nu-du*[*mar*] *a-ši-i*[*b*]. Koschaker's interpretation of this tablet as a self-sale (*NRUA*, p. 131 n. 6) is based upon his erroneous reading of line 7 as [*kīma?*] 1 ÌR [I]*Nu-du-*[*mar*] *a-ši-*[*ib*] "He shall stay as the slave of *PN*." Lewy's reading of this line (*Or*, N.S. *10* [1941], 317 n. 3) as [*ana*] 3 ITU *i-na* É[I] *Nudu*[*mar*] *a-ši-*[*ib*] "He shall stay in the house of PN for three months" is difficult since the duration clause (lines 9–13) does not recapitulate such a fixed term.

c. This personal name is restored from the seal on line 35 and should be added to the *NPN* entries on pp. 86b and 120b.

d. Koschaker's *Bürgschaftsrecht* is the classic work on Mesopotamian suretyship and guaranty. For the role of the guarantor in Nuzi, see Cassin, *RA*, *34* (1937), 154–68.

e. The name of the witness on line 27 may be restored as [*Še-eš?*]-*me-ek-ka*$_4$ by comparing it to line 33 and the *NPN* entry sub *Šešwikka* (p. 133a). Note that this personal name is not listed in *NPN* (cf. p. 256b).

f. *NPN* (p. 318) lists this name as one which was actually pronounced as Sumerian. Cf. text 26, note d.

33. SMN 1598

(1) Document of *tidennūtu* of Teḫib-sissa, son of Ḫanaya. [Accordingly], he caused [himself to enter] into [the house] of Pai-tešub, son of Za . . . (6) [Teḫib-sissa receiv]ed ten . . . (and) forty . . . belonging to [Pai-tešub]. (10) If Teḫi[b-sissa][a] neglects [the work in] the house [of] Pai-[tešub f]or a single day, Teḫib-sissa shall pay to Pai-tešub one mina of cop[per]—his hire (for a replacement) per day.

(16) Thus (declares) Teḫib-sissa: "If I die or disappear, then my six ho[mers of land] in the city Z[izza (?)],[b] to the ea[st of the dis]trict of the *mami . . . riḫe*[c] (23) shall be [guar]antors for m[e]; Paitešub may retain them in lieu of [the money].

(26–31) four witnesses, two lines destroyed

(32) Taki,[d] the scribe

(33) [Whoever a]mong them violates the agreement shall pay a fine of . . .

(35–39) six seals

a. According to the copy, [I]*Te-ḫi-*[*ib-si-is-sa*] (line 11) seems to have been written as an indented line.

b. For the location of the city Zizza, see Oppenheim, *RA*, *35* (1938), 139–40; and H. Lewy, *JAOS*, *88* (1968) [= AOS, 53], 158 f.

c. The name of the district apparently ends with the Hurrian adjectival suffix *-ḫe* (Speiser, *Introduction to Ḫurrian*, p. 114–15; F. Bush, *A Grammar of the Hurrian Language* [Ph.D. diss., Brandeis University, 1964], pp. 163–66).

d. The personal name should perhaps be read as *Ta-ki-*⟨*ya*⟩ (lines 32, 35 f.) Cf. *NPN*, p. 145b.

34. *AASOR*, *16*, No. 60

Pfeiffer and Speiser, *AASOR*, *16* (1936), 109

(1) Document of *tidennūt*[*u*][a] of Silib-kušuḫ, [son of A]ḫuya. Accordingly, he has caused himself to enter into the house of Uznā, wife of Enna-madi, for ten years in *tidennūtu*; (7) and Uznā has given to Silib-

kušuḫ thirty-five minas of tin, one homer of barley and one homer of wheat likewise in *tidennūtu.* (11) When the ten years in the house of Uznā have elapsed, Silib-kušuḫ shall return to Uznā the thirty-five minas of tin, the one homer of barley and the homer of wheat—the money specified in the document; and thus free himself[b] from the house of Uznā. (19) If Silib-kušuḫ neglects the work of Uznā for a single day, Silib-kušuḫ shall pay to Uznā one mina of copper, his hire (for a replacement) per day.

(25) Thus (declares) Silib-kušuḫ: "If I am not present, then Uznā may seize [c]my sons and daughters and wife."[c] They shall restore the money and his hire (for a replacement) to Uznā. (29) The buildings of Silib-kušuh are guarantors for Silib-kušuḫ.

(31) The tongue of Silib-kušuḫ—he has declared thusly before [witnesses]: "I have received[d] the money specified in the document from Uznā."

(34–41) eight witnesses

(42–47) six seals, including the seal of Turar-tešub [the scribe].[e]

a. *ṭuppi tidennāti.* For the form of this superscription see above, p. 13 n. 13.

b. *ušeṣṣu/ušeṣṣi.*

c–c. Speiser has noted (*AASOR, 16* [1936], 110) the un-Semitic limitation of the possessive suffix *-ya* to the last of the three nouns, *aššataya/aššatī.*

d. *ilqemi/elqemi.* This same confusion occurs in *AASOR, 16,* No. 25:16 and SMN 1067:8 (texts 51, and 38).

e. Turar-tešub is neither a witness nor one of the contracting parties. The presence of his seal on this tablet may best be explained by assuming that he is the scribe Turar-tešub, son of Itḫ-abiḫe (cf. *AASOR, 16,* No. 52:33).

35. SMN 2102

(1) Document of *tidennūtu* of Madib-abu and of Agib-tešub, sons of Tarmiya. (5) We have received[a] twenty-nine minas of bronze belonging to Utḫab-tae, son of Ar-tura in *tidennūtu* for four years. (9) In lieu of the twenty-nine mi[nas] of bronze, Agib-tešub, being a *tidennu,*[b] is to stay[c] in the house of Utḫab-tae and per[form] his task. (13) When four years have elapsed Madib-abu and Agib-te[šub] shall return the twenty-nine minas of bronze to Utḫab-tae and Agib-tešub will go free. (18) If Agib-tešub hides[d] from the service of Utḫab-tae, Madib-abu and Agib-tešub shall pay to Utḫab-tae one mina of cop[per]—his hire (for a replacement) per day.

(26) The tongue of Agib-tešub—he has de[clared] in the presence of witnesses:

"Of my own free will I have been consigned; I shall stay in the house of Utḫab-tae."

(30) Until he returns the aforementioned bronze, he will perform his task.

(32) Genni, son of Ḫubida, and Ḫanadu, son of Ar-tešub are guarantors for Madib-abu and for Agib-tešub. If they cannot find them,[e] then Utḫab-tae may seize Ḫanadu and Genni.

(38–42) five witnesses, one seal

(43) Pui-tae, the scribe

(44–46) six seals

a. *nilteqū/nilteqe*. In Nuzi, the first person plural verbal forms often exhibit the suffix *-u* in addition to the prefix *ni-* (Goetze, *Language*, *14* [1938], 141).

b. *tidenna*. Goetze has observed that in Nuzi Akkadian the predicative noun often appears in the accusative case (ibid., p. 140 n. 49). The accusative ending of the form may therefore indicate that it is to be understood predicatively.

c. *ašbu/ašib*. The other examples of the confusion between singular and plural verbal forms in this tablet are *utār/utarrū* (line 27) *umalla/umallū* (line 25) and *ipušū/ipuš* (line 32).

d. The verb *ḫesū* "to hide" occurs in two other contexts in Nuzi. One refers to the concealing of stolen sheep (*HSS*, *9*, 143:9) and the other refers to one's failure to substantiate his claim in a lawsuit (*JEN*, *4*, 344:39 and 355:24). In the latter context, the defendant fails to produce his witnesses. The judges then declare that the defendant loses the case *kī illik u uḫtessi* "since he came and covered up (the matter)." Cf. *CAD*, Ḫ, p. 177 which posits two different bases for these two contexts.

e. *-šunu/šunūti*. See Gordon *Or*, N.S. 7 (1938), 40 for other examples of this interchange in the Nuzi dialect.

36. *JEN*, *3*, 306

Cassin, *RA*, *34* (1937), 162

(1) Document of [*tidennūtu*] of Teḫib-tilla, [son of Puḫi-šenni.] Muš-[šenni], son of Šadu-kewi[a] received ten homers of barley; in li[eu of the barley], he is to stay ten years in the house of Teḫib-tilla. (6) When the ten years elapse, he shall return the ten homers of barley and go free. (9) The guarantor of Muš-šenni is Tur-šenni, son of Arik-kani; if Muš-šenni departs from work for a single day, Tur-šenni shall pay one mina of copper per day. (15) If Tur-šenni and Muš-šenni violate the agreement, they shall pay a fine of one mina of silver.

(18–25) eight witnesses

(26–29) four seals, including seal of the scribe

a. Note that Muš-šenni's brother, Ḫalu-šenni son of Šadu-kewi, also entered into a *tidennūtu* arrangement with Teḫib-tilla, son of Puḫi-šenni (*JEN*, *3*, 293, text 16). The set of witnesses to both these transactions is the same.

37. *AASOR*, *16*, No. 29

Pfeiffer and Speiser, *AASOR*, *16* (1936), 88.

(1) The tongue of Šug-tešub,[a] the weaver—he has declared in the presence of witnesses: "I am a *tidennu* of Tulbun–naya and there is no

guarantor for me. (6) Therefore, by my own free will, I have cast[b] myself into bondage."[c]

(9) Thus (declares) Šug-te[šub]: "If [I] raise a compl[aint[d] against] Tulbun-[naya, con]cerning the bo[nda]ge, I shall pay a fine of [one mina of gold] (and) one mina of sil[ver to] Tulbun-[naya]."

(15–32) seventeen witnesses including Urḫiya, the scribe

(33–39) six seals and one witness

a. The personal name should perhaps be read as Šug⟨ri⟩-tešub (*NPN*, p. 137b).

b. *iddānni.* The base of this verbal form is *nadū* "to cast," although orthographically it appears to have been derived from an initial weak base. (Similar orthographies of verbal forms from the base *ndn* occur in *JEN*, *1*, 19:13, 19, and 90:6.) The translation of the verb in the first person singular is based upon the occurrence of the reflexive pronoun *ramāni* (line 6).

c. Literally *šeršerētu* means "chains." For the placing of a person in chains as a sign of enslavement, see *MSL*, *1*, 28:11′ with Landsberger's discussion on p. 136. Cf. Ebeling, "Urkunden des Archivs von Assur aus mittelassyrischer Zeit," *MAOG*, 7/1–2 (1933), p. 5 note a.

d. *isa*[*ssi*]/*išassi*. For the *š*/*s* interchange in Nuzi, see Berkooz, *Nuzi Dialect.*, p. 63.

38. SMN 1067

(1) Document of *tidennūtu* of Šullum-Adad, son of Tuḫmi-tešub. (4) Accordingly, Šullum-Adad, himself, has entered[a] into the estate of Ibša-ḫalu, son of Unaya in *tidennūtu*. (9) And Ibša-ḫalu

four ewes, twice plucked,
one dyed[b] ram,
one dyed ewe,
one ram, once plucked,
one ewe, once plucked,
two male goats, *ḫuššubāte*[c](?)
one female goat, twice shorn,

(14) a total of eleven small livestock[d] (and) two minas thirty shekels of bronze Ibša-ḫalu gave[e] to Šullum-Adad. (18) When Šullum-Adad returns the money specified in this[f] document to Ibša-ḫalu, he, himself, may go free. (24) If Šullum-Adad performs *šattetaumma*[g] for the *ilku*-duty[h] of Kirib-šarri, then Nula-zaḫi and Wur-te shall clear Utḫab-tae for Ibša-ḫalu. (30) If Šullum-Adad abandons the work of Ibša-ḫalu, he shall pay a fine of one m[ina] of copper—the hire (for a replacement)—to Ibšaḫalu . . .

(34–39) six witnesses

(40) Ḫurbi-tešub, the scribe

(41–45) seven seals

(46) The tablet was written after a proclamation in the city of Dūr-ubla[i] [at] the gate.

(47) The year ????[j]

a. *ēterub/īterub.*
b. The term *ṣarīpu* was first connected with *ṣarāpu* "to dye" by Gadd in *RA, 23* (1926), 140. *CAD* (Ṣ, p. 111) equates the term *ṣarīpu* with the related phrase *sime ṣarīpu* "marked with a dye" as interpreted by Goetze (*Property*, p. 26, n. 38). Cross, however, derives *sime* from *siāmu*, "to become red–brown," thus translating the phrase "red-dyed" (ibid.). This would refer to the process of dyeing the wool prior to plucking. But cf. Landsberger, *JCS, 21* (1967), 145 n. 30.
c. The meaning of the descriptive term *ḫuššubāte* (?) is obscure. The base *ḫšb* is only attested in a grammatical text, in the D stem (*CAD*, Ḫ, p. 138a and *AHw, 1*, 332).
d. udu: *immeru*. In this context, the term refers to both sheep and goats (Cross, *Property*, p. 31; *CAD*, I–J, p. 133).
e. sì[nu]/*iddin.*
f. *annītu/annīti.* The forms of *annū* "this" are frequently misused with regard to case, number, and gender (Gordon, *Or*, N.S. 7 [1938], 41 f.). Cf. text 41, note d.
g. *šattetaumma eppuš/ippuš.* For the Hurro-Akkadian construction x-*umma epēšu*, see Speiser, *Introduction to Hurrian*, p. 129; and Bush, *A Grammar of the Hurrian Language*, p. 171. Such phrases usually mean "to become or to perform x." The meaning of the Hurrian element of the hybrid construction is obscure. However, the context indicates that a person who becomes *šatteta* is physically drafted into service. Cf. *CAD*, A/2, p. 511 sub *attataumma*.
h. The *ilku*-duty denotes feudal services performed for a higher authority in return for land held (*CAD*, I–J, pp. 73 and 80). The Hurrian synonym for *ilku* is *irwišši* (ibid., p. 188; *AHw, 1*, 248).
i. For the location of the city Dūr-ubla, see H. Lewy, *JAOS, 88* (1968) [= AOS, 53], 158 f.
j. mu-meš[ti] ŠA IGI IA ḪU UR[. . .] The word mu:*šattu* "year" usually introduces a year formula and has therefore been understood as a singular despite the occurrence of the plural indicator MEŠ. The interpretation of the remaining signs is difficult. They may be rendered as the personal name *Ša-lì-ya* which would represent either an alternate spelling for the Hurrian name Šalliya (*NPN*, p. 123a) or a hypocoristicon for an Akkadian Šalim-x name (*NPN*, p. 123a, b). The remaining two syllables may perhaps be the beginning of the name Hurra (cf. *NPN*, p. 218a). Note that the preceding line lacks two final signs.

39. *HSS, 13*, 418

(1) Document of *tidennūtu* of Agawatil, son of Itḫib-tilla, and of Elmaše, wife of Itḫib-tilla. (4) They have given Pizunne,[a] daughter of Itḫib-tilla, to Uznā, daughter of Ḫašiya,[b] in *tidennūtu*; (7) And Uznā
seven full-grown rams,[c] thrice[d] plucked, including one dyed, full-grown ram[e];
three ewes, thrice plucked;
(12) one ewe, once plucked;
two full-grown goats,[f] thrice sheared;
one female goat, twice sheared;
and one male goat, once sheared;

(17) a total of fifteen sheep and goats belonging to Uznā, she has given to Agawatil and to Elmaše in *tidennūtu.* (22) When Agawatil and Elmaše return[g] the small livestock specified in this document to Uznā, they may then ta[ke] back Pi[zu]ne. (28) If Pizune becomes the object of a claim, Agawa[til and] Elmaše shall clear (her). (30) And if Pi[zu]ne neglects[h] the work [of] Uznā, Agawatil and Elmaše shall pay one mina of co[pper], her [hi]re (for a replacement) per day. (35) The document[i] was written at the gate of the city of Turša.

(36–40) five witnesses

(41) Ḫuziri, son of Sunzu, the scribe

(42–49) eight seals

a. Pizune, daughter of Itḫi-tilla, also appears in *HSS, 13,* 595.
b. Uznā, daughter of Ḫašiya, is to be identified with Unzā, the wife of Enna-madi (*HSS, 19,* 38:2).
c. Cross (*Property,* p. 24) interprets udu-nita-gal as a "castrated ram." But cf. below, note e, and *CAD* I-J, p. 131a.
d. [a-]ta-an/ta-àm
e. udu-gal: *immeru rabū* (*MSL, 8*/1, 16:105).
f. más-gal: ŠU-lum (*MSL, 8*/1, 30:216; *JNES, 4* (1945), 167). Cf. Cross *Property,* p. 31 and *MSL, 8*/1, 58.
g. *utārma*/*utarrūma.* The use of the singular verbal forms for the required plural also occurs in line 30 (*uzakka*[*ma*]/*uzakkū*[*ma*]) and line 34 (si-a-meš[la]/ *umallū*).
h. *uzzib*/*izzib.* Cf. *AHw, 1,* 268; *CAD,* E, p. 423.
i. *ṭuppi*/*ṭuppu.*

40. *AASOR, 16,* No. 61

Pfeiffer and Speiser, *AASOR, 16* (1936), 110.

Case: [Document of] Elḫib-tašenni

(1) Document of *tidennūtu* of Urḫiya, son of Agib-tilla. Accordingly, he has given his son, Elḫib-tašenni, to Kula-ḫubi, son of Ar-teya in *tidennūtu* for five years; (7) and Kula-ḫubi has given forty minas of tin (and) ten minas of bronze likewise in *tidennūtu* to Urḫiya. (10) If Elḫib-tašenni becomes the object of a claim, then Urḫiya shall clear him for Kula-ḫubi. (14) If Elḫib-tašenni neglects the work of Kula-ḫubi for a single day, Urḫiya shall pay to Kula-ḫubi, one mina of copper—his hire (for a replacement) per day. (20) When the five years (of) Elḫib-tašenni in the house of Kula-ḫubi have elapsed, Urhiya shall return the forty minas of tin and ten minas of bronze to Kula-ḫubi and thus free his son from the house of Kula-ḫubi. (29) Whoever violates the agreement shall pay a fine of one sound ox. (30) The document[a] was written after a proclamation in the city of Nuzi at the palace gate. (33) If Elḫib-tašenni runs away or disappears, then Urḫiya must make full payment.

(36–44) seven witnesses and Tarmi-tešub, son of Itti-šarri, the scribe
(45–53) nine seals

a. *ṭuppi*/*ṭuppu*.

41. Gadd, *RA*, *23* (1926), No. 32

Ibid., 110.

(1) The tongue of Ni[ngiya,] son of Puḫi-šenni,—he has de[clared before the]se witnesses as follows:

(5) "I have received two new cloths two(+?)[a] *kuduktu* in weight,[a] and thirty minas of tin from Ḫumer-n[aya,] daughter of Itḫin-na[war]; (10) and I have gi[ven] Ḫudiya, my son, to Ḫumer-naya in *tidennūtu*. (14) When I return the two cloths and the thirty minas of tin to Ḫumer-naya, I may then take back my son Ḫudiya."

(18) If Ḫudiya becomes the object of a claim, Ningiya shall clear (him) for Ḫumer-naya. (24)[b] If Ningiya dies beforehand,[c] then Ḫudiya may [re]turn the money specified in this document to Ḫumer-naya[b] and thus fr[ee himself] from the house of Ḫumer-naya. (31) This[d] document was written after [a proclamation] at the *ḫamru*-precinct of [D]IM(!).

(34–39) six witnesses

a–a. Read line 6 as *ku-duk!-tu*₄ *šu-qú-ul!-ti-*[*šu*]. Gadd's transliteration [túg]*e-tap-tum* (*RA*, *23* [1926], 110), which was accepted by von Soden (*AHw*, *1*, 185a sub *edaptum*), is untenable in this context. Furthermore, the tablet stipulates the return of only two garments in line 14. Cross's reading (*Property*, p. 51) *ku-duq-qa-tu*₄ *šu-qú-ul-ti*[ti] is also difficult in view of the copy, and in view of the attested plural *kudkētu* for *kuduktu* (*AHw*, *1*, 499a). In the transliteration presented here, the unit of measure appears in the singular even though more than one unit was specified (cf. *HSS*, *13*, 245:2).

b–b. This entire clause has been misinterpreted by Koschaker (*NRUA*, p. 121) because of an erroneous transliteration of line 26 which is to be read as *ù* [[I]*Ḫ*]*u-dì-ya* kù-babbar!-meš.

c. *ḫamutta*. Note that this line has been placed in the wrong entry in *CAD* (Ḫ, p. 75 sub *ḫamut*).

d. *annūtu*/*annītu*.

42. *HSS*, *5*, 82

Speiser, *JAOS*, *53* (1933), 35.

(1) Document of *tide*[*nnūtu* of] Tarmiya, son of . . .; Tarmiya has given his son, Kunna, in *tidennūtu* for three years to Ilānu, son of Tayuge, in *tidennūtu*; (7) and Ilānu

three ewes, thrice plucked,
one ram, thrice plucked,
one male spring lamb, plucked in the month of Kurillu,[a]
one new cloth weighing six minas,

this money he has given to Tarmiya. (13) Whenever three years have elapsed, Tarmiya shall return the money specified in this document to Ilanu, and take back his son. (19) If Kunnu has a claimant, Tarmiya will clear (him) for Ilānu. (23) And Ilānu will give two minas of wool per year to Tarmiya, as the wool-ration[b] of Kunnu. (28) If Kunnu neglects[c] the work of Ilānu for a single day, Tarmiya shall pay to Ilānu one mina of copper, his daily hire (for a replacement). (33) Whoever between them violates the agreement must pay a fine of one ox.

(35–41) six witnesses

(42) scribe

(43–45) six seals

a. The month *kurillu* is specified as falling after the harvest (Gordon and Lacheman, *ArOr, 10* [1938], 55). The term also occurs in Nuzi and Middle Assyrian texts as the name of a harvest festival (cf. *AHw, 1,* 513a).

b. The term síg-ba: *lubultu* designates the "wool ration" and is to be differentiated from túg-ba: *nalbašu* which designates the "clothing-ration" (*MSL, 5,* 10). For the socio-economic implications of the term "ration," see Gelb's discussion of the Mesopotamian ration system in the second half of the third millennium B.C. ("The Ancient Mesopotamian Ration System," *JNES, 24* [1965], 230–43).

c. *ezzib/izzib.*

43. *AASOR, 16,* No. 27

Pfeiffer and Speiser, *AASOR, 16* (1936), 87

(1) Document of *tidennūtu.* (2) Uqari, his father, gave Taena, son of Uqari, to Tulbun-naya in *tidennūtu* for six years; and Tulbun-naya gave one homer of barley to Uqari. (6) And whenever the six years elapse, Uqari shall return one homer of barley to Tulbun-naya and take back his son, Taena. (10) But if Taena departs from the work of Tulbun-naya for a single day, Uqari must give one mina of copper, his hire (for a replacement) per day to Tulbun-naya. (15) As for Taena, Tulbun-naya shall provide barley and wool rations for him.

(17–30) fourteen witnesses[a]

(31–41) nine seals including seal of Urḫiya, the scribe.

a. For the restoration of the patronymic *A-kib-t[e!-šub]* (line 25), see *NPN*, p. 105b; for the reading of the personal name *Ur!-ḫi!-ya* (line 30), see *NPN*, p. 82a.

44. *JEN, 3,* 319

(1) Document of *tide[nnūtu]* of Teḫib-tilla, son of [Puḫi-šenni]. Teḫib-tilla gave twenty shekels[a] of gold to Unab-še, son of Tubki-tilla.[b] (5) In lieu of the twenty shekels of gold, Unab-še is to stay in the house of

Teḫib-tilla in *tidennūtu*. (8) (As long as) Unab-še [does not gi]ve back the tribute(?)[c] of twenty shekels of gold to Teḫib-tilla and does not go free, Teḫib-tilla shall provide barley and wool rations to [Unab]-še.

(13–14) two witnesses including Artašenni,[d] the scribe

(15–17) three seals

a. This form of the *šiqlu* sign is very similar to that in *JEN*, *5*, 552:2.

b. Note that these contracting parties also appear together in the sale adoption contract *JEN*, *1*, 20.

c. gu-un^{tu_4}:*biltu*. The term *biltu* denotes tax and rent payments as well as tributary payments (*CAD*, B, pp. 232 ff.). However, such usage of this term is unattested in Nuzi. Another possibility is to render the first sign as *šu*!, thus forming the subordinating conjunction *šu!-un-tu*$_4$.

d. Artašenni the scribe is probably the son of Apil-sīn (*JEN*, *1*, 77:29) and hence the brother of Taya. For a listing of the members of the scribal school of Apil-sīn, see Wilhelm, *Untersuchungen zum Ḫurro-Akkadischen von Nuzi*, p. 10.

45. *JEN*, *3*, 303

Gordon, "Fifteen Nuzi Tablets Relating to Women," *Le Muséon*, *48* (1935), 131.

(1) Document of *tidennūtu* of Agab-tukke, son of U[ge; accordingly], he gave[a] his [son], Šugriya, to [Te]ḫib-tilla, son of Puḫi-še[nni], for *tidennūtu* in lieu of twenty shekels of gold. (6) Whenever Agab-tukke re[tur]ns the twenty shekels of gold to Teḫib-tilla, he shall then [tak]e back his son, Šugriya. (10) [b]If Agab-tukke [cannot re]turn (it), Šugriya, his son shall [re]turn (it) and [go] wherever he pleases. (13) If Šugriya [cannot re]turn (it), the sons (and) daughters of Šugriya shall return (it) to Teḫib-tilla and thus go free.[b] (19) But if the sons (and) daughters of Šugriya cannot re[turn] these twenty ⟨shekels⟩ of gold, then in lieu of the twenty ⟨shekels⟩ of gold, they must stay in the house of Teḫib-tilla and his son.

(25–29) five witnesses

(30) one seal preserved

a. *idden*/*iddin*. Although the vowels *e* and *i* are usually distinguished from each other, their interchange is by no means rare (Berkooz, *Nuzi Dialect*, pp. 30 ff.).

b–b. This translation follows the readings supplied by H. Lewy (*Or*, N.S. *10* [1941], 319 n. 1) who corrected Gordon's restorations (*Le Muséon*, *48* [1935], 131) on the basis of parallel terminology of the *tidennūtu* contracts.

46. *JEN*, *3*, 302

(1) [Document of *ti*]*dennūtu* of Alpuya, son of Unaya. [He has re]ceived [twenty sh]ekels of gold from the house of Teḫib-tilla; (4) and in lieu of the twenty shekels of gold, [Al]puya is to [sta]y in the house of Teḫib-tilla. (6) When he returns the twenty shekels of gold, he may then go free.

(8) [If] Alpuya dies, [his] sons shall give back the twenty shekels of gold and [thus] may go (wherever they please).[a] (10) If Alpuya neglects the work of Teḫib-tilla, then the money shall ac[crue in]terest. (13) And if Alpuya violates the agreement, he shall then pay two minas of gold.

(15–24) ten witnesses including scribe, Taya

(25–27) three seals

a. The verb *illakū* is used elliptically for the fuller expression *ašar ḫadū illakū* "they may go wherever they please." Cf. *JEN*, 309:9 and 308:15 (texts 19, and 8).

47. *JEN*, *5*, 489

[Document of *tidennūtu* of Taya, son of Šeḫliya. From the house of Teḫib-tilla,][a] (1) he has recei[ved twenty] shekels of gold; and in lieu of the twenty shekels of gold, [Taya] is to stay in the house of Teḫib-tilla. (4) Whenever he pleases, Taya may give back the twenty shekels of gold [and go free]. If Taya di[es], then his sons may gi[ve back] the twenty shekels of gold [and thus go (wherever they please)]. (8) The gold does not bear interest and Taya does not re[ceive his] hi[re]. (10) If Taya [neglects] the work of Teḫib-tilla, then the gold [shall accrue] interest.

(13–21) nine witnesses including scribe Taya, son of Apil-sīn

(22) one seal

a. On the basis of *JEN*, *3*, 302:1–4 (text 46), the opening lines of this text may be restored as follows: *ṭup-pí di-te-en-nu-ti ša Ta-a-a* dumu *Še-eḫ-li-ya uš-tu* é *Te-ḫi-ib-til-la*.

48. *JEN*, *6*, 609

(1) Document of *tidennūtu* of Tieš-ši[mi]ga, son of Awīlu. [From the house of] Teḫib-tilla, son of Puḫi-še[nni he has received] twenty shekels of gold; (4) in lieu of the twenty shekels of gold he gave [his son, Ar]-sarwa. (5) When he [wishes to][a] go (wherever he pleases), [he may give ba]ck the twenty shekels of gold and thus go free. (7) If Ar-[sarwa] dies, his sons may gi[ve back the twenty shekels of gold] and go (wherever they please). (9) The gold does not b[ear] interest and(!) [Ar-sarw]a does not receive his hire. (11) [If] Ar-sarwa is [absent] from the w[ork] of Teḫib-tilla, then the gold shall accrue interest.

(14–27) fourteen witnesses including scribe Taya, son of Apil-sīn

(28–30) three seals

a. *ina ūmi š*[*a ḫadū u*]. Cf. *JEN*, *5*, 489:4 (text 47).

49. SMN 1418

(1) Three talents of copper belonging to Kainanni and to Ennaya,

Ḫanaya, son of Abiššeya received in *tidennūtu*. Ḫanaya is to stay[a] in the house of Ar-teya. (5) When Ḫanaya returns the three talents of co]pper to] Ar-te[ya] . . .

(rev. 1–4) four seals

a. *ašbu/ašib*.

50. SMN 2047

(1) Document of *tidennūtu*. In lieu of twelve minas of [ti]n belonging to Tai-tilla . . . received by [a]Ibša-ḫalu, son of Te[ḫu]ya(?). (5) Accordingly, the sons of Kib-ta⟨lili⟩ are to stay[b] in the house of Tai-tilla in [*tid*]*ennūtu*. (8) Whenever Kib-talili re[tu]rns the twelve minas of tin to Ta[i-til]la, he may take back [his s]ons [from the house of] Tai-[tilla]. (12) Kibtalili, [x hom]ers of land . . . Tai-ti[lla]. . . . Ki[bta]lili . . .

rest of obverse almost completely illegible

(21–28) seven witnesses

(29–33) seven seals including that of Nirḫi-tilla, the scribe.

a. For the difficult construction *leqū ana* PN "to receive to PN," see text 10, note a.

b. *ašib/ašbu*.

51. *AASOR*, *16*, No. 25

Pfeiffer and Speiser, *AASOR*, *16* (1936), 86.

(1) Document of *tidennūtu* of Aril-lu, son of . . .; he caused himself to enter the estate of Tulbun-naya, daughter of Šeldun-naya, in *tidennūtu*. (5) Aril-lu received ten homers of barley, one ox, one sheep, two *tallu*[a] of sesame[b] oil, and one cloth from the estate of Tulbun-naya. (9) When the years have elapsed, Aril-lu shall return the money specified in this document to the estate of Tulbun-naya and thus go away.[c]

(13) Thus (declares) Aril-lu: "The king assigned me to Kuru-adal for a tributary payment[d]; but I have received[e] the money from Tulbun-maya and g[ave] (it) to Kuru-adal."

(17) And thus (declares) Kuru-adal: "As for the remaining money of the tributary payment, I have assigned (it) to Tulbun-naya."

(19) Aril-lu . . . Eḫli-tešub . . . Aril-lu . . .

(22) [If Ku]ru-adal raises a complaint, [he shall pay a fine of] one mina of silver and one mina of gold to Tulbun-naya.

(24) one seal

(25–43) nineteen witnesses[f] including scribe Attilammu

(44–49) six seals

a. The *tallu* measure of capacity, probably based upon the size of a certain vessel (cf. *ŠL* 86:56), contained eight *qa* (Cross, *Property*, p. 15).

b. Kraus has rejected Helbaek's theory that the term *šamaššammu* applies to linseed rather than sesame ("Sesam im alten Mesopotamien," *JAOS, 88* (1968) [= AOS, 53], 112 ff.). But A. L. Oppenheim has pointed out to me in a personal communication that the matter is complicated by the fact that sesame seed has to be boiled to obtain its oil while linseed has only to be pressed.
c. The verb *rēqu* "to distance oneself" is used here in the same sense as *waṣū* "to go out," denoting freedom from servitude. For a different usage of this verb, see *JEN, 3*, 312:20 (text 20), which Oppenheim would connect with *rēqu* "idle, without work."
d. The term *ṭātu* "tribute, bribe" also occurs in *AASOR, 16*, No. 8:26. The range of meaning of this term in the Old Assyrian texts is discussed by Larsen, *Old Assyrian Caravan Procedures*, pp. 170 f.
e. *ilteqemi/elteqemi.*
f. Read the personal name in line 27 as *Ša!-at-tu-mar-di* (*NPN*, p. 120b); in line 39, as *Še-eh!-li-te-šub* (*NPN*, p. 130a); and in line 43 as ⸢*A!*⸣*-ti-la-am-mu* (*NPN*, p. 40a).

52. *AASOR, 16*, No. 62

Pfeiffer and Speiser, *AASOR, 16* (1936), 111.

(1) Document of *tidennūtu* of Agib-tilla, son of Šarriya.[a] Agib-tilla has given his son, Kinniya, to Urḫi-kušuḫ, son of the king, in *tidennūtu* for five years; (7) Urḫi-kušuḫ has given three homers of emmer (and) one homer five seah of barley to Agib-tilla. (10) When the five years elapse, Agib-tilla shall return the three homers of emmer (and) the one homer five seah [of barley] to Urḫi-kušuḫ, taking back his son, Kinniya. (15) If Kinniya neglects[b] the work of Urḫi-kušuḫ for a single day, Agib-tilla shall pay to Urḫi-kušuḫ one mina of copper, the hire (for a replacement) per day.

(21) The tongue of Agib-tilla—he has declared before witnesses as follows: "(24) I have received three homers of emmer (and) one homer five seah of barley from Puḫi-šenni, son of Mu[š-a]bu, the representative(?)[c] of Urḫi-kušuḫ, and I am sa[tis]fied.

(30–35) six witnesses, including scribe Elḫib-tilla

(36) The document [was writt]en at the gate.

(37–43) seven seals

a. For the reading of the patronymic as *Šar!-ri-ya*, see *NPN*, p. 125a.
b. *ezzib/izzib.*
c. On the basis of context, the term *amumiḫḫuru* has been tentatively translated as "representative" (Speiser, *AASOR, 16* [1936], 111–12). The usage of the Hurrian element *-ḫuri* appears to be similar to that of *-uḫli*, designating officials and occupational terms (Speiser, *Introduction to Hurrian*, p. 130; Bush, *A Grammar of the Hurrian Language*, p. 113; and Dietrich and Loretz, "Die soziale Struktur von Alalaḫ und Ugarit, 1: Die Berufsbezeichnungen mit der ḫurritischen Endung *-ḫuli*," *WO, 3* [1964–66], 189 ff.). For the suggested meaning of the Hurrian root *amum*, see *NPN*, p. 200.

NOTE: While preparing this manuscript for publication, A. L. Oppenheim called my attention to the unpublished Nuzi material in the Oriental Institute of the University of Chicago. There were two fragmentary tablets dealing with personal *tidennūtu*; they are presented below in translation:

53. JENu 118

several lines destroyed

(1) [Tarmi-. . ., son of . . .]ib-tilla[a] [gave] nineteen mi[nas of tin for fifteen ye]ars in *tiden[nūtu* to] Akkul-enni. (4) When fifteen ye[ars have elapsed], Akkui-enni shall return the nineteen minas of tin to [Tarmi-. . .], and thus free[b] hi[mself] from the house of Tarmi-[. . .]. (9) [If] Akkul-enni neg[lects] the work of Tar[mi-. . .], Akku[l-enni shall pay to Tarmi-. . .] one mina of copper—the daily hire (for a replacement).

several lines destroyed

seven witnesses, the rest destroyed

a. The name of the contracting party may have been Tarmi-tilla, son of Agib-tilla. Cf. *NPN*, p. 149.

b. *ú-še-ez-ze-eb*/*ušeṣṣi*. This confusion may have resulted from the occurrence of the verb *ezēbu* in the following clause.

54. JENu 627

(1) [The tongue] of Wunni—[he has declared before] wit[nesses:] "I have received from Paik[ku sixteen homers of barley".] (5) Accordingly, he [himself] has entered into the house of Paikku in *tidennūtu*. (8) Whenever Wunni shall return the sixteen homers of barley, then Wunni shall free himself from the house of Paikku. (13) If Wunni shall neglect the work of Paikku, [then he shall pay] the daily hire (for a replacement) to Paikku. (18) The document [was written . . .]

several lines destroyed

nine witnesses including scribe Arib-šarri.

APPENDIX 2

Prosopographic Data[1]

Agab-tukke son of Uge
D of Teḫib-tilla son of Puḫi-šenni (*JEN*, *3*, 303).
Agawatil son of Ellu
C of Sige son of Tai-tilla; c is tin (*HSS*, *5*, 40).
Agawatil son of Itḫib-tilla
D of Uznā daughter of Ḫašiya (*HSS*, *13*, 418).
Agib-tašenni
D and t of Muš-abu son of Burna-zini (*SMN* 2803).
Agib-tešub son of Tarmiya; brother of Madib-abu
D and t of Utḫab-tae son of Ar-tura (*SMN* 2102).
Agib-tilla son of Šarriya
D of Urḫi-kušuḫ son of the king (*AASOR*, *16*, No. 62).
Akkul-enni
D and t of Tarmi- . . . (JENu 118).
Akkul-enni son of Tuniya
D and t of Tešub-madi son of Šerta-ma-ilu (*SMN*, 2144).
Algi-tilla son of Kainnuya; brother of Zunnaya
Held as t by Šilwa-tešub son of the king (*HSS*, *9*, 13).
Alpuya son of Unaya
D and t of Teḫib-tilla (*JEN*, *3*, 302).
Amqa son of Ambi-zina
D of Uznā (*JEN*, *2*, 192).
Appuzizi son of Keliya
Held as t by Šeḫal-tešub son of Teḫub-šenni (SMN 2013).
Arib-šarri
Scribe of Paikku and Wunni (JENu 627).

[1] C = creditor
c = borrowed commodity
D = debtor
t = antichretic pledge (*tidennu*)

Aril-lu

D and t of Tulbun-naya daughter of Šeldun-naya (*AASOR*, *16*, No. 25).

Ar-šanta son of Anneya

D and t of Kel-tešub son of Ḫudiya (*JEN*, *3*, 316).

Ar-šarwa son of Tieš-šimiga son of Awīlu

Held as t by Teḫib-tilla son of Puḫi-šenni (*JEN*, *6*, 609).

Artašenni

Carpenter of Wur-tešub son of Agib-tašenni; held as t by Ḫud-arrapḫe son of Tišam-mušni (*JEN*, *3*, 290).

Artašenni

Scribe of Teḫib-tilla son of Puḫi-šenni and Unab-še son of Tubki-tilla (*JEN*, *3*, 319).

Ar-tešše son of Ḫanaya

D and t of Šugriya son of Ri. . . (*AASOR*, *16*, No. 63).

Ar-teya

C of Ḫanaya son of Abiššeya; c is copper (SMN 1418).

Ar-tidi son of Ḫalu-šenni son of Šadu-kewi

Held as t by Teḫib-tilla son of Puḫi-šenni (*JEN*, *3*, 293). Litigant in lawsuit with Šurgi-tilla son of Teḫib-tilla concerning *tidennūtu* contract *JEN*, *3*, 293 (*JEN*, *4*, 387).

Ar-tirwe son of Taya

Held as t by Tulbun-naya daughter of Šeldun-naya (*AASOR*, *16*, No. 28).

Attilammu

Scribe of Aril-lu and Tulbun-naya daughter of Šeldun-naya (*AASOR*, *16*, No. 25).

Ay-abāš father of Wandiš. . .

D of Tarmiya (SMN 2493).

Bēlaya son of Tae son of Agawatil

Held as t by Tulbun-naya (*AASOR*, *16*, No. 38).

Elḫib-tašenni son of Urḫiya

Held as t by Kula-ḫubi son of Ar-teya (*AASOR*, *16*, No. 61).

Elḫib-tilla son of Ibšaya

D and t of Takku son of Enna-madi (*JEN*, *3*, 308).

Elḫib-tilla

Scribe of Agib-tilla son of Šarriya and Urḫi-kušuḫ son of the king (*AASOR*, *16*, No. 62).

Elḫib-tilla son of Wurrikunni

Scribe of Enna-madi and Šilwa-tešub (*HSS*, *9*, 15).

Elmaše wife of Itḫib-tilla

D_2 of Uznā daughter of Ḫašiya (*HSS*, *13*, 418).

Eniš-tae son of Ikkiu

D and t of Teḫib-tilla (*JEN*, *3*, 309).

Enna-madi father of Ḫudiya

D of Šilwa-tešub son of the king (*HSS*, *9*, 15).

Enna-madi son of Teḫib-tilla

C of Itḫin-nawar son of Ar-šanta; c is tin (*JEN*, *3*, 304). C of Ḫanadu son of Ar-teya; c is two slaves (*JEN*, *3*, 312). C of Innigi son of Tae; c is a slave (*JEN*, *3*, 317).

Enna-madi son of Unaya

Weaver held as t by Teḫib-tilla son of Puḫi-šenni (*JEN*, *3*, 299).

Ennaya

Prior creditor(?) of Ar-teya (SMN 1418).

Genni son of Ḫubida

Guarantor of Agib-tešub and Madib-abu sons of Tarmiya (SMN 2102).

Ḫabil-damqa father of Ḫanadu

D of Tulbun-naya daughter of Šeldun-naya (*AASOR*, *16*, No. 24).

Ḫalu-šenni son of Šadu-kewi

D of Teḫib-tilla son of Puḫi-šenni (*JEN*, *3*, 293, *JEN*, *4*, 387).

Ḫanadu son of Ar-tešub

Guarantor of Agib-tešub and Madib-abu sons of Tarmiya (SMN 2102).

Ḫanadu son of Ar-teya

D and t of Enna-madi son of Teḫib-tilla (*JEN*, *3*, 312).

Ḫanadu son of Ḫabil-damqa

Held as t by Tulbunaya daughter of Šeldun-naya (*AASOR*, *16*, No. 24).

Ḫanaya son of Abiššeya

D and t of Ar-teya (SMN 1418).

Ḫanaya son of Tiwirra

Held as t by Mušeya son of Ḫašiya (*JEN*, *3*, 301).

Ḫašib-. . . son of . . .-enni

Scribe of Zirra and Pai-tešub (SMN 1592).

Ḫašiya

Scribe of Kubi-šarri son of Milkuya and Turar-tešub son of Agib-tašenni (*HSS*, *9*, 28).

Ḫašše son of Adad-ēriš; brother of Iluya and Kaniya

D of Kirib-šeri son of Ḫud-tešub (SMN 3587).

Ḫud-arrapḫe son of Tišam-mušni

C of Wur-tešub son of Agib-tašenni; c is silver, barley (*JEN*, *3*, 290).

Ḫudiya son of Enna-madi

Held as t by Šilwa-tešub son of the king (*HSS*, *9*, 15).

Ḫudiya son of Ningiya

Held as t by Ḫumer-naya daughter of Itḫin-nawar (Gadd, *RA*, *23* (1926), No. 32).

Ḫudiya son of Uta-mansi

Scribe of Ḫurbiya son of Tauga and Nudumar, the *šellintānu* (*TCL*, *9*, 10).

Ḫumer-naya daughter of Itḫin-nawar

C of Ningiya son of Puḫi-šenni; c is cloth and tin (Gadd, *RA*, *23* (1926), No. 32).

Ḫurbi-tešub

Scribe of Šullum-adad son of Tuḫmi-tešub and Ibša-ḫalu son of Unaya (SMN 1067).

Ḫurbiya son of Tauga

D and t of Nudumar, the *šellintānu* (*TCL*, *9*, 10).

Ḫuziri son of Sunzu

Scribe of Agawatil son of Itḫib-tilla and Elmaše wife of Itḫib-tilla and Uznā daughter of Hašiya (*HSS*, *13*, 418).

Ibša-ḫalu son of Teḫuya

Prior creditor(?) of Kib-talili who receives c from Tai-tilla (SMN 2047).

Ibša-ḫalu son of Unaya

C of Šullum-adad son of Tuḫmi-tešub; c is sheep, goats, and bronze (SMN 1067).

Ilānu son of Tayugi

C of Tarmiya father of Kunnu; c is sheep and cloth (*HSS*, *5*, 82).

Ilī-abī son of Tiwirra

Held as t by Mušeya son of Ḫašiya (*JEN*, *3*, 301).

Iluya son of Adad-ēriš; brother of Ḫašše and Kaniya

D of Kirib-šeri son of Ḫud-tešub (SMN 3587, SMN 3719).

Innigi son of Tae

D and t of Enna-madi son of Teḫib-tilla (*JEN*, *3*, 317).

Iriri

Scribe of Tešub-madi son of Šerta-ma-ilu and Akkul-enni son of Tuniya (SMN 2144).

Itḫ-abiḫe

Scribe of Teḫib-tilla son of Puḫi-šenni and Ḫalu-šenni son of Šadu-kewi (*JEN*, *3*, 293).

Itḫin-nawar son of Ar-šanta

D and t of Enna-madi son of Teḫib-tilla (*JEN*, *3*, 304).

Kainanni

Prior creditor(?) of Ar-teya (SMN 1418).

Kainnuya father of Algi-tilla and Zunnaya

D of Šilwa-tešub son of the king (*HSS*, *9*, 13).

Kaniya son of Adad-ēriš; brother of Iluya and Hašše

Held as t by Kirib-šeri son of Ḫud-tešub (SMN 3587).

Kel-tešub son of Ḫudiya

C of Ar-šanta son of Anneya; c is cow and barley (*JEN*, *3*, 316).

Kibaya son of Sate

Guarantor of Ḫurbiya son of Tauga (*TCL*, *9*, 10).

Kib-talili

D of Tai-tilla (SMN 2047).

Kib-talli

Scribe of Mušeya son of Ḫašiya and Tiwirra son of Ede-ya (*JEN*, *3*, 301).

Kinniya son of Agib-tilla

Held as t by Urḫi-kušuḫ son of the king (*AASOR*, *16*, No. 62).

Kinniya son of Ar-tešša

Scribe of Elḫib-tilla son of Ibšaya and Takku son of Enna-madi (*JEN*, *3*, 308).

Kirib-šeri son of Ḫud-tešub

C of Iluya and Ḫašše sons of Adad-ēriš; c is barley, tin, ewes, rams, and cloth (SMN 3587). C of Iluya son of Adad-ēriš; c is ewe, barley, and cloth (SMN 3719).

Kubi-šarri son of Milkuya

D and t of Turar-tešub son of Agib-tašenni (*HSS*, *9*, 28).

Kula-ḫubi son of Ar-teya

C of Urḫiya son of Agib-tilla; c is tin and bronze (*AASOR*, *16*, No. 61).

Kunnu son of Tarmiya

Held as t by Ilānu son of Tayugi (*HSS*, *5*, 82).

Kuru-adal

Prior creditor(?) of Aril-lu (*AASOR*, *16*, No. 25).

Madib-abu son of Tarmiya; brother of Agib-tešub

D of Utḫab-tae son of Ar-tura (SMN 2102).

Minaš-šuk son of Keliya

D of Šeḫal-tešub son of Teḫub-šenni (SMN 2013).

Muš-abu son of Burna-zini

C of Agib-tašenni; c is copper and barley (SMN 1418).

Mušeya son of Ḫašiya

C of Tiwirra son of Ede-ya; c is copper (*JEN*, *3*, 301).

Muš-šenni son of Šadu-kewi

D and t of Teḫib-tilla son of Puḫi-šenni (*JEN*, *3*, 306).

Mušuya son of Eḫliya

D and t of Teḫib-tilla son of Puḫi-šenni (*JEN*, *3*, 305).

Nabū-nāṣir

Scribe of Ḫabil-damqa and Tulbun-naya daughter of Šeldun-naya (*AASOR*, *16*, No. 24).

Nanna-adaḫ

Scribe of Šugriya son of Ri. . . and Ar-tešše son of Ḫanaya (*AASOR*, *16*, No. 63).

Niguya son of Tarmi-šarri

Scribe of Šilwa-tešub son of the king and Kainnuya (*HSS*, *9*, 13).

Ningiya son of Puḫi-šenni

D of Ḫumer-naya daughter of Itḫin-nawar (Gadd, *RA*, *23* (1926), No. 32).

Nirari son of Taya

Scribe of Sige son of Tai-tilla and Agawatil son of Ellu (*HSS*, *5*, 40).

Nirḫi-tilla

Scribe of Tai-tilla and Kib-talili (SMN 2047).

Nudumar

Designated as *šellintānu*; C of Ḫurbiya son of Tauga; c is copper (TCL, *9*, 10).

Nula-zaḫi

Specified as a substitute for Šullum-adad son of Tuḫmi-tešub (SMN 1067).

Paikku

C of Wunni; c is barley (JENu 627).

Pai-tešub son of Za...

C of Teḫib-sissa son of Ḫanaya (SMN 1598).

Pai-tešub

Designated as the *šellintānu* of Šilwa-tešub; C of Zirra; c is wheels and asses (SMN 1592).

Pal-tešub son of Zirra

Held as t by Pai-tešub the *šellintānu* of Šilwa-tešub (SMN 1592).

Pizune daughter of Itḫib-tilla

Held as t by Uznā daughter of Hašiya (*HSS*, *13*, 418).

Puḫi-šenni son of Muš-abu

Designated as the *amumiḫḫuru* of Urḫi-kušuḫ (*AASOR*, *16*, No. 62).

Puḫi-šenni son of Wardu-kēnu

D and t of Tulbun-naya (*AASOR*, *16*, No. 26).

Pui-tae

Scribe of Madib-abu and Agib-tešub sons of Tarmiya and Utḫab-tae son of Ar-tura (SMN 2102).

Šamaš-damiq son of Itḫ-abiḫe

Scribe of Uznā and Amqa son of Ambi-zina (*JEN*, *2*, 192).

Šeḫal-tešub son of Teḫub-šenni

C of Minaš-šuk son of Keliya and Unuš-kiaše wife of Keliya; c is tin and ewes (SMN 2013).

Šeršiya

Scribe of Puḫi-šenni son of Wardu-kēnu and Tulbun-naya (*AASOR*, *16*, No. 26).

Sige son of Tai-tilla

D and t of Agawatil son of Ellu (*HSS*, *5*, 40).

Silib-kušuḫ son of Aḫuya

D and t of Uznā wife of Enna-madi (*AASOR*, *16*, No. 60).

Šilwa-tešub son of the king

C of Kainnuya father of Algi-tilla and Zunnaya; c is a slave-boy (*HSS*, *9*, 13). C of Enna-madi father of Ḫudiya; c is barley (*HSS*, *9*, 15).

Sīn-iqīša

Scribe of Taya son of Ar-tamuzi and Tulbun-naya daughter of Šeldun-naya (*AASOR*, *16*, No. 28).

Sīn-nādin-šumi

Scribe of Teḫib-tilla son of Puḫi-šenni and Zikaya son of Kutukka (*JEN*, *6*, 607).

Sīn-uballiṭ son of Šamaš-ummāni

D and t of Teḫib-tilla son of Puḫi-šenni (*JEN*, *3*, 295).

Šugriya

Scribe of Teḫib-tilla son of Puḫi-šenni and Sīn-uballiṭ son of Šamaš-ummāni (*JEN*, *3*, 295).

Šugriya son of Agab-tukke

Held as t by Teḫib-tilla son of Puḫi-šenni (*JEN*, *3*, 303).

Šugriya son of Ri. . .

C of Ar-tešše son of Ḫanaya; c is slave (*AASOR*, *16*, No. 63).

Šuk-tešub

Weaver held as t and D by Tulbun-naya (*AASOR*, *16*, No. 29).

Šullum-adad son of Tuḫmi-tešub

D and t of Ibša-ḫalu son of Unaya (SMN 1067). He may have to perform *šattetaumma* for the *ilku*-duty of Kirib-šarri.

Sunzu

Scribe of Itḫin-nawar son of Ar-šanta and Enna-madi son of Teḫib-tilla (*JEN*, *3*, 304). Scribe of Innigi son of Tae and Enna-madi son of Teḫib-tilla (*JEN*, *3*, 317).

Šurgi-tilla son of Teḫib-tilla

Litigant in lawsuit with Ar-tidi son of Ḫalu-šenni concerning *tidennūtu* contract *JEN*, *3*, 293 (*JEN*, *4*, 387).

Tae son of Agawatil; brother of Utḫab-še son of Kaliya

D of Tulbun-naya (*AASOR*, *16*, No. 38).

Taena son of Uqari

Held as t by Tulbun-naya (*AASOR*, *16*, No. 27).

Taḫirišti son of Zikaya

Held as t by Teḫib-tilla son of Puḫi-šenni (*JEN*, *6*, 607).

Tai-tilla

C of Kib-talili; c is tin (SMN 2047).

Taki

Scribe of Teḫib-sissa son of Ḫanaya and Pai-tešub son of Za. . . (SMN 1598).

Takku son of Enna-madi

C of Elḫib-tilla son of Ibšaya; c is sheep (*JEN*, *3*, 308).

Tarmi-. . .

C of Akkul-enni; c is tin (JENu 118).

Tarmi-tešub son of Itti-šarri

Scribe of Ḫud-arrapḫe son of Tišam-mušni and Wur-tešub son of Agib-tašenni (*JEN*, *3*, 290). Scribe of Urḫiya son of Agib-tilla and Kula-ḫubi son of Ar-teya (*AASOR*, *16*, No. 61).

Tarmiya

C of Ay-abāš father of Wandiš. . . (SMN 2493).

Tarmiya father of Kunnu

D of Ilānu son of Tayugi (*HSS*, *5*, 82).

Taya

Scribe of Teḫib-tilla and Alpuya son of Unaya (*JEN*, *3*, 302). Scribe of Teḫib-tilla and Eniš-tae son of Ikkiu (*JEN*, *3*, 309).

Taya son of Apil-sīn

Scribe of Mušuya son of Eḫliya and Teḫib-tilla son of Puḫi-šenni (*JEN*, *3*, 305). Scribe of Taya son of Šeḫliya and Teḫib-tilla (*JEN*, *5*, 489). Scribe of Tieš-šimiga son of Awīlu and Teḫib-tilla son of Puḫi-šenni (*JEN*, *6*, 609).

Taya son of Ar-tamuzi

D of Tulbun-naya daughter of Šeldun-naya (*AASOR*, *16*, No. 28).

Taya son of Šeḫliya

D and t of Teḫib-tilla (*JEN*, *5*, 489).

Teḫib-sissa son of Ḫanaya

D and t of Pai-tešub son of Za. . . (SMN 1598).

Teḫib-tilla

C of Alpuya son of Unaya; c is gold (*JEN*, *3*, 302). C of Eniš-tae son of Ikkiu; c is men and women (*JEN*, *3*, 309). C of Taya son of Šeḫliya; c is gold (*JEN*, *5*, 489). (Cf. Teḫib-tilla son of Puḫi-šenni).

Teḫib-tilla son of Puḫi-šenni

C of Ḫalu-šenni son of Šadu-kewi; c is barley (*JEN*, *3*, 293). C of Sīn-uballiṭ son of Šamaš-ummāni; c is copper (ibid., 295). C of Unaya son of Agib-šarri; c is copper (ibid., 299). C of Agab-tukke son of Uge; c is gold (ibid., 303). C of Mušuya son of Eḫliya; c is a slave (ibid., 305). C of Muš-šenni son of Šadu-kewi; c is barley (ibid., 306). C of Unab-še son of Tubki-tilla; c is gold (ibid., 319). C of Zikaya son of Kutukka; c is a female slave (*JEN*, *6*, 607). C of Tieš-šimiga son of Awīlu; c is gold (*JEN*, *6*, 609).

Tešub-madi son of Šerta-ma-ilu

C of Akkul-enni son of Tuniya; c is tin (SMN 2144).

Tiam-biri

Scribe of Teḫib-tilla son of Puḫi-šenni and Unaya son of Agib-šarri (*JEN*, *3*, 299).

Tieš-šimiga son of Awīlu

D of Teḫib-tilla son of Puḫi-šenni (*JEN*, *6*, 609).

Tiwirra son of Ede-ya

D and t of Mušeya son of Ḫašiya (*JEN*, *3*, 301).

Tulbun-naya daughter of Šeldun-naya

C of Ḫabil-damqa father of Ḫanadu; c is a slave (*AASOR*, *16*, No. 24). C of Aril-lu; c is barley, ox, sheep, oil, and cloth (ibid., 25). C of Puḫi-šenni son of Wardu-kēnu; c is barley (ibid., 26). C of Uqari father of Taena; c is barley (ibid., 27). C of Šuk-tešub the weaver (ibid., 29). C of Taya son of Ar-tamuzi; c is barley (ibid., 28). C of Tae son of Agawatil and Utḫab-še son of Kaliya; c is slave and sheep (ibid., 38).

Turar-tešub

Scribe of Silib-kušuḫ son of Aḫuya and Uznā wife of Enna-madi (*AASOR*, *16*, No. 60).

Turar-tešub son of Agib-tašenni; brother of Wur-tešub

C of Kubi-šarri son of Milkuya; c is barley (*HSS*, *9*, 28).

Tur-šenni son of Arik-kani

Guarantor of Muš-šenni son of Šadu-kewi (*JEN*, *3*, 306).

Unab-še son of Tubki-tilla

D and t of Teḫib-tilla son of Puḫi-šenni (*JEN*, *3*, 319).

Unaya son of Agib-šarri

D of Teḫib-tilla son of Puḫi-šenni (*JEN*, *3*, 299).

Un-teya son of Iluya

Held as t by Kirib-šeri son of Ḫud-tešub (SMN 3719).

Unuš-kiaše wife of Keliya

D of Šeḫal-tešub son of Teḫub-šenni (SMN 2013).

Uqari father of Taena

D of Tulbun-naya (*AASOR*, *16*, No. 27).

Urḫi-kušuḫ son of the king

C of Agib-tilla son of Šarriya; c is emmer, barley (*AASOR*, *16*, No. 62).

Urḫiya

Scribe of Uqari and Tulbun-naya. Scribe of Šuk-tešub the weaver and Tulbun-naya (*AASOR*, *16*, No. 29).

Urḫiya son of Agib-tilla

D of Kula-ḫubi son of Ar-teya (*AASOR*, *16*, No. 61).

Uthab-še son of Kaliya

Brother and *ewuru*-heir of Tae son of Agawatil. D of Tulbun-naya (*AASOR*, *16*, No. 38).

Utḫab-tae

Scribe of Iluya and Ḫašše sons of Adad-ēriš and Kirib-šeri son of Ḫud-tešub (SMN 3587).

Utḫab-tae son of Ar-tura

C of Madib-abu, Agib-tešub sons of Tarmiya; c is bronze (SMN 2102).

Uznā

C of Amqa son of Ambi-zina; c is a slave (*JEN*, *2*, 192).

Uznā daughter of Ḫašiya; wife of Enna-madi

C of Agawatil son of Itḫib-tilla and Elmaše wife of Itḫib-tilla; c is sheep and goats (*HSS*, *13*, 418). C of Silib-kušuḫ son of Aḫuya; c is tin, barley, and wheat (*AASOR*, *16*, No. 60).

Wandiš. . . son of Ay-abāš

Held as t by Tarmiya (SMN 2493).

Wunni

D and t of Paikku (JENu 627).

Wur-te

Specified as a substitute for Šullum-adad son of Tuḫmi-tešub (SMN 1067).

Wur-tešub son of Agib-tašenni; brother of Turar-tešub

D of Ḫud-arrapḫe son of Tišam-mušni (*JEN*, *3*, 290).

Zikaya son of Kutukka

D of Teḫib-tilla son of Puḫi-šenni (*JEN*, *6*, 607).

Zini

Prior creditor(?) of Ḫanadu son of Ar-teya (*JEN*, *3*, 312).

Zirra father of Pal-tešub

D of Pai-tešub the *šellintānu* of Šilwa-tešub (SMN 1592).

Zunnaya son of Kainnuya; brother of Algi-tilla

Held as t by Šilwa-tešub son of the king (*HSS*, *9*, 13).

TABLE 1. INDEX OF TIDENNŪTU TEXTS

Gadd, *RA*, *23* (1926), 146 ff. Nos. 2–4, 26, 30, 32, 43, 45, 47, 48, 62.
TCL, *9*, 8–10, 16, 29, 32.
JEN, *2*, 102, 103, 111, 189, 192.
JEN, *3*, 289–312, 315–320.
JEN, *4*, 340, 364, 387.
JEN, *5*, 489–491, 513.
JEN, *6*, 568, 573, 606–609.
JEN unpubl. (cf. JAOS, 55 [1935], 430–31) 4, 7, 118, 119, 295, 627, 632, 703, 775, 791, 792, 799, 818, 829, 851, 921, 924, 972, 974, 979, 1164.
AASOR, *16*, Nos. 7, 24–29, 38, 60–67.
Peredneagiatskii Sbornik: Voprosi Hettologii i Hurritologii (1961), pp. 424 ff. Nos. 10–23, 92.
HSS, *5*, 4, 12, 18, 22, 33, 38–41, 66, 81–91.
HSS, *9*, 13, 15, 20, 27, 28, 97–107, 118, 155, 156.
HSS, *13*, 91, 171, 340, 376, 418.
HSS, *14*, 619.
HSS, *19*, 12, 121.
SMN (to be published in a forthcoming HSS volume, *Excavations at Nuzi*, *9*) 672, 703, 798, 825, 1043, 1062, 1067, 1176, 1212, 1418, 1592, 1598, 1711, 2002, 2013, 2047, 2102, 2109, 2112, 2132, 2138, 2139, 2144, 2179, 2194, 2245, 2301, 2311–2313, 2338, 2345, 2388, 2426, 2443, 2476, 2479, 2493, 2511, 2519, 2520, 2557, 2568, 2574, 2582, 2591, 2599, 2608, 2622, 2628, 2631, 2646, 2649, 2658, 2660, 2666, 2696, 2703, 2719, 2772, 2803, 2823, 3175, 3472, 3476, 3485, 3495, 3586–3588, 3590, 3594, 3597, 3599, 3600, 3601, 3609, 3613, 3614, 3617, 3719, 3755.

TABLE 2. DISTRIBUTION OF CLAUSES IN THE PERSONAL TIDENNŪTU CONTRACTS

Text	Duration Clause	Specified Work	Delinquency Clause	Dth/Disapp. of *tidennu*	Support of *tidennu*	Clear Title Clause	Dth/Disapp. of *D*	Penalty Clause	*Šūdūtu* Clause
1	Indefinite								
2	Indefinite								
3	Definite								x
4	Indefinite								
5	Definite			x					
6	Definite							x	
7	Indefinite		x						
8	Indefinite		x						x
9	Definite		x					x	x
10	Indefinite		x						x
11	Definite		x						
12	Definite		x						
13	Definite		x					x	x
14	Definite								
15	Indefinite		x	x			x		
16	Definite		x	x				x	
19	Indefinite							x	
20	Definite		x					x	
21	Indefinite			x					
22	Indefinite		x					x	
23	Indefinite		x				x		
24	Indefinite		x					x	x
25	Definite								
26	Definite		x						x
27	Indefinite	x					x		

(continued

TABLE 2 (*cont.*)

Text	Duration Clause	Specified Work	Delinquency Clause	Dth/Disapp. of *tidennu*	Support of *tidennu*	Clear Title Clause	Dth/Disapp. of *D*	Penalty Clause	*Šūdūtu* Clause
28	Definite	x	x						
29	Definite		x			x		x	x
30	Definite							x	
31	Definite	x	x					x	
32	Definite	x	x	x			x		
33			x	x			x	x	
34	Definite		x	x			x		
35	Definite	x	x	x			x		
36	Definite		x					x	
38	Indefinite		x						x
39	Indefinite		x			x			
40	Definite		x	x		x		x	x
41	Indefinite					x	x		x
42	Definite		x		x	x		x	
43	Definite		x		x				
44	Indefinite		x		x				
45	Indefinite								
46	Indefinite		x	x			x	x	
47	Indefinite		x	x			x		
48	Indefinite		x				x		
49	Indefinite								
51	Definite							x	
52	Definite		x						
53	Definite		x						
54	Indefinite		x						

Bibliography

For a comprehensive bibliography of the Nuzi texts and related studies and articles, consult M. Dietrich, O. Loretz and W. Mayer, *Nuzi-Bibliographie*, Alter Orient und Altes Testament-Sonderreihe, 11 (Neukirchen-Vluyn, Kevelaer, 1972). Only references to works relating to Mesopotamian legal material utilized in this study have been listed in the selected bibliography below.

Bottéro, J., *Le Problème des Ḫabiru à la 4e Rencontre Assyriologique Internationale*, Cahiers de la Société Asiatique, 12, Paris, Imprimerie Nationale, 1954.

Boyer, G., *Textes juridiques*, Archives Royales de Mari: Textes, 8, Paris, Imprimerie Nationale, 1958.

Cassin, E. M., *L'Adoption à Nuzi*, Paris, Maisonneuve, 1938.

——, "La Caution à Nuzi," *RA*, *34* (1937), 154–168.

——, "Tablettes inédites de Nuzi," *RA*, *56* (1962), 57–80.

Chiera, E., "A Legal Document from Nuzi," *AJSL*, *47* (1930–31), 281–286.

Chiera, E. and Speiser, E. A., "Selected Kirkuk Documents," *JAOS*, *47* (1927), 36–60.

Cohen, B., "Antichresis in Jewish and Roman Law," *Alexander Marx Jubilee Volume*, New York, Jewish Theological Seminary, 1950, pp. 179–202.

Cross, D., *Movable Property in the Nuzi Documents*, American Oriental Series, 10, New Haven, American Oriental Society, 1937.

Cuq, E., "Les actes juridiques susiens," *RA*, *28* (1931), 47–71.

——, "Le droit élamite d'après les actes juridiques de Suse," *RA*, *29* (1932), 149–182.

——, *Études sur le droit babylonien, les lois assyriennes, et les lois hittites*, Paris, Geuthner, 1929.

——, "Les Tablettes de Kerkouk," *Journal des Savants* (1927), 337–346, 393–403.

David, M. and Ebeling, E., "Assyrische Rechtsurkunden," *Zeitschrift für vergleichende Rechtswissenschaft*, *44* (1929), 305–381.

Draffkorn, A., "*Ilāni/Elohim*," *JBL*, *76* (1957), 216–224.

Driver, G. R. and Miles, J. C., *The Babylonian Laws*, 2 vols. Oxford, Clarendon Press, 1952, 1955.

Eisser, G. and Lewy, J., "Die altassyrischen Rechtsurkunden vom Kültepe, I," *MVAG, 33* (1930); "II," *MVAG, 35/3* (1935).

Falkenstein, A., *Die neusumerischen Gerichtsurkunden, 1–3,* München, Bayerische Akademie der Wissenschaften, 1956.

Finkelstein, J. J., "Ammiṣaduqa's Edict and the Babylonian 'Law Codes'," *JCS, 15* (1961), 91–104.

——, "Cuneiform Texts from Tell Billa," *JCS, 7* (1953), 111–176.

——, "The Edict of Ammiṣaduqa: A New Text," *RA, 63* (1969), 45–64.

——, "The Middle Assyrian Šulmānu Texts," *JAOS, 72* (1952), 77–80.

Gadd, C. J., "Tablets from Chagar Bazar and Tall Brak, 1937–1938," *Iraq,* 7 (1940), 22–61, plates I–V.

——, "Tablets from Kirkuk," *RA, 23* (1926), 49–161.

Garelli, P., *Les Assyriens en Cappadoce*, Bibliothéque archéologique et historique de l'Institut français d'Archéologie d'Istanbul, Paris, Adrien Maisonneuve, 1963.

Goetze, A., *The Laws of Eshnunna*, Annual of the American Schools of Oriental Research, New Haven, American Schools of Oriental Research, 1956.

Gordon, C. H., "Biblical Customs and the Nuzu Tablets," *BA, 3* (1940), 1–12. Reprinted in The Biblical Archaeologist Reader, 2 (ed. D. N. Freedman & F. Campbell, Jr.) Garden City, Doubleday 1964, pp. 21–33.

——, "Fifteen Nuzi Tablets Relating to Women," *Le Muséon, 48* (1935), 113–132.

——, "Nuzi Tablets Relating to Women," *AnOr, 12* (1935), 161–184.

——, "Parallèles nouziens aux lois et coutumes de l'ancien testament," *Revue Biblique, 44* (1935), 34–41.

Greenberg, M., "Another Look at Rachel's Theft of the Teraphim," *JBL, 81* (1962), 239–248.

——, *The Ḫāb/piru*, American Oriental Series, 39, New Haven, American Oriental Society, 1955.

Harris, R., "The Archive of the Sin Temple in Khafajah (Tutub)," *JCS, 9* (1955), 31–88.

Hayden, R., *Court Procedure at Nuzu*, Unpublished Ph.D. Dissertation, Brandeis University, 1962.

Hirsch, H., "Akkadisch (altassyrisch) *mazzāzum* 'Pfand, Verpfändung'," *WZKM, 62* (1969), 52–61.

Kienast, B., "Zum altbabylonischen Pfandrecht," *SZ, 83*/2 (1966), 334–338.

Klíma, J., "Parerga Mariaca," *Ivra, 16* (1965), 11–26.

——, "Zu *manzazānum*-Garantien nach den altbabylonischen Urkunden," *ArOr, 36* (1968), 551–562.

Klíma, J., Petschow, H. et al., "Gesetze," *RlA*, *3*/4 (1966), 243–297.

Kohler, J., Peiser, F. E., Ungnad, A. and Koschaker, P., *Hammurabi's Gesetz*, *1–6*, Leipzig, Pfeiffer, 1910–1928.

Korošec, V., "Keilschriftrecht," *Orientalisches Recht*, Handbuch der Orientalistik, *1*/3 (Leiden, Brill, 1964), 49–219.

Koschaker, P., *Babylonisch-assyrisches Bürgschaftsrecht*, Leipzig, Teubner, 1911.

——, "Cuneiform Law," *Encyclopedia of the Social Sciences*, *9* (1932), 211–219.

——, "Drei Rechtsurkunden aus Arrapḫa," *ZA*, *48* (1944), 161–221.

——, "Fratriarchat, Hausgemeinschaft und Mutterrecht in Keilschriftrechten," *ZA*, *41* (1933), 1–89.

——, *Über einige griechische Rechtsurkunden aus den östlichen Randgebieten des Hellenismus*," Abhandlungen der Sächsischen Akademie der Wissenschaften, 42, Leipzig, Hirzel, 1931.

——, *Neue keilschriftliche Rechtsurkunden aus der El-Amarna-Zeit*, Abhandlungen der Sächsischen Akademie der Wissenschaften, 39, Leipzig, Hirzel, 1928.

——, "Randnotizen zu neueren keilschriftlichen Rechtsurkunden," *ZA*, *43* (1936), 196–210.

Kraus, F. R., *Ein Edikt des Königs Ammi-ṣaduqa von Babylon*, Studia et Documenta ad Iura Orientis Antiqui Pertinentia, 5, Leiden, Brill, 1958.

——, Ein Edikt des Königs Samsu-iluna von Babylon, *Studies in Honor of Benno Landsberger*, Assyriological Studies, 16, Chicago, University of Chicago Press, 1965, 225–231.

Landsberger, B., "Neue Lesungen und Deutungen im Gesetzbuch von Ešnunna," *Symbolae Iuridicae et Historicae Martino David Dedicatae*, vol. II, Leiden, Brill, 1968, 65–105.

——, "Bemerkungen zu San Nicolò und Ungnad, *Neubabylonische Rechts- und Verwaltungsurkunden* Bd. I, *1*/2," *ZA*, *39* (1929–30), 277–294.

Larsen, M. T., *Old Assyrian Caravan Procedures*, Uitgaven van het Nederlands Historisch-Archaeologisch Instituut te Istanbul, 22, Istanbul, Nederlands-historisch-archaeologisch Instituut in het Nabije Oosten, 1967.

Lautner, J. G., *Altbabylonische Personenmiete und Erntearbeiterverträge*, Studia et Documenta ad Iura Orientis Antiqui Pertinentia, 1, Leiden, Brill, 1936.

Leonhard, R., "Antichresis," *Paulys Realencyclopädia der classischen Altertumwissenschaft*, Stuttgart, Metzler, *1*/2, 2396.

Lewy, H., "The Nuzian Feudal System," *Or*, N.S. *11* (1942), 1–40, 209–250, 297–349.

——, "The *Titennūtu* Texts from Nuzi," *Or*, N.S. *10* (1941), 313–336.

Lewy, J., "The Biblical Institution of Deror in the Light of Akkadian Documents," *Eretz-Israel*, *5* (1958), 21–31.

Liebesny, H., "The Administration of Justice in Nuzi," *JAOS*, *63*, (1943), 128–144.

——, "Evidence in Nuzi Legal Procedure," *JAOS*, *61* (1941), 130–142.

——, "The Oath of the King in the Legal Procedure of Nuzi," *JAOS*, *61* (1941), 62–63.

Matouš, L., "Quelques remarques sur les récentes publications de textes cunéiformes économiques et juridiques," *ArOr*, *27* (1959), 438–446.

Mendelsohn, I., "On Slavery in Alalakh," *IEJ*, *5* (1955), 65–72.

——, *Slavery in the Ancient Near East*, New York, Oxford University Press, 1949.

Muffs, J. Y., *Studies in the Aramaic Legal Papyri from Elephantine*, Studia et Documenta ad Iura Orientis Antiqui Pertinentia, 8, Leiden, Brill, 1969.

Oppenheim, A. L., *Catalogue of the Cuneiform Tablets of the Wilberforce Eames Babylonian Collection in the New York Public Library. Tablets of the Time of the Third Dynasty of Ur*, American Oriental Series, 32, New Haven, American Oriental Society, 1948.

——, "Untersuchungen zum babylonischen Mietrecht," *WZKM*, Beiheft 2 (1936), 1–149.

Petschow, H., *Neubabylonisches Pfandrecht*, Abhandlungen der Sächsischen Akademie der Wissenschaften, 48, Berlin, Akademie Verlag, 1956.

Pfeiffer, R. H. and Speiser, E. A., *One Hundred New Selected Nuzi Texts*, Annual of the American Schools of Oriental Research, 16, New Haven, American Schools of Oriental Research, 1936.

Purves, P. M., "Additional Remarks on Nuzi Real Property," *JNES*, *6* (1947), 181–185.

——, "Commentary on Nuzi Real Property in the Light of Recent Studies," *JNES*, *4* (1945), 68–86.

Saarisalo, A., *New Kirkuk Documents Relating to Slaves*, Studia Orientalia, 5/3 (1934), 1–101.

Samuel, A. E., "The Role of Paramone Clauses in Ancient Documents," *Journal of Juristic Papyrology*, *15* (1965), 221–311.

Scheil, V., *Actes juridiques susiens*, Mémoires de la Mission Archéologique de Perse, *22*, Paris, Leroux, 1930.

——, *Actes juridiques susiens*, Mémoires de la Mission Archéologique de Perse, *23*, Paris, Leroux, 1932.

Shaffer, A., "Hurrian **kirezzi*, West-Semitic *krz*," *Or*, N.S. *34* (1965), 32–34.

——, "*kitru*/*kiterru*: New Documentation for a Nuzi Legal Term," *Studies Presented to A. Leo Oppenheim*, Chicago, Oriental Institute (1964), 181–194.

Simmons, S. D., "Early Old Babylonian Tablets from Harmal and Elsewhere," *JCS*, *13* (1959), 71–93, 105–119; *JCS*, *14* (1960), 23–32, 49–55, 75–87, 117–125.

Skaist, A., "The Authority of the Brother at Arrapha and Nuzi," *JAOS*, *89* (1969), 10–17.

Speiser, E. A., "Cuneiform Law and the History of Civilization," *PAPS*, *107* (1963), 536–541.

——, "Leviticus and the Critics," *Yehezkel Kaufmann Jubilee Volume*, Jerusalem, Magnes Press, 1960, 29–45.

——, "New Kirkuk Documents Relating to Family Laws," *AASOR*, *10* (1928–29), 1–74.

——, "New Kirkuk Documents Relating to Security Transactions," *JAOS*, *52* (1932), 350–367; *JAOS*, *53* (1933), 24–46.

——, "A Significant New Will from Nuzi," *JCS*, *17* (1963), 65–71.

——, "The Wife-Sister Motif in the Patriarchal Narratives," *Philip W. Lown Institute of Advanced Judaic Studies, Brandeis University Studies and Texts*, *1* (1963), 15–28.

Steele, F. R., *Nuzi Real Estate Transactions*, American Oriental Series, 25, New Haven, American Oriental Society, 1943.

Weil, H. M., "Gage et Cautionnement dans la Bible," *AHDO*, 2 (1938), 171–241.

Wiseman, D. J., *The Alalakh Tablets*, Occasional Publications of the British Institute of Archaeology at Ankara, 2, London, 1953.

——, "The Tell Al Rimah Tablets, 1966," *Iraq*, *30* (1968), 175–205.

Yaron, R., *The Laws of Eshnunna*, Jerusalem, Magnes Press, 1969.

General Index

GN—Geographic name
MN—Month name
PN—Personal name
RN—Royal name

Index of Translated Texts